The Stories I Never Told You

John Rozema

The Stories I Never Told You

A MEMOIR

JOHN ROZEMA

REDEMPTION PRESS

© 2010 by John Rozema. All rights reserved.
2nd Printing 2014.

Published by Redemption Press, PO Box 427, Enumclaw, WA 98022.

No part of this publication may be reproduced, stored in a retrieval system, or transmitted in any way by any means—electronic, mechanical, photocopy, recording, or otherwise—without the prior permission of the copyright holder, except as provided by USA copyright law.

Unless otherwise noted, all Scriptures are taken from the *Holy Bible, New International Version®, NIV®*. Copyright © 1973, 1978, 1984 by Biblica, Inc.™ Used by permission of Zondervan. All rights reserved worldwide. WWW.ZONDERVAN.COM

Scripture references marked KJV are taken from the *King James Version* of the Bible.

Permission by Workman Publishing Company to reprint the authorized short version of Dorothy Law Nolte's poem, *Children Learn What They Live*, is gratefully acknowledged.

Excerpted from the book *Children Learn What They Live*, Copyright © 1998 by Dorothy Law Nolte and Rachel Harris. Used by permission of Workman Publishing Co., Inc., New York. All Rights Reserved.

ISBN 13: 978-1-63232-544-0 (Print)
        978-1-63232-545-7 (ePub)
        978-1-63232-546-4 (Mobi)
Library of Congress Catalog Card Number: 2009908344

You wouldn't know it by peeking at my bank account or by looking at my material possessions, but I'm a very rich man! God has blessed me undeservedly and beyond my wildest dreams—with four wonderful treasures.

These include my love and my loyal companion, my wife and my best friend of more than thirty years, Janneke, (a common Dutch name, pronounced Yanukkah);

and my three dear sons,

Dennis, Kevin, and Darren.

Except where otherwise noted, the stories in this book were affectionately written for, and are lovingly dedicated to them.

Amazing grace! How sweet the sound
That saved a wretch like me!
I once was lost, but now am found;
Was blind, but now I see.

—John Newton, 1725–1807

Author's Note

The stories in this book are true; however, I have changed the names of those who have crossed my path during my life's journey, with the following exceptions: the names of my immediate and extended family members, as well as the names of those dear people who have given me their consent to use their names. In addition, with the kind permission of his family, I have included the name of Richard Lee Fisher, an architect from Southern California who had a bright and promising future. A great friend, Richard tragically died from a brain tumor in 1991 at age thirty-eight.

I have not changed the names of the Commander of the United States Military Assistance Command, Vietnam (MACV), the first American soldier killed in combat in Quang Tri Province, Vietnam, and the name of my commander who was killed in action at Khe Sahn just prior to the onset of the 1968 Tet Offensive battles in the Republic of Vietnam.

Finally, the names of an African American celebrity and an Irish composer, as well as the names of the founders of the Christian ministry Licht im Osten (Light in the East), with its headquarters in Stuttgart-Korntal, Germany, remain unchanged.

Contents

Acknowledgments xiii
Foreword xvii

PART ONE: PREPARATORY SCHOOL
One: How it All Began. 1
Two: When Time Stood Still 11
Three: Preparing the Soil 17
Four: A Mariner's Calling. 23
Five: Fly Away 29
Six: Living the Dream 37
Seven: A Different Kind of Fireworks. 43
Eight: You're in the Army Now 49
Nine: A Shattered Picture. 59
Ten: Life at Kilroy Compound. 69
Eleven: The Snare of Death 79
Twelve: A Wrong Turn 87
Thirteen: On the Run 99
Fourteen: Miracle on Meisenweg 111

Part Two: In the School of the Most High

Fifteen: A Long, Sweet Honeymoon............119
Sixteen: A Flower in the Desert 129
Seventeen: End of a Honeymoon............141
Eighteen: Not-So-Quiet Time 151
Nineteen: When Johnny Comes Marching Home 157
Twenty: My Golden Calf............165
Twenty-One: An Opportunity Squandered 173
Twenty-Two: The Fire of Affliction 181
Twenty-Three: A Spiritual Transformation............195
Twenty-Four: A Church in Peril............201
Twenty-Five: No Place Like Home............217
Twenty-Six: A Time to Cry............225
Twenty-Seven: "This Thing is from Me" 233
Twenty-Eight: Jehovah Jireh............241

Part Three: Graduation

Twenty-Nine: No Fear of Death 253
Thirty: A Rude Awakening............259
Thirty-One: The Miracle Boy 265
Thirty-Two: On a Hill Far Away 275

Supplement to "The Miracle Boy" 285
Endnotes............289

Acknowledgments

FOR NEARLY HALF a century, I have lived with an inexplicable, inward drive to chronicle the journey of my life. What I present here was mostly written from memory. My ability to vividly recall detailed accounts, especially from my early childhood years, can only be called a gift from God. It is therefore proper and fitting that I should begin by thanking the Lord for allowing me to preserve these memories and for enabling me to express and write down on paper what has been on my heart all these years.

Fundamentals of English Grammar and English Composition 101 were not my favorite topics in school. I think that's because as a student at Pasadena City College in California during the late sixties and early seventies, my mind was notorious for wandering off subjects that didn't tickle my fancy. Writing a collection of short stories and compiling them in book form required the help of my friends. I would like to recognize them here, listing them in the order in which the manuscript was edited.

Many people have encouraged me to write a book, but Dr. John Wine, MD, was the impetus around the time of the 2004 Thanksgiving holiday for me to start writing my life's story. Without my asking, both John and his wife, Barbara, volunteered to proofread my work. They did so on top of carrying a heavy day-to-day workload at the Burkeville

Medical Clinic in southside Virginia, and home schooling their two teenage children.

In April 2007, while I was in a virtual comatose state due to an adverse reaction to chemotherapy, doctors had little hope of my recovery. But I remember Barbara at my bedside, firmly and repeatedly telling me, "You can't go yet! You must finish writing your book first!" John and Barbara's efforts were not limited to editing and proofreading; they spent much time praying and seeing the book to its completion. For this I will always be grateful. These two wonderful people, who are pillars at my church, have blessed my family and me in ways I will never forget.

I would also like to thank my friend and former colleague Beth Nutter. While employed with the Department of Social Services, I never permitted official correspondence to leave my desk without first asking Beth to peruse it and make certain that what I had written was error free—for good reason. Beth has a natural, uncanny ability to detect grammatical imperfections. Among the many documents she carefully scrutinized was my yearly, seventy-five-page Employment Services Annual Plan. Beth has sometimes—and rightly so—accused me of being a "comma freak." Each time I envision Beth looking over my work, I visualize her sitting at her desk behind a machine gun with her finger on the trigger, aiming for those commas. Over the years I have much appreciated her using critical literary eyes and sharing with me her deep thoughts and feelings about the account of my life.

Among those who helped with editing and proofreading the manuscript was Roberta "Bobbi" Page, a homeschooler parent of three boys. Together with her husband, Tom, Bobbi is co-publisher of three weekly community newspapers in southside Virginia: *The Monitor*, *The Sussex-Surry Dispatch*, and *The Prince George Journal*. In fall 2004, when I casually mentioned my intention to write my testimony, she responded, "May I please read it?" She also agreed to be part of our little editing circle. I'm so grateful for her expertise and the many contributions she has made to my writing efforts.

Janet Loeser, assisted by her daughter, Alyce, an English major and a recent graduate of Bluefield College in Virginia, put the finishing touches on the manuscript before submitting it to the publisher. Janet, who once taught English and writing to homeschooled children, sometimes made me feel like I was a student in her class. She once confided to me that editing and proofreading the manuscript were her ministry. I much appreciate Janet and Alyce's investment in this book based on their keen literary insight and their many recommendations for improvement.

In addition to my editorial friends listed above, I would be remiss if I didn't mention Peter Geudeke from Emmen, the Netherlands, who taught me to minimize superlatives and to "say more with less." Peter assisted me with proofreading and editing the *Rozemagram*, a four-page newsletter published three to four times per year, when we lived in the Netherlands from 1991 to 1994.

Someone else who deserves special recognition is Lonnie Smith, who without giving as much as the slightest hint, volunteered to underwrite the publishing costs. He didn't know that I often asked the Lord where the money was going to come from for the publishing fees. Both Lonnie and his wife, Traci, are two very special people with huge hearts! Lonnie's kind and overly generous offer was an affirmation that the Lord wanted me to proceed with writing and publishing this testimony.

Last but not least, I express my undying love and gratitude to Janneke, who has been my staunchest supporter since the day we fell in love more than thirty-two years ago. Perhaps I should have listed her first because she, the first to see the rough draft, didn't hesitate to point out areas that needed correction or improvement. Janneke also helped me find appropriate Scriptures and was a constant source of encouragement during this extended letter-writing campaign. Without her many prayers, patience, and gentle nudging, these stories would never have been recorded.

To the Lord, under whose wings I have taken refuge, and to all the wonderful people mentioned above, I owe my profound gratitude.

Foreword

THIS IS A book worth reading! *The Stories I Never Told You* is a series of letters that invite you on a journey worth taking. The letters are a reminder that each of us is a story and that God has written who we are into every detail. Every chapter is like looking into a mirror and reflecting a sense of the hopes and heartaches, tragedies and triumphs, most of us encounter. On several occasions I found myself thinking, *This is* my *story.* I suspect you will do the same. The author, John Rozema, found a way to write down stories that reflect God's authorship of his life. Recalling past experiences was an invitation to allow God to co-author the rest of his life's story.

Here is a preview of some of the themes that run throughout his letters: every young boy longs for his father's acceptance and approval; our earthly fathers often fail us, but our heavenly Father will forever be faithful; abandoned by his natural father and emotionally abused by his stepfather, John desperately wanted to experience the joy of God-given fatherhood. Instead, he grew up living in fear, rejection, and intimidation.

Though he disliked the home he grew up in, he fell in love with America. John found a warm, inviting home in his new country. For the first time in his life, thanks to his Aunt Julie, he heard the words, "I love you!" John writes, "All the tears that had been bottled up inside me since I was a little boy—and there must have been an incalculable number—continued to pour out of me with loud weeping and wailing."

Another theme emerges when John enters the United States Army. Travel with him to Vietnam and listen to how he meets God in a foxhole and later attempts to visit the Vietnam War Memorial while emotionally paralyzed. The memories are agonizing. He says, "With each new day, I was fully cognizant of the possibility that I might not make it back home alive."

A third theme of mega proportion saturates the last chapters of John's letters to a "dear friend." Overcoming his fierce anger against his stepfather and being selected to attend the school of architecture, he proved to himself that he wasn't "the dumb, stupid, ignorant kid" with big ears he had been made out to be. He had value. More importantly, God heard John's cry for help; and he has been forever changed. He states, "I was basking in sin, always looking for something to fill that void in my life. And the more I sinned, the greater the void!"

While John lets his readers know that he was a master at wearing many masks, he couldn't hide from God. Under the terrible weight of sin and guilt, he cried out to God. His fourteenth letter describes the miraculous encounter he experienced. Today he is a real man who by God's grace has cultivated godly character we would do well to emulate. John wants everyone to hear the gospel of Jesus Christ and to experience forgiveness of sin.

John was searching for a father, for freedom, for a family, for a country, and for God. Finding the longings of his heart, he ends his book with letters to a "dear friend" that detail his spiritual transformation and his insatiable desire to be a witness of God's love to his family in Holland.

The Bible says that a wife is a gift from God. John describes another longing of his heart, God's gift—Janneke van de Koot—on his wedding day: "To be in that idyllic, picturesque church building with a radiant, beautiful young bride standing at my side, looking like a princess in a fairytale, was almost too much for me to handle."

His agonizing bout with cancer and the loving support of his church, New Covenant Fellowship, will warm your heart. Throughout each story is the truth that God is sovereign and personally involved in the affairs of men. You will be challenged to recall your own past experiences and to find the meaning God has written there. I suspect that by the end of John's letters, you will gain a clear sense of how God has written the chapters of his life. Conversely, you will see how God is leading you into the rest of *your* story.

What a privilege it has been to write this foreword about the life of a man who demonstrates such awesome humility! John, *you* are a real man, a spiritual man, one with whom God is obviously pleased; and a man whom I greatly admire and respect. Thank you for the gift of your life's stories.

Your friend, pastor, and counselor,

David "Kirk" Kirkendall
Crewe, Virginia

Part One
Preparatory School

There is a time for everything,
and a season for every activity under heaven:
a time to be born and a time to die,
a time to plant and a time to uproot,
a time to kill and a time to heal,
a time to tear down and a time to build,
a time to weep and a time to laugh,
a time to mourn and a time to dance,
a time to scatter stones and a time to gather them,
a time to embrace and a time to refrain,
a time to search and a time to give up,
a time to keep and a time to throw away,
a time to tear and a time to mend,
a time to be silent and a time to speak,
a time to love and a time to hate,
a time for war and a time for peace.

—Ecclesiastes 3:1–8

One

How it All Began

My dear friend,

The Japanese invasion of Java Island in March 1942 shattered the tranquility of the beautiful, pristine, tropical paradise of the eastern shores of Java in the Netherlands' East Indies, where my mother lived with her parents, Hein and Isah Rozema.

During World War II, the Imperial Japanese Army confiscated all homes and properties belonging to Dutch citizens and confined them to detention centers under cruel and harsh conditions. During these difficult circumstances I was born.

Grandfather Hein was serving as a nineteen-year-old conscript in the Royal Dutch Army when he was shipped to the Dutch East Indies (now Indonesia) around the turn of the twentieth century. He and thousands of other young soldiers were transported to the tropical islands to wage war against native "savages" in an effort to colonize the islands. Like many of its western European neighbors, Holland was a colonial power.

A Shy Native Girl

Soon after his arrival, Grandfather met Isah, a beautiful, shy native girl. Birth records are silent, but by best estimates she must have been fifteen or sixteen when she met my grandfather and fell in love with him.

Leaving her native village and family, she accompanied him wherever the army sent him, often to hostile fire zones.

Not until after the birth of their third child did they decide to get married. My mother was the eighth child born into this happy family of fourteen children—seven boys and seven girls—along with several adopted children. Mother often remarked that the days of her youth were golden years.

My grandfather was the recipient of Holland's highest military decoration for valor, an honor that enabled him to retire at a relatively young age and receive a small pension. In 1920 Hein and Isah chose to settle down in the town Situbondo, where he was appointed chief of police until the outbreak of hostilities with Japan in World War II.

Emmy

My dear mother, Emmy, was twenty-one when she became pregnant with me in November 1942. Only nineteen, my father was unprepared to take on the responsibilities of fatherhood. After much persuasion from an older sister, he decided not to marry my mother. Although I don't specifically recall Mother talking about her relationship with my father or her love for him, I know that his abandoning her broke her heart. I always sensed that somewhere deep inside, she harbored affection for him for all the remaining days of her life.

Several times during her pregnancy, Mother's older sister, Juliana (Aunt Julie), pressured Mother to get an abortion. Abortions during those days were not only rare and illegal; they were very risky. Unskilled local natives, lacking any form of medical knowledge or training, performed them in back alleys for a lucrative fee, using the most primitive methods imaginable. Mother steadfastly refused, and I was born on August 8, 1943. Ironically, Aunt Julie would later become a great influence in my life.

Immediately after my birth, my mother asked Uncle Roelof ("Ralph"), her second-oldest sibling, to report my birth to the local town office. Mother explicitly told him that my first name was to be "Guy." She should have written the name down because by the time he arrived at the office of vital statistics, he had forgotten it.

Without giving the matter much thought, Uncle Roelof decided to give me his name. At the time, all privately owned automobiles and motorcycles had been confiscated, and telephones were no longer in working order. Going home to tell Mother that he had forgotten my name, and then returning to the town office a second time seemed like too much effort for him.

He probably figured that Mother wouldn't object to my being named after him, but he was wrong. Mother was anything but happy when he returned home and told her that I was registered under the name Roel, a common Dutch name and abbreviated form of Roelof.

Ears

While growing up, my name was Guy, but I never liked it. I also despised the name my uncle had given to me.

When I was an infant, Mother was unhappy with my ears. They seemed too large. According to her stories, they protruded awkwardly, almost perpendicularly to my little head. To remedy this problem, she taped both ears to my head with bandages each night before going to sleep. She hoped my ears would eventually grow at a normal angle and didn't realize that this procedure nearly flattened the upper edges of my ears, making them appear larger than normal size. Later, others often ridiculed me because of my ears.

The Father Mistake

Soon after the war, Mother decided to find a suitable father for me. Employed as a chauffeur for VIPs at a nearby military installation, she met many eligible bachelors. Mother assumed that the man who showed any affection for me would obviously make a wonderful father and a suitable husband. She dated several men, but only one demonstrated the desired affection.

On February 27, 1948, after a two-year courtship, Mother married Gerrit Jan Valk, a soldier in the Royal Dutch Army stationed in the Dutch East Indies. My friendly relations with this man soured almost immediately after they were married, and Mother's decision to marry him proved to be one of the most tragic mistakes of her life. During this period, my stepfather relished teasing me and usually didn't know when to quit—only to become incensed when I began to cry. Mother's gentle attempts to intervene did little to alleviate the problem.

"We need to make a man out of him, not a sissy!" were his frequent replies. He demanded that I stop wailing. "Crying is for girls and little old ladies, not for boys!"

Realizing that I couldn't live up to my stepfather's expectations, I soon became afraid of him. Whenever possible, I kept my distance and avoided him at all costs.

One episode in particular stands out in my mind. On one long weekend, my parents rented a vacation home in the mountains near Bandung. While on this outing, my stepfather took me for a walk one afternoon on a deserted mountain trail. In an area surrounded by lush tropical vegetation, he ordered me to sit on a narrow ledge high above a deep pool of crystal clear water. My stepfather sternly told me not to move and to await his return.

I don't know how long I sat there, petrified and frozen in place. The slightest move, I realized, would cause me to fall into the water below. Because I was unable to swim, such an accident would have been the end of me. Eventually, my stepfather returned to pick me up and took me home.

Not until years later did I begin harboring strong suspicions that my stepfather may have tried to kill me that day and make it look like an accident. I believe that much of his harsh behavior toward me stemmed from the fact that he was a jealous man; he wanted all my mother's affection for himself.

My half sister, Hanna, was born in June 1948. During the winter of 1950, my family embarked on a twenty-one-day journey by ocean liner to the Netherlands, where I would live for the next twelve years. Indonesia had become an independent, sovereign nation, and most Dutch citizens were migrating back to their homeland.

Because of my stepfather's repeated and excessive angry outbursts at me during this voyage, I became convinced that Mother had married a monster. The trip marked the beginning of many years of emotional trauma that caused deep wounds in my soul and scars on my heart. I feel the pain to this day and lick the wounds even as I write these words on paper.

SKATING MISADVENTURE

We temporarily lived with my stepfather's parents in Deventer until a permanent home became available in Ede, where he was stationed as a professional soldier.

Transitioning from a hot, tropical climate to cold, harsh winter conditions wasn't easy. The winter of 1950 was exceptionally cold, and I preferred to stay indoors where it was cozy and warm. My stepfather, however, angrily insisted that I play outside despite the frigid temperatures. Like all good Dutch boys, I needed to grow up and be tough, he said. Playing outside in freezing temperatures for hours was part of the toughening process.

Every boy and girl in Holland learns to ice skate, and I was no exception. Without asking if I was even interested, my stepfather took me out on the ice one day and tried to teach me how to skate. The experience was nothing short of disastrous. By today's standards, the skates were old-fashioned. Except for the steel blades, they were fabricated out of wood and fastened to shoes with ordinary shoe strings.

By the time we reached the frozen waters, my fingers were so painfully cold and stiff that I could hardly bend them, let alone tie skates to my shoes. Mittens or gloves didn't keep my little fingers warm. Under my stepfather's critical, watchful eye, I strapped the skates to my shoes with great difficulty.

"Watch the other children," he ordered, "and keep your balance before lifting your foot off the ice!"

"But I'm too cold," I lamented. "I can't move."

"Stop your whining! Get out there and skate like the others!" he snarled.

As expected, I failed miserably at my first and subsequent attempts to gracefully move on ice. My legs and feet moved in one direction, but my skates in another. I slipped, and my face smacked on the hard, frozen ice—much to my stepfather's chagrin.

"Can't you ever do anything right?" he repeatedly shouted. His verbal abuse amused nearby children, many of whom had already mastered the sport.

I was embarrassed, my cheeks flaming red. Though I loved the beauty of the winter scenery, I dreaded being outside in bone-chilling temperatures for hours. Despite my tearful objections, he was determined to see me skate flawlessly on the ice "like every good Dutch boy." As a result of his anger and impatience, coupled with my clumsiness, all my efforts resulted in a painful, intimidating experience. Much to my delight, he became exasperated and eventually gave up hope of ever seeing me become an accomplished skater.

The Bicycle Disaster

The following summer, my stepfather must have had an exceptionally good day because he surprised me with a bicycle. I encountered one slight problem, however; my feet couldn't reach the pedals even when he adjusted the seat to its lowest position. Children's bicycles were simply not manufactured in Holland after the war.

To solve this height problem, my stepfather built two wooden blocks and bolted one to each pedal so my feet could reach. Though this idea may sound clever, pedaling this single-gear bicycle with this modification wasn't easy. With my outstretched toes I could barely touch one block at its lowest point, while the other block at its highest point tended to spin and slip out from under my foot whenever I applied pressure to create momentum. I found myself concentrating more on keeping my feet planted on the improvised pedals than on steering the bicycle in a straight direction.

As a result, I often landed on the cobblestone pavement and frequently hit many unseen obstacles. My stepfather jogged behind me, working up a sweat, and shouting instructions along with expletives not fit for publication. To many onlookers this scene must have been an amusing spectacle. Though I suffered no serious injuries, I disliked riding the bike because it was simply another exercise in public humiliation.

The Butcher of Ede

During the summer of 1951, we settled in a permanent dwelling, a two-story, brick row house at Lombok Lane 22 in Ede. Not long after this move, our family physician introduced me to the "Butcher of Ede," an ear, nose, and throat specialist, because I needed to have a nasal polyp removed.

I soon learned why this man had received his nickname. His medieval methods of performing routine medical procedures were classic acts of sheer torture. Notorious for his short-fused temper, the doctor considered the use of locally administered anesthesia for the removal of a nasal polyp a waste.

I was very nervous when my mother accompanied me to the hospital that morning. After the doctor tightly strapped my waist and ankles to a chair, a muscular nurse pulled my head back as if in a headlock and held it firmly in place. Then, while this woman held one arm and another nurse tightly held the other, the "Butcher" slowly but firmly chipped away deep into my nasal cavity with what seemed like a hammer and chisel.

When he burned my nostril with a heated surgical tool to widen my nasal passage's opening, I began to cry. In response he became angry with me.

"Stop your crying!" he ordered. "And stop acting like a baby!"

Terrified, I broke out in a cold sweat. The pain was intense, and I was bleeding and choking while the nurses still held me in their viselike grip. It was like a frightening, nightmarish scene from a Hollywood horror movie.

Fear turned to panic, and my wailing escalated to loud screaming. The doctor retaliated by cursing with loud, profane language, trying either to scare me or to quiet me. But this tactic didn't work either. I don't know how long this horrible ordeal lasted, but it seemed to go on for a lifetime.

Life at Lombok Lane 22

Though my stepfather didn't inflict physical pain to the Butcher of Ede's level, life at Lombok Lane 22 became increasingly intolerable as a result of his continued emotional abuse. For reasons that baffle me to this day, he threatened to place me in a children's home or orphanage where I would never see my mother again. Those were his exact words! I never figured out what I had said or done to merit such a drastic reaction, but I believed every word he said. Being taken away from my mother was the most terrifying threat imaginable. To me, death would have been more tolerable.

While I grew up under these difficult circumstances, my mother kept me going from one day to the next. She was my rock, my refuge, my joy, and the only person I could go to for comfort. Being taken away from my mother and never seeing her again would have been a punishment I couldn't bear—and my stepfather knew it.

For many years I desperately tried not to say or do anything to irritate or anger my stepfather for fear that he would act on his threats. I lived in constant fear, and despite my best efforts to gain his approval, they were never good enough. He frequently reminded me of how stupid I was. He told me that I was "no good," "would never amount to anything," and would "always be a miserable failure!" It didn't take me long to believe those words, and my grades in school proved it.

Almost all these painful ordeals took place when Mother was absent. I never shared my anguish with her, nor did I tell her what her husband was doing to me. Instead, I learned to suffer alone in silence. My mean-spirited stepfather, a strict disciplinarian, was apparently oblivious to the long-term irreparable, emotional damage he was causing. I stayed silent because I figured my mother had her own pain to deal with. I wanted to protect her the best I could and didn't wish to add more to her plate.

No Coward

Two more siblings were born to this marriage: Martin was born not long after we moved into our new home in October 1951, and Rita was born in December 1955. No one escaped the emotional injuries inflicted by my stepfather. Being the oldest child, however, I believe I received the brunt of his outrage.

Mother was a master at hiding her feelings. I suspect that under different circumstances she would have divorced this man; however, while I was growing up in Holland, dissolving a marriage simply wasn't an option. Divorce was virtually nonexistent and in some circles shameful even to mention. It meant potentially becoming a social outcast. I don't believe Mother was prepared to pay such a heavy price.

And being married *did* have its advantages. A hard worker, my stepfather paid the bills on time and kept food on the table. He was, in fact, a good provider. As far as society was concerned, that was all that mattered.

Though Mother was good at hiding her feelings, she was no coward. She wasn't afraid to stand up to my stepfather when she thought he had overstepped the bounds of his parental authority. She did so at least once when she saw my stepfather slap me across the face for no good reason.

She stopped what she was doing and approached him without hesitation, pointing her finger between his eyes. Angrily but calmly, she said, "If I ever see you do that again, I will pack my suitcase, take the children, move out, and never come back!"

Mother meant what she said. Surprisingly, without further confrontation, he turned and walked away.

Making Excuses

My stepfather had spent most of his wartime years as a prisoner of war in Japanese prison camps. Shipwrecked off the coast of Burma, he had spent several days in shark-infested waters, only to be rescued by a Japanese freighter. He and many other survivors had been taken prisoner and transported to Japanese slave labor camps. There he had been instrumental in building the now-infamous railroad through the treacherous, dense, and mountainous jungles of Burma.

He seldom spoke of his life as a prisoner of war, but I learned enough in school to know that allied nation soldiers working on the railroad had been exposed to insufferable tropical diseases, hunger, cruelty beyond imagination, and death at the hands of their Japanese captors. As a child, I always made excuses and rationalized my stepfather's abusive conduct because of his wartime experiences.

In all my years living with this man, I cannot recall a single instance of warmth, friendship, or affection. Though I know others loved and cared for me, my stepfather's ominous presence overshadowed all else. His insidious hostility toward me left a black mark on my life. In a few short years, I had changed from a happy toddler with my mother, safe and secure in my grandparents' loving home, to a boy with a shameful, humiliated life.

I hated my world! Humiliation, shame, and hatred were deeply entrenched in my heart and remained carefully hidden there. Sometimes I even thought of killing myself. Then I believed the answer to my problem was to leave home at my earliest convenience. In fact, that goal became the driving force of my young life.

> You intended to harm me, but God intended it for good.
> —Genesis 50:20

It wasn't until many years later that I learned the truth of this Bible passage.

Your friend,
John

Two

When Time Stood Still

My dear friend,

Life wasn't always as miserable as I have portrayed it thus far. I experienced plenty of happy moments. The times I spent with my grandparents during my Easter, summer, and Christmas breaks were happy, and I will always treasure them. Weeks before the start of my school vacation, I lay in bed at night awake and counted the days until I left home, when I stepped on the bus and began the almost-two-and-a-half-hour journey to my grandparents' home. Sometimes I missed my connection in Apeldoorn and waited an hour or more for the next bus, but the delay didn't bother me.

THE LOOK OUT

Grandfather Hein and Grandmother Isah lived in a large, three-story, brick and thatch-roofed villa built in the early nineteen hundreds. It was on the outskirts of the historic, picturesque town of Hattem, an area of Holland that attracted many vacationers and tourists alike. The house stands to this day and overlooks beautiful, green pasturelands and grazing Holstein dairy cattle.

I don't know if naming homes is an exclusively Dutch practice, but many houses in Holland bore names. Some homes are affectionately named after people, while others are named after whatever reflected the home's character. Some homes, like my grandparents' house, which was aptly named De Uitkijk or The Look Out, were named after a unique topographic feature. Most of these names are beautifully carved in wood and prominently displayed, usually above the home's main entrance. My grandparents' sign simply read "The Look Out."

GRANDFATHER AND GRANDMOTHER

I can still see Grandfather, a towering figure who was always in a happy mood, comfortably sitting in his oversized chair in front of a large picture window, smoking his pipe or chewing tobacco, and singing popular marching songs from days gone by. Many songs, however, weren't always in good taste.

One song I still remember was about a girl named Sarah, whose skirt always slid off her hips. He happily sang this song dozens of times throughout each day. Grandfather, who by then was suffering from Alzheimer's disease, probably had no idea what he was singing. Much to Grandmother's dismay and embarrassment, he kept singing his colorful tunes, even when we had visitors, but most were not bothered or offended by the lyrics because they knew about Grandfather's health.

Grandmother, who couldn't read or write, was the best cook, especially in preparing exotic Indonesian dishes. In all my travels I have yet to savor a meal that matches or comes close in flavor to an Indonesian "Rijst Tafel." Its accompanying forty-five side dishes are eaten over the course of several hours, each possessing its own unique and exotic flavor. Grandmother didn't cook a meal with forty-five side dishes every day; however, the kitchen was her domain, and there she spent most of her time creating elaborate, fancy, and delicious meals to perfection. She painstakingly ensured that all her guests were satisfied with plenty to eat.

She warmly welcomed visiting family, friends, and neighbors with the traditional question—had they had something to eat, or were they hungry? When someone replied that he or she hadn't eaten in a while or was hungry, she hurried off to her kitchen and prepared a wonderful meal. Her guests didn't wait long to satisfy their appetites, regardless of the time of day.

Barbaric Methods

Grandmother raised her own chickens. Once in a while, she allowed us youngsters the thrill of catching them, chopping off their heads, and helping her clean these birds in preparation for a great dinner feast. Whenever she gave us permission to kill a couple of her chickens, we made sure Grandmother wasn't nearby—she wouldn't have approved of our barbaric methods.

After chopping off their heads, we let them go so we could watch them fly, flutter, and run erratically around the chicken coop, blood splattering and feathers flying in every direction. Afterward, we were often covered in chicken blood from head to toe. A great spectacle was watching the panic and commotion among the remaining chickens who had escaped the hatchet. I'm sure some of those poor chickens lived under great duress, knowing that their turn would come one day.

The Hands

My grandparents had forty-two grandchildren, many of whom were my age and also spent their vacations at The Look Out. During one particular visit, I shared a double bed in the attic with my cousin, Matthew, who was three years older than I. I don't remember the events of that typically fun day. As usual, we played all day, stayed up late, took a bath, and went to bed around midnight.

I awoke sometime in the middle of the night when two, unusually large, adult-size hands mysteriously protruded through the mattress and held me firmly in place. I clearly felt four fingers on each side of my stomach and two thumbs in my kidney area. Frozen, I lay on the mattress in a panic, wondering what to do.

A partially opened window stood directly in front of the bed. The cool breeze drifting through the window caused the lace curtains to gently sway back and forth. Puffs of white clouds slowly rolled across a bright, moonlit sky.

Yet the hands didn't let go.

This wasn't a dream or a nightmare, I realized. It was real and I was wide awake. I don't know how long I lay there, but every second seemed like an eternity. Time stood still.

To say that I was in torment and overcome with fear is an understatement. Physically immobilized, I wished I was dead. As I lay there, petrified, I tried to strategize what to do next. I desperately wanted to struggle out of this frightful situation, scream, and wake the entire household. But my vocal chords were mysteriously paralyzed. Physically powerless, I was aware of every single drop of cold sweat that poured out of my body's pores onto my bed sheets and pillowcase. Soon I was drenched in sweat.

Not the slightest movement did I detect from those two hands. Since I had never been confronted by such a horrifying encounter, I thought I was going insane. Nothing had happened or been said the day or evening before that could have led to such a terrifying phenomenon.

While lying there, I discovered that I could move my fingers and decided that the only way to escape the dreadful situation was to wake Matthew. Slowly and cautiously, I moved my right hand across the bed sheet toward my cousin, who slept about two feet from me. Deathly fearful of what might happen next, I dared not speed the process. I moved my hand more slowly than the time a wounded snail would have needed to reach Matthew.

At the precise moment the little finger of my right hand touched my cousin's pajama shirtsleeve, the hands instantly vanished.

As if the bed sheets and pillowcase weren't already wet enough from my sweat, I began to sob silently on them. I decided not to wake Matthew. If I told him what had happened, I feared he would be convinced that I had freaked out. He certainly would have mocked me. Afraid to fall asleep, I lay there soaked in sweat and in great distress until daylight.

The next morning, I told Grandmother that I wasn't feeling well and would take the next bus home. I didn't tell her the real reason for my wanting to leave. In fact, fearful of being ridiculed or humiliated, I never shared my story with anyone.

Not until almost twenty years later, while living in the United States with Aunt Julie, her husband, Uncle Hendrik, and my cousin Jake, did I discuss the details of that horrible night. A student at Cal Poly in San Luis Obispo, California, I didn't have a lot of money in those days because I went to school on the GI Bill. Going home each weekend spared me the expense of buying meals.

After we watched a scary movie on TV late one Saturday evening, Aunt Julie said, "Something strange and very scary happened to me while we stayed at Grandma's home in Holland."

To my astonishment, she described an event that was nearly identical to what had happened to me almost two decades earlier. Aunt Julie's account differed in that one hand, not two, had terrorized her in the night.

She had awoken and found herself lying on one side. Wanting to roll over on her other side, she had been unable to do so. A mysterious, large hand had firmly held her down so she wasn't able to move. Stricken with great fear, she too had been paralyzed. Like me she hadn't been able to scream. Aunt Julie had escaped the frightful confrontation in similar fashion. She had moved her hand across the mattress and touched my uncle who slept beside her.

I experienced tremendous relief when I shared my story for the first time without being labeled as someone who had gone off the deep end.

> For our struggle is not against flesh and blood, but against the rulers, against the authorities, against the powers of this dark world and against the spiritual forces of evil in the heavenly realms.
> —Ephesians 6:12

Not a night went by that I didn't think about this horrifying encounter, and nearly twenty-five years later, I was still unable to fall asleep while lying on my back.

Your friend,
John

Three

Preparing the Soil

My dear friend,

In the Netherlands, separation of church and state doesn't exist as we know it in America. While the state doesn't meddle with the affairs of the church, all schools—whether Protestant, Catholic, or public—are funded by the central or federal government. To my knowledge, private schools were nonexistent when I lived there, but parents had the freedom to choose which school their child attended. Interestingly, the northern half of the Netherlands is primarily Protestant, while the southern half is predominantly Catholic. Because my parents were unbelievers, they naturally chose for me to attend public school.

Children attending public schools in the Netherlands have a noncompulsory opportunity to become educated about the different religious and nonreligious groups that make up Dutch society. My stepfather, who embodied nothing religious, insisted that I attend Christian religious education classes twice per month. I don't know why other than perhaps to keep me off the streets and out of trouble, even though I rarely got into trouble. I didn't believe his intent was that I learn anything about Christianity; he didn't hide his immense distaste for anything affiliated with the church. I always pitied the poor soul who rang our doorbell, soliciting funds for a Christian charity. I wondered why all local churches didn't blacklist us as the result of my stepfather's blatantly rude conduct.

CHRISTIAN RELIGIOUS EDUCATION CLASSES

A Dutch Reformed Church minister taught the Christian religious education classes I attended in fifth grade. I can still visualize this man before me: tall, slender, in his late fifties. He had a somewhat pointy, balding head; thin lips; and a pale complexion. He wasn't someone who inspired excitement about things in the Bible, and no more than five or six students attended his class.

These unstructured classes primarily consisted of a Bible story, followed by a question-and-answer session. Incredible as it may sound, this man by his own admission admitted that he didn't believe everything written in the Bible. Moreover, he thought some Bible stories were fictitious. I didn't learn much in these classes, but I remember engaging in long discussions about creation and Adam and Eve.

QUESTIONS ABOUT GOD

During third or fourth grade, I befriended Patrick, who attended Catholic Mass every week with his family. The Catholic school was located too far away, so his parents had enrolled him in the nearest public school. Each time I played at my friend's house, his mother sternly warned us that God was watching our every move and wouldn't hesitate to punish us severely if we did something wrong. She also frequently cautioned us that if we sinned, we would be in danger of the fires of hell. I didn't know what to make of her words, but her comments about God frightened me. As a result, my friendship with Patrick was short-lived.

My parents never talked about religion. In fact, the name of God was never mentioned except when my stepfather cursed. I naturally assumed that all soldiers cursed because many of his friends and colleagues used similar language. He once casually remarked that he wouldn't want the privilege of a military funeral when he died. Oddly enough, he said he couldn't bear the thought of a bunch of cursing soldiers having to march in his funeral procession.

Even with all the negatives in my life concerning religious matters, after hearing the comments Patrick's mother had made and attending the religious education classes, I began to seriously consider God's existence. I had heard enough to convince me that God was real. My problem, however, was that my concept of God was poor at best. I imagined an angry God sitting on His throne somewhere in heaven, enraged at this world. I had no clue what heaven was like and concluded that only good people went there when they died, a thought that pretty much excluded me. Someone also explained to me that all bad people ended up in hell. The little bit I had heard about hell—if the place was even real—convinced me that I didn't want to go there.

I learned about the theory of evolution; however, I couldn't accept its assertion that nature in all its splendor and beauty was the product of a process that had lasted hundreds of millions of years. Moreover, I refused to accept the notion that what I observed in nature had come about by an act of mere coincidence. Evolution simply didn't make a lot of sense to me. As far as I was concerned, someone who possessed a great amount of intellectual brilliance should also reach the same conclusion. How was it possible for a microscopic cell to develop into a completely formed human being in less than nine months, or for a caterpillar to be transformed into a butterfly in a matter of weeks? All these theories about evolution and coincidences seemed preposterous. I reasoned that somewhere in the universe a Creator must have designed the natural order and beauty I discovered in the world around me.

STEPPING INTO ANOTHER WORLD

A two-acre open field in front of our house separated us from a large, newly built Dutch Reformed Church. Most neighborhood people affiliated with that church walked to services nearly every Sunday. Holland, about twice the size of New Jersey, is a small country. Walking a reasonable distance wasn't unusual for many people—weather permitting, of course. Except for major highways, virtually every street offered a sidewalk and a bicycle path on both sides.

Many families who lived on our street and were members of that church passed our house each Sunday morning and routinely became objects of ridicule. While eating breakfast, my stepfather made sarcastic comments about those "poor fools wasting their time, energy, and money on that church."

Many of my friends, however, belonged to that church and occasionally invited me to come along. It was a beautiful, contemporary, brick church building with seating for at least six hundred. Each time I visited—I attended no more than four or five times—I was amazed to find the building packed to capacity. Looking back at my visits, I remember feeling completely lost and out of place. It was like stepping into another world.

Dressed in a long, black, flowing robe with a fancy, white collar, the minister stood high in his beautifully carved, ornamental oak pulpit like a stern presiding judge admonishing the people. I didn't understand anything he read from his Bible. Therefore, listening to his long, boring sermons was like listening to someone speaking in a foreign language. I had difficulty concentrating and sitting still. I hadn't the slightest idea what the people there were doing, why they were doing it, and what it was that drew these people to that building every Sunday. I also couldn't understand why so many returned for a second service late Sunday afternoon. A somber, solemn atmosphere permeated the Sunday services, and the organ music sounded morbidly depressing. Though I didn't hear fire-and-brimstone sermons, I was still turned off by it all.

I was obviously a stranger to many, and I didn't like people staring at me as if to say, "Who are you, and what are you doing here?" As a result I never felt at ease in that church.

Except for taking a leisurely walk, my friends were not permitted to do activities on Sunday after church, including riding a bicycle or going swimming on hot Sunday afternoons. Doing anything but resting was considered a sin. It was obvious to me that my friends didn't enjoy going to church; they went because their parents had forced them to.

Vocational School

When I reached sixth grade, my parents had an important decision to make about my further education. They had basically two options—vocational school or regular high school. In addition to these two schools, there was also an advanced high school intended for children who exhibited superior academic abilities. Besides learning French, German, and English, students at the advanced school were required to learn classical languages such as Latin and Greek. Those students were later groomed to be doctors, lawyers, ministers, and politicians. My grades disqualified me from attending that school.

My stepfather insisted that I attend vocational school. According to him, I wasn't smart enough to make good grades anywhere else. I asked his permission, however, to attend regular high school because most of my friends were going there. To my surprise, he agreed to let me attend the school of my choice but with one condition: if I failed to pass one grade, he wouldn't hesitate to transfer me to vocational school.

As I've already described, his frequent disparaging remarks caused my defeat on many fronts. Not being able to make passable grades in high school was a foregone conclusion in his mind. And as usual, he was right. After one year in regular high school, he transferred me to vocational school to learn a trade. Only one vocational school, the Christian Vocational School of Ede, was located in the city where we lived. Out of all the basic technical professions to choose from, I decided to become an apprentice machinist.

Vocational school was a very different environment for me. Each morning began with a prayer. Before being dismissed in the afternoon, we prayed again. On Friday afternoons after the last class, we attended a mandatory school assembly for all students and teachers. There we listened to a Scripture reading, a devotional, and a prayer by the school's principal, but everything the principal said went way over my head.

Everything at the vocational school was regimented with strict rules; no one dared to break those rules for fear of severe punishment. I once fumbled with a piece of machinery. Observing me from a distance, my teacher came up behind me and roughly whacked my fingers with the edge of a long ruler. I'm surprised he didn't break any of my fingers. The pain was so bad that I couldn't use them for several days. I had no intention of breaking the equipment. Though I may not have been paying close enough attention to safely operate the piece of machinery, his physical punishment and oral reprimand in front of my classmates seemed incredibly evil to me.

Wrestling with Religion

I didn't know what to make of Christianity, Christians, or the church. My friends who had invited me to church in the past couldn't answer my questions about what I had observed in their place of worship. I simply couldn't identify myself with their lifestyle, nor did I want to. As far as I was concerned, nothing about Christianity attracted me to it. The example of my machine shop teacher certainly did little if anything to make Christianity more appealing to me.

In spite of my not-so-favorable impression of the Christian faith, I learned to pray. Let me hasten to add, however, that I prayed only when in dire need or in deep anguish because of something my stepfather had said to me. I remember lying awake in bed many nights, wounded and teary eyed, crying out to God and asking Him to explain the reasons behind my stepfather's harsh and cruel treatment. There was no answer. I never saw his behavior change toward me or anyone else in my family.

Looking back at my childhood and knowing what I know today, I can only surmise that God was working behind the scenes, preparing the soil of my heart, and directing me on a path that would eventually cause me to flee into His gentle, loving, and wide-open arms.

> A farmer went out to sow his seed. As he was scattering the seed, some fell along the path, and the birds came and ate it up. Some fell on rocky places, where it did not have much soil. It sprang up quickly, because the soil was shallow. But when the sun came up, the plants were scorched, and they withered because they had no root. Other seed fell among thorns, which grew up and choked the plants. Still other seed fell on good soil, where it produced a crop—a hundred, sixty or thirty times what was sown. He who has ears, let him hear.
> —Matthew 13:3–9

On the journey of my life, people crossed my path and planted seeds. But it was God who in His time caused those seeds to grow and flourish.

Your friend,
John

Four

A Mariner's Calling

My dear friend,

I have been a dreamer for much of my life. When I was a little boy, I dreamed of someday becoming the captain of a ship and sailing the oceans of the world.

Our voyage from Indonesia to Holland on the passenger liner MS *Willem Ruys* in February 1950 made a big impression on me. The trip took us through the Indian Ocean, the Red Sea, the Mediterranean Sea, the Atlantic Ocean, and the English Channel. I can still see myself as a scrawny six-year-old leaning on the ship's handrail, mesmerized, daydreaming for hours, savoring the fresh and gentle ocean breeze, and looking out over the vast expanse of the seemingly endless waters.

Our cabin was located on the ship's lower deck. My bunk bed was positioned in such a way that I could easily look out the cabin's porthole and see a breathtaking, close-up view of the ocean. When my parents weren't around, I sometimes lay flat on my stomach, carefully unscrewed the large, brass wing nuts, stuck the upper part of my body out the open porthole, and gazed at the high waves with outstretched arms. During my little escapades, it was a thrill to be showered with a million tiny, airborne droplets of salty ocean spray.

OUT TO SEA

Three of my older cousins had joined the Dutch merchant fleet. After listening to many exciting stories upon their return from overseas travels, I too decided someday to join their ranks, sail the world's vast oceans, explore uncharted territories, and visit exotic places.

My opportunity came when I graduated from vocational school as a sixteen-year-old apprentice machinist. Much to my delight, I received permission from my parents to join the Dutch merchant marines. Wasting no time, I immediately registered with a maritime employment agency in Amsterdam.

When the man processing my application asked if I could cook, my answer was, "No, sir." He must have sensed that I desperately wanted to sail the oceans. With a smile on his face, he said, "I don't think that'll be a big problem. I'm certain someone on that ship will gladly show you how to master the art of cooking."

Except for a cook position, no vacancies were available for someone with my limited qualifications. Even though I knew nothing about cooking, I was eager to take on the assignment and leave home. I figured that in whatever little time was left before reporting for duty, Mother could teach me all I needed to know about becoming a ship's chef. Unfortunately, there wasn't time.

When I completed all the administrative formalities, I was told to report in two days to a ship that was in the process of being loaded with steel destined for Sweden. I naturally assumed that the man at the maritime employment agency had known what he was talking about; someone on that ship would provide the required on-the-job-training.

I was filled with excitement and enthusiasm when my stepfather took me to the train station early that morning. Three hours later, I triumphantly and proudly marched up the narrow gangplank and reported to the ship's captain for duty. To my disappointment, the ship's appearance was unimpressive. It resembled an old rust bucket. Despite the ship's unpleasant, less-than-perfect nautical features, I was determined to maintain a good attitude and become the best sailor in the entire Dutch merchant fleet.

The ship's crew consisted of the captain, first mate, a sailor, and me. Immediately after my arrival, we set out to sea.

Sleeping quarters came at a premium. Not surprisingly, I was assigned the last vacant bunk directly above the engine compartment. The constant loud and annoying clanging noise of the ship's engine was so overwhelming that continuous exposure could have permanently damaged one's hearing. I had no hot running water, and except for the captain's quarters, the vessel lacked any form of comfort.

No Leisurely Vacation

Once we were out at sea, it didn't take long for Captain Josef van der Graaf to discover that I couldn't so much as boil a pot of potatoes. I carefully explained to him what I had been told, to which he angrily replied, "I run a ship, not a floating cook school on the ocean!" (expletives deleted). The captain had good reason to be upset, but for him to make my life miserable didn't seem fair. He was no friendly chap and had nothing good to say to me throughout my ordeal on the ship.

The captain instructed the first mate that in addition to his regular duties he would now function as cook with me as his helper. He assigned me the additional unpleasant role as deck swabber. I sensed that the captain was determined to get even with me by making sure this journey wasn't going to be a leisurely vacation.

I quickly became seasick and felt miserable for days. The captain took no pity on me and put me to work. The ship was so heavily weighed down with steel that the upper deck was virtually below sea level. Frankly, I didn't think we were going to survive the trip to Sweden; not much time passed before the Dutch coastline disappeared beyond the horizon. By nightfall, I almost wished that I'd stayed home and didn't want to continue on what I perceived to be a potentially perilous journey.

The captain, who must have been in his mid to late forties, didn't fit my image of a ship's captain. He never wore a shirt; seldom combed his dark, bushy hair; possessed a beer belly that hung ten inches below his belt; smoked like a chimney; and drank Dutch gin flavored with slices of fresh lemon from morning till night. Remarkably, I never saw the man inebriated. He spent most of his time at the helm, sipping his favorite beverage and dishing out orders. Amazingly, he kept the old rust bucket afloat and on course.

Whenever possible, I kept my distance from this man—and for good reason. He took great pleasure in harassing me at every turn. When things didn't go his way, he threatened to throw me overboard. He also had an unpleasant demeanor, was quick to anger, and used a selection of words that would have made a drunken sailor blush.

When I wasn't helping the first mate prepare meals, I spent a lot of time on my knees, scraping rust off with an old, worn-out steel brush or painting the "old rust bucket." The almost four-week journey took us to Germany, Denmark, Sweden, Finland, and back to Holland. Lacking a friend on this boat, I sometimes felt very lonely.

Fried Rice

One day our newly appointed cook prepared a dish of freshly cooked green beans, along with meat, gravy, and potatoes. After the meal, I mistakenly commented to the captain that the beans tasted pretty good.

"Good!" he exclaimed. In a not-so-pleasant tone, he added, "Since you like them so much, you get to eat every stinking green bean left in the pot, and I will stay here to make sure that you eat every one of them! I don't care if they start falling out of your nose or ears!"

I was so scared of that man that I ate—with great difficulty, I might add—the remaining two to three pounds of green beans. Feeling miserable afterwards, I definitely wished that I had stayed home.

I had watched my mother cook fried rice a few times and hoped to gain the first mate's favor one day by offering to prepare a sumptuous meal of fried rice. He reluctantly agreed to let me give it a try on the condition that he would carefully observe every move I made. Midway through the process, he angrily shoved me aside, grabbed whatever I had already prepared, and ordered me to throw the concoction overboard.

"You know as much about cooking fried rice as I know about swimming the ocean with a two-ton brick around my neck!" he yelled.

Our chef then proceeded to demonstrate to me how to properly cook a sailor's version of fried rice. When he was almost done, he mixed his creation of "stimulating flavor" with a half bottle of cooking oil, causing everyone to experience diarrhea within hours after our evening supper. Naturally, I was blamed for the mishap.

A Profound Mistake

After we unloaded the ship of its cargo in Sweden, we crossed the Baltic Sea for Finland, where the vessel was loaded with timber. To my amazement, the cargo was stacked so high on the upper deck that it almost obstructed the view of whoever was at the helm. I panicked at the thought of getting lost at sea and never seeing my mother and siblings again.

The rusty, old freighter didn't travel very fast, and on her journey home sailed by a number of beautiful, densely wooded, small islands along the Swedish coastline. Long bridges connected many of these islands. As we approached the first bridge, while still at a considerable distance from it, I casually remarked to the captain that the ship might not be able to clear the bridge because of the cargo. As usual, my comment to him was a profound mistake.

He angrily reached for a battery-powered bullhorn and ordered me to stand on the bow of the ship and shout in English, "Raise the bridge! Raise the bridge!" I wasn't to stop shouting until we had reached our objective. The incident was embarrassing because our destination was almost an hour away. By the time we arrived, I had lost all strength in my jaws and had no breath left—much to the amusement of the captain and crew.

In spite of its enormous pile of cargo, our ship had sufficient room to clear the bridge. I was thankful that no one on the bridge had observed my humiliating performance.

Longing for Home

Despite the many problems at home, I longed for my mother, my siblings, and my friends. I began to count every minute left on the journey.

Late one afternoon, after having been away from home for nearly four weeks, which seemed like a lifetime, I saw the approaching Dutch coastline on the distant horizon. I had never realized until then that

Holland held such a strong appeal for me. I was overjoyed when I learned that we would sail to a seaport on the northeastern shore and unload our cargo.

Without requesting permission, I wasted no time and ran below deck to pack my personal belongings in anticipation of going home. I had no question in my mind that I would disembark this ship with or without pay and with or without anyone's permission.

Soon after the ship docked in Harlingen and cleared customs, the captain handed me three cartons of cigarettes and a small envelope with pay. He wished me well and said he was sorry things hadn't worked out. The money was barely enough to purchase a taxi ride to the train station and a one-way train and bus ticket to my grandmother's home.

I caught the last train out. When I finally arrived at her house in the middle of the night, I crawled into a real bed and slept continuously for almost two days.

Yet man is born to trouble as surely as sparks fly upward.
—Job 5:7

As I closed my eyes that night, my dreams of becoming captain of a ship vanished forever.

Your friend,
John

Five

Fly Away

My dear friend,

Grandfather Hein, my hero, died on February 18, 1958, at the age of seventy-six. The day was very sad for me because I adored him. All my life, I greatly respected and admired this kindhearted man who had always demonstrated his love and affection for his grandchildren.

As a war hero from his early colonial days, Grandfather was entitled to a military funeral with pomp and circumstance, a grand affair to which the townsfolk of Hattem were not accustomed. I wanted to attend my grandfather's funeral and say my last farewell as well as witness and be part of the solemn pageantry, but my stepfather ordered me to stay home and go to school.

"You have no business being there!" he said.

As always, his remarks fueled the fires of deep hatred I harbored toward him.

AN UNEXPECTED INVITATION

Not long after Grandfather's death, Grandmother moved in with Aunt Julie, Uncle Hendrik, and their son, Jake, in another part of Hattem. Throughout my teen years, I visited Grandmother regularly, and Jake and I became good buddies. During one of these visits, Aunt Julie approached me.

"We're moving to California," she said. "Would you like to come live with us?" Her facial expression told me she wasn't joking.

I almost fell out of my chair. I was seventeen and so eager to flee from home that I would have enthusiastically moved anywhere with them. Besides, moving to America was a boyhood dream.

When I was younger, other boys and girls spent their money on candy and ice cream. But I saved a portion of my meager weekly allowance to buy something much more intriguing: a copy of *Life* magazine. I didn't know one word of English, but I sure enjoyed looking at pictures of life in America. Once a month I jumped on my bike, pedaled to the local bookstore, and purchased the latest copy, treating it with utmost care.

I can still see myself lying on my stomach on my bedroom floor, looking at the pictures, and daydreaming about when I would live in America—far away from my stepfather. My tiny bedroom, measuring about eight feet by ten feet, was the safest place in the whole world; it was my little shelter. I felt threatened within the confines of our home if I was anywhere outside my bedroom door.

What sparked my interest in America even more than *Life* magazine were movies about cowboys and Indians. Nothing was more exciting on a Saturday or Sunday afternoon than going to Rheehorst, the local theater, and seeing John Wayne, Burt Lancaster, Gregory Peck, Gary Cooper, Richard Widmark, and many other great actors starring in a Western movie. During the days following our seeing one of these movies, my friends and I acted out what we'd seen on the big screen. One day I was a gunslinging cowboy; another day I played the role of an Indian with my makeshift bow and arrow.

During this time, Mother frequently took me to a friend's house to watch the TV show *Father Knows Best*. I naively assumed that the show portrayed the life of a typical American family and wanted so much to be part of it. I didn't have a loving father who cared for his wife and children the way Robert Young did in that show.

During my teen years, I also listened to popular American music: Bill Hailey and the Comets, Patsy Cline, Fats Domino, the Everly Brothers, Elvis, The Platters, Pat Boone, and Jim Reeves, to name a few. Each time I visited my grandparents, Aunt Connie tried to teach me how to dance the rock and roll. Each year on New Year's Eve, many friends, neighbors, and family members converged at The Look Out to eat and dance to American music throughout the night until early on New Year's Day.

As you can see, I had fallen in love with America long before I ever set foot on its soil. I had also heard stories about California from family members who had moved there and had fallen in love with the place. So when Aunt Julie invited me to live with her family there, it was like being struck by a bolt of lightning—except this bolt felt wonderful.

Like most of my relatives, Aunt Julie wasn't aware of the full extent of my home troubles. However, I'm certain she suspected that something wasn't right. It was common knowledge that she wasn't particularly fond of my stepfather. Once she openly scolded him after he slapped me across my face for something that had seemed trivial to her.

Immigration

Returning home after my visit, I excitedly told my parents about Aunt Julie's offer and described how much I wanted to move to California. The thought had never occurred to me that they might object; thankfully, they didn't. My stepfather's only comment was that I'd be back in no time because I wouldn't be able to survive without his support.

Those words became the impetus for me to do something constructive with my life and to prove to him and myself that I wasn't the stupid idiot he always made me out to be. I was determined to show him that I didn't need his help or advice, no matter how rough things became. I also made up my mind never to return home again.

Uncle Hendrik explained in great detail the steps I needed to take to immigrate to the "land of the free" and the "home of the brave." Another piece of great news was that Aunt Connie and her husband, Henk, who were my good friends, had learned of my new adventure and agreed to finance my move across the ocean without my asking.

Like most western European nations, Holland was recovering from World War II. Unemployment was high, and many migrated to foreign lands—the majority moving to Canada, Australia, and New Zealand—hoping to find a better future. Many families also relocated to South Africa while others made a new living in Brazil, Argentina, or the United States. It wasn't unusual to learn that some of my school friends were suddenly packing their belongings and moving to a remote part of the world. It was an accepted fact that once you moved, you'd probably never see your friends again.

My first step on this journey was to visit the United States consulate general in Rotterdam and obtain the necessary information and documentation needed to immigrate to America. This process can sometimes take up to a year before approval is granted and the individual or families are issued necessary visas for permanent residence in the United States. It was an exhilarating feeling to receive a letter in the mail one day from the U.S. consulate general, informing me that my application to immigrate to the United States had been approved.

Since Uncle Hendrik had already started his own process, he and his family moved ahead of me. They left Holland in March of 1962 and moved to California. I followed them three months later, on June 26th.

Temptation

The evening before my departure, Mother cooked one of my favorite meals: juicy steak, fried potatoes, buttered peas and carrots, a great salad, and dessert. As usual, my stepfather dominated the dinner table conversation. He said something about American immigration procedures that prompted me to reply and disagree. As was his custom, he cruelly dismissed my remark with sarcasm.

At that moment—and for the first time in my life—I literally wanted to explode because I'd endured all I could take from this man. His cruel remark was the icing on the cake. I became so angry that I longed to reach for an eight-inch-long kitchen knife, which was within arm's reach, lunge across the dining room table, and go for his throat.

I was overcome with great anguish. In a split second I thought of the consequences and reasoned that the act wasn't worth the price. Going to prison for the better part of my life didn't bother me, but I couldn't stand the thought of not stepping on the airplane the following day and flying across the great ocean to the land of my dreams. As usual, I kept my cool, suppressed my vengeful feelings, and remained silent for the rest of the evening.

I shamefully confess that I often fantasized about murdering my stepfather. The only thing that prevented me from acting on my wild fantasies was that I loved my mother and simply couldn't bear to add more grief and misery to her already-difficult life. Though opportunities for revenge were plentiful, I'm very thankful that I never acted on those emotions.

READY TO GO

The next morning, on our way to Schiphol International Airport in Amsterdam, we stopped at a photographer's studio in town for a family portrait. Sponsored by the Episcopal Church USA, I had been sent a button to wear so the representative from that organization would recognize me upon my arrival in New York and assist me with immigration formalities. I proudly wore the button on my suit for the family portrait.

All I could think about during our one-hour drive to the airport was stepping on the airplane, trying hard to forget the past, looking to the future, and never coming back. Nothing about visiting the home where I had grown up appealed to me. No one, not even my mother, suspected how much anger, hatred, and bitterness were bottled up inside me. I figured this problem would gradually subside as time went on.

A few other family members joined us at the airport to say their farewells. Thankfully, we didn't have much time to waste. Soon after I checked in at the airline ticket counter, I received my ticket and boarding pass, and then hurriedly said good-bye to everyone there. I fully expected Mother to become emotionally distraught at my departure, but if she was, she didn't show it. Mother must have figured that this move was best for all of us. To my astonishment, of all my family members assembled at the airport, the only one crying was my stepfather.

I couldn't believe what I was seeing; I had never seen this man cry before. This coldhearted man, who was responsible for inflicting life-long injuries, was wishing me well with tears streaming down his face. I had no sympathy and couldn't understand what had gotten into him. For a brief moment I thought his emotional reaction might be an act of remorse, but being sorry for anything wasn't characteristic of him.

Flying

I flew with no more than twenty passengers on a KLM Royal Dutch Airlines DC-7C airplane across the great Atlantic Ocean. I still possess a copy of my airline ticket and boarding pass. Flying in those days was a luxury, and I received the royal treatment. We departed Amsterdam in the afternoon, made a brief stop in Ireland, and arrived in New York the following morning.

Upon arriving at Idlewild Airport, now JFK International, one of the first things that caught my eye was a tall, muscular, uniformed New York City police officer. His arms were folded across his chest, his sleeves were rolled up, and a pistol dangled from his hip. He looked like a cop who had walked off the set of a gangster movie; someone you didn't want to tangle with in a dark alley.

When I had lived in Holland, the police officers were unarmed. Because crime was virtually nonexistent then, they must have had boring jobs. I once spent an afternoon at the police station because my friends and I had been caught stealing a few apples from a nearby orchard. We had gotten off easily, however. Our punishment had consisted of writing the sentence "I will never steal apples again" one hundred times.

At the airport a kind lady representing the Episcopal Church USA greeted me, escorted me through customs and immigration, and asked if I wanted to take an earlier flight to Los Angeles. My response was an emphatic yes since I wanted to get there as soon as possible. She escorted me to the TWA ticket counter, where I was issued another ticket, this one for a plane leaving within the hour.

Flying on a DC-8 jetliner was a thrill after enduring an almost-thirteen-hour-long flight on a noisy, four-engine, propeller-driven airplane. I arrived at the Los Angeles International Airport almost three hours earlier than expected. Overcome with excitement, I didn't think of calling my relatives to let them know I was catching an early flight. When I arrived, no one was there to greet me.

Monrovia

Instead of waiting, I decided to take a taxi to what was to become my new home in Monrovia, approximately thirty miles east of L.A. The burly cab driver had never met someone from Holland and gave me a grand tour of the city as a special treat. After an almost-two-hour excursion, he dropped me off at Aunt Julie and Uncle Hendrik's modest, two-bedroom home near the foothills of the beautiful San Gabriel Mountains.

I instantly fell in love with everything I saw—from the drive-in theaters, banks, and restaurants, to the eight-lane freeways, skyscrapers, and fancy automobiles. Upon my arrival at Aunt Julie's house, the cab driver insisted that I pay him no more than twenty-five dollars for the entire trip.

Because no one was home, I patiently waited on the front porch for Aunt Julie and her family. The wait lasted more than a couple of hours because they were frantically searching the L.A. airport for me and checking other airlines to see if my flight had been switched to another carrier. When they gave up hope of finding me and decided to return home, they were surprised to find me sitting on their front porch.

It was a happy reunion. I knew I was going to love living with my new family in my newly adopted country. My cousin Jenny, one year older than I, later picked me up in her brand-new Chevrolet Corvair, which featured an unconventional, two-inch gearshift lever on the dashboard, and gave me a tour of Monrovia and its surrounding area.

> The Lord had said to Abram, "Leave your country, your people and your father's household and go to the land I will show you."
> —Genesis 12:1

By bedtime, I realized my boyish daydreams of living in America were no longer just dreams. I was convinced that I had died and gone to heaven!

Your friend,
John

Six

Living the Dream

My dear friend,

When I moved to California at age eighteen, everything I had dreamed of as a young boy became reality. These were times of innocence, and I didn't have a worry in the world. For the first time in many years, I was no longer living a life subjected to fear, ridicule, rejection, and intimidation. Aunt Julie and Uncle Hendrik took good care of me and life was sweet.

One of the first things I observed upon arriving in this great country was the friendliness of the American people. Most people with whom I came in contact seemed outgoing, friendly, and carefree. That's not to say that Dutch people were unfriendly, but they tend to be more reserved and to a degree somewhat stoic, especially when meeting people for the first time.

Everywhere I went, people treated me as if I were a good friend. I noticed this friendliness immediately after I stepped off the plane in New York and met the U.S. Immigration and Naturalization authorities, the customs officials, the representative from the Episcopal Church USA, the TWA airline employees, and even the cab driver at the L.A. airport.

To this day I remember the man who sat beside me on my flight from New York to Los Angeles. He portrayed the typical fifty-ish, friendly, outgoing American gentleman: conservatively dressed with a crew cut and an Ivy League appearance. He was the personification of someone pictured in *Life* magazine. This man welcomed me to America and made me feel right at home.

Many people went out of their way to help me. This helpful spirit was evident one hot summer day when my car overheated. As I pulled to the side of the road, steam billowed from under the hood, and several motorists stopped to offer assistance.

LIKE A PERMANENT VACATION

Life in America during the early sixties was fun and carefree. Living in Southern California with its hot summer climate, beautiful coastline, blooming deserts, and vast mountain ranges was like being on a permanent vacation.

During the first three months after my arrival, Aunt Julie insisted that I not rush in finding a job so I could adjust to a new life and culture and have an opportunity to explore Southern California. I loved visiting Disneyland, Knott's Berry Farm, Hollywood, Beverly Hills, and many other famous tourist attractions, most of which were within an hour's drive. I spent Saturday mornings watching Bugs Bunny, Daffy Duck, the Road Runner, Tom and Jerry, Sylvester, Tweety, and many other famous TV cartoon characters.

My first New Year's Eve was spent with a few thousand other people who were partying, camping out on the sidewalk of Colorado Boulevard in Pasadena, and awaiting the seventy-fourth annual Rose Parade.

I remember driving down the San Diego Freeway for an occasional one-day excursion to Tijuana, Mexico, and seeing virtually no traffic on those Sunday mornings.

One of my favorite pastimes was driving up the winding mountain roads behind our home. On a clear night I enjoyed a spectacular view of the San Gabriel Valley and portions of the Los Angeles Basin. There in front of me sparkled a seemingly endless sea of lights.

Each year Uncle Frank, who had immigrated with his family to the United States two years earlier, took me, Jake, and others deer hunting during the hot summer hunting season. Hunting was something I had never done before. Except for air pellet guns, ownership of any type of firearm had been strictly forbidden in Holland. The little bit of hunting that did occur had been reserved for a select few.

Although we seldom saw or killed a deer, I had a great time listening to Uncle Frank's wild war stories and exaggerated fishing tales. I savored many delicious meals prepared over campfires in the mountains high above Ventura, California.

Buying a Car and Finding a Job

In no time I felt settled and right at home in my newly adopted country. Soon after my arrival, I began taking driving lessons from a local driving school because I needed a car so I could get around and eventually find a job. Learning how to drive in an AMC (American Motors Corporation) Rambler in the area where we lived and to maneuver my way through busy traffic on the Los Angeles freeways was a cinch. I passed my written exam and driving test on my first attempt. I was as proud as I could be.

The next step was to buy a car. It was extremely exciting to go out one day and buy my first car. Uncle Frank was the family's car expert and was a little biased toward Chevrolet. At his strong urging, he suggested that I buy a Chevy from a nearby dealer. I arrived with an entourage of family members early one evening and selected a vehicle in excellent shape, a light blue 1953 Chevrolet Bel-Air for three hundred dollars.

During my first day as owner, I drove the car continuously throughout the night and into early the next morning, exploring Los Angeles and the surrounding area. At that time in Holland, having a driver's license—let alone a car—at age eighteen was unthinkable. I kept the vehicle for one year, then traded it in for a V-8 1957 Chevrolet Bel-Air.

I found a job as a welder at a factory in nearby Irwindale, where contemporary office furniture was manufactured. I proudly drove my fancy, white '57 Chevy with a chrome-encased spare tire mounted on the rear bumper. Unlike my first automobile, this one had cost $750 and had come equipped with power steering, power brakes, and power windows. It had come in nearly perfect condition without so much as a dent or scratch. Even the upholstery had looked like new.

Adjusting to a New Culture

Nearly every Friday or Saturday evening, my family and I loaded up the car and went to Big Sky, a nearby drive-in theater where we watched two movies for only a few dollars. The movies were called "double features" in those days. At the drive-in snack bar, I developed a taste for hot tamales, tacos, burritos, enchiladas, hamburgers, hot dogs, and popcorn.

We often went to the grocery store together and piled up a big shopping cart with groceries. Less than thirty dollars provided plenty for the four of us to eat in an entire week. At the time, whoever bagged our groceries also took them to our vehicle and loaded them into our trunk. I was amazed at the size of grocery stores and the variety of food products stocked on the shelves. I soon became addicted to Swanson's TV Dinners.

Self-serve gas stations were nonexistent then. The station's attendant gassed up our vehicle, cleaned the front windshield, and checked the oil level and tire pressure.

I earned $325 per month at my job and felt like a king. I saved enough money to pay for my mother's visit during the summer of 1963. The round-trip airfare from Amsterdam to Los Angeles was approximately five hundred dollars.

It was great seeing Mother again. She spent a month with us and had an opportunity to see much of the great state of California. She loved to shop at Sears & Roebuck, visit Hollywood and Beverly Hills, and admire the homes of famous movie stars. Mother couldn't believe her eyes when she saw the giant sequoia trees at Yosemite National Park. After she returned to Holland, I regularly stayed in touch with her and my siblings through letters; however, I didn't directly communicate with my stepfather.

The Assassination

President John F. Kennedy was my new hero, and I took every opportunity to watch him on television. I saw the movie *PT-109* twice in the theater and saw it a few more times on television. I'm certain that you've heard the famous question, "Where were you when President Kennedy was shot?" I worked the third shift and usually slept during the day. Therefore, I was asleep in bed when the news flash came that JFK had been shot on Friday, November 22, 1963, in Dallas, Texas.

Aunt Julie was ironing clothes and watching television when the program was interrupted by the announcement that JFK had been shot.

My aunt immediately woke me when she heard the horrible news. I quickly got dressed and with the rest of the family remained glued to the television for three days until his burial at Arlington National Cemetery.

The whole nation was in shock. His death seemed completely unbelievable. I was terribly disappointed that such an awful thing could happen in this great, wonderful land of ours. I simply couldn't fathom why anyone would want to murder such a great man and do so in such a cowardly fashion.

The death of President Kennedy and the events immediately following his assassination had a profound, lasting effect on me. It was a great tragedy I will remember until my dying day.

Citizenship

Despite the horrible events surrounding the death of our president, I was proud to be part of the American scene and couldn't wait to become an American citizen. Much inspired by President Kennedy, I was determined to "earn" my American citizenship. I will always remember that famous line in his inaugural address: "Ask not what your country can do for you; ask what you can do for your country!"

Those words inspired me to obtain my citizenship but not in the ordinary way—submit an application, answer the proverbial U.S. citizenship test questions, raise my right hand, and recite the oath. No, I was going to do something to contribute to the good of our nation, but how that would work itself out, I didn't know. I figured by the time I was eligible for U.S. citizenship I would have a better picture of how to demonstrate my love for and devotion to my newly adopted country.

> When times are good, be happy;
> but when times are bad, consider:
> God has made the one
> as well as the other.
>
> —Ecclesiastes 7:14

Your friend,
John

Seven

A Different Kind of Fireworks

My dear friend,

Of all my aunts—and I had quite a few—I was closest to Aunt Julie. Before our move to America, she often secretly slipped me spending money or surprised me with an occasional gift. She cautioned me not to mention her generosity to my stepfather because he certainly wouldn't have approved. Once she purchased me a new suit, including a nice pair of shoes and a matching tie. When I arrived home, proudly wearing my new outfit, my stepfather became unglued.

Living with Aunt Julie's Family

Family members criticized Aunt Julie for inviting me to live with her and her family in California, but I will always think of her as someone who cared enough to take me under her wing.

Her husband, Uncle Hendrik, was of noble birth—in fact, he was a direct descendant of the city of Amsterdam's thirteenth-century founder. More important than his noble birth was his exemplary character; he was a kind, soft-spoken, and patient man. In fact, to this day I consider him to be the most patient man I've ever known. It was not in his nature to exhibit anger or resentment. He never complained, was never moody, and always seemed to be in good spirits. What a striking contrast Uncle Hendrik was to my stepfather!

I will always be grateful to Aunt Julie and Uncle Hendrik, whom I considered my surrogate parents, for welcoming me into their home and including me as part of their family. Their son, Jake, was not only like a younger brother but also a good friend.

Many Festering Wounds

Though time and distance now separated me from my stepfather's humiliating words and actions, years of emotional abuse left many festering, unhealed wounds. Of course, I was always careful to hide my persistent hatred and bitterness toward my stepfather. An expert at disguising myself behind a thousand masks and erecting walls around my heart, I limited my friendships to only a handful of people. They were those with whom I felt closely connected, those who wouldn't pose a threat.

Beneath my defenses lingered a negative view of myself. I learned to believe most of what my stepfather had told me over the years, beliefs that contributed to my poor self-esteem. Naturally, I assumed that everyone I met, particularly adults, would see me as my stepfather had—stupid, inept, and ignorant.

Silenced

As a young adult, I had become oversensitive to criticism, and my feelings were easily hurt. On those rare occasions when someone hurt my feelings, regardless of whether the hurt was intentional, I was profoundly wounded and retreated deeply inside myself, unable to talk as if my jaws were clamped shut. No matter how hard I tried to verbalize what was on my heart, I couldn't utter a sound, as if my brain experienced a chemical reaction over which I had no control.

I have struggled with this problem of withdrawal for much of my adult life, and thankfully it was not an everyday occurrence at that time. But when it did return, Aunt Julie didn't know what to make of it. In fact, all her valiant attempts at getting me to talk inevitably failed. I simply couldn't discuss my feelings with her or anyone else.

In turn, these episodes—sometimes lasting as long as two, three, or four days—only increased my negative feelings about myself and made me feel sorry for those affected by my strange behavior. I would have given anything to have been able to open up and share my feelings with someone—anyone—but nothing seemed to solve my problem. I wished I could run to the local drug store and buy a supply of "talk pills." *They would have solved my problems*, I thought. Sadly, in spite of all the advances in the field of modern medicine, such a product remains conspicuously absent from store shelves.

I also wished I was able to cry, an emotional release that perhaps would have solved many problems. But, you see, my stepfather forbade me to cry. He taught me at a very young age that boys do not cry. Crying was only for girls and sissies, he said. Well, I wasn't about to let anyone label *me* a sissy, no matter what. And because I was so afraid of my stepfather's punishment, I had conditioned myself not to cry no matter how painful the circumstances.

THREE SIMPLE WORDS

But one day when I was twenty-one, everything changed. I again suffered another painful episode of withdrawal, but this time Aunt Julie had reached her limit of patience and could endure my problem no longer.

I remember that I was outside in her backyard, emotionally paralyzed, while she was inside the house. Several times she had already gently prodded me to talk, but as usual her efforts hadn't gone anywhere. She must have been at her wit's end. Perhaps that's why she tried a different approach this time.

She tapped on the kitchen window and motioned me to come inside.

As I entered the kitchen, she said in a stern voice, "Follow me into the living room."

I obeyed her, wondering what she had in mind.

"I want you to sit on the sofa," she said.

As I sat, she took her place beside me. Then she put her arm around me and said something no one else in my entire life, not even my own mother, had told me up to that point. To make certain that I understood her words, she said in a firm but gentle voice, briefly pausing between each word, "I . . . love . . . you!"

Even now, my eyes well up with tears when I remember that intense, dramatic moment.

Because of what happened next, I no longer imagined running to the local drug store and seeking a remedy for people like me. At twenty-one years of age, I was sobbing, crying my heart out. I made no attempt to stop the tears and allowed them all to come.

The crying felt so good! All the tears that had been bottled up inside me since I was a boy—and there must have been an incalculable number—continued to pour out of me with loud weeping and wailing.

Aunt Julie, now with both arms wrapped around me, joined me in joyful chorus. I can best describe that moment as beautiful fireworks going off all around me. I never wanted them to end because the emotional release felt so wonderful.

After Aunt Julie uttered those three simple but profound words, I immediately thought, *How is it possible that anyone would love* me? That thought is a fair description of how I felt about myself at the time. I hadn't the slightest idea that people were supposed to *love* each other. No one else had ever told me that he or she *loved* me.

I assumed that we were born into this world to make the best of this life, to die, and then to see what comes next. Love had never entered the picture. My parents had never said those words to me, and I had never heard anyone else say them other than in a Hollywood movie. And then I figured those words were exclusively reserved for young couples in love to utter to each other in the bedroom. But what does 1 Corinthians 13 say?

> If I speak in the tongues of men and of angels, but have not love, I am only a resounding gong or a clanging cymbal. If I have the gift of prophecy and can fathom all mysteries and all knowledge, and if I have a faith that can move mountains, but have not love, I am nothing. If I give all I possess to the poor and surrender my body to the flames, but have not love, I gain nothing. Love is patient, love is kind. It does not envy, it does not boast, it is not proud. It is not rude, it is not

self-seeking, it is not easily angered, it keeps no record of wrongs. Love does not delight in evil but rejoices with the truth. It always protects, always trusts, always hopes, always perseveres.

—vv. 1–7

I'm amazed at how three short, simple, yet incredibly powerful words forever changed my outlook on life! I became more conscious of my emotional imperfections and determined to work on them, knowing that it was not easy for those around me to deal with my inward struggles.

Your friend,
John

Eight

You're in the Army Now

My dear friend,

The letter in my hand said to bring three sets of clean underwear, extra socks, shaving gear, a toothbrush, and toothpaste. It said to report the following month to the U.S. Armed Forces Entrance and Examination Station (AFEES) in Los Angeles. I received this notice from the local draft board in early March 1965, informing me of my imminent induction into the United States Armed Forces. The letter also informed me that I would undergo a thorough medical examination and a battery of tests to determine if I was physically and mentally fit to serve.

Fears

Though I don't like to admit it, the letter scared me to death. I assumed that everyone who wore a soldier's uniform was a carbon copy of my stepfather, and I wasn't sure if I was prepared or willing to be subject to more abuse.

For weeks I kept scheming how I could avoid the draft. I knew that at some point in the future I would be drafted into military service, but I had no idea that it would come so soon. I wasn't yet eligible for U.S. citizenship and couldn't understand why the United States wanted me to serve. I also understood that not reporting for duty was a violation of federal law, which meant I could be prosecuted and sent to prison or be deported back to the Netherlands. Neither of these were options I considered. I had no intention of spending time in prison or going back to Holland.

I was so unsettled by this letter that I couldn't sleep. Nearly every night, I lay awake in bed for hours, tossing and turning and pondering my next move. This sleeplessness went on for several weeks until early one morning, having run out of a thousand excuses, I said to myself, *You know what? Millions went before me, they did it, and I can do it too!* Miraculously, it seemed as if a heavy burden were lifted off my shoulders. I was able to sleep again, and life gradually returned to normal. Isn't it strange how attitudes affect our lives?

Processing

Approximately three weeks later, before dawn on April 20, 1965, Uncle Hendrik dropped me off at the AFEES station. I was shaking in my boots as I said good-bye. Between 150 and 200 men, mostly my age or younger, were there in a similar predicament. I quickly learned that I wasn't the only one who was scared. Thankfully, making a few new friends didn't take me long.

The old AFEES station was a drab, lifeless, three-story office building situated in the heart of Los Angeles. Like so many of its neighboring structures, its appearance wasn't very attractive. The facility was used to process new recruits for service in the U.S. Army, Navy, Marines, and Air Force. The hallway floors were painted with lines, each of a distinct color.

I quickly learned what these lines were for. We were divided into four separate groups. To minimize congestion and unnecessary delays at each processing point, each group was instructed to follow a specific line color. My group was told to follow the yellow line. I don't think the yellow line was intended for cowards even though I may have felt a little cowardly that morning. It was a simple, clever idea because you'd never get lost in the maze of hallways and offices if you followed your designated line and went from one station to the next. At one particular station I underwent a lengthy interview; at another I completed a myriad of forms; at yet another I underwent a series of tests.

The doctors' station was humiliating because that's where we had to drop our shorts in front of everyone and make our way from one medical expert's desk to the next. There was no privacy, and the examination process resembled an assembly line. I was glad when it was over.

We all got a good taste of the "hurry up and wait" administrative military formalities. We learned that two prospective recruits had been sent home for medical reasons. The rest of us were assigned to the four different branches of the service, the vast majority inducted into the U.S. Army.

Late that afternoon, everyone assembled in a special office. We were ordered to stand at attention and raise our right hands as the AFEES commander administered the oath of enlistment. Those individuals destined to become soldiers in the United States Army were told that they would be transported to the Los Angeles International Airport for a flight to Fort Polk, Louisiana, for basic training. As we boarded the bus for the airport, two men handed each of us a pocket-sized New Testament. I kept the little, green-colored Gideon Bible but saw no need to read it.

Fort Polk

The army must have faced a logistical nightmare. Since Fort Ord was closed due to a meningitis outbreak, recruits were transported to different training bases across the nation. Thousands of other recruits and I would have ordinarily been shipped to Fort Ord. Instead, we flew in three modified, World War II, vintage, DC-3 propeller-driven airplanes to an airfield in the vicinity of Fort Polk in Louisiana.

The flight was long, noisy, and uncomfortable. I was thankful when we made a one-hour refueling stop in Dallas, Texas, and were able to take a stretch break. These aircraft belonged to Texas International Airlines, which was under contract to the U.S. Army to transport new recruits. I couldn't figure out why the state of Texas had its own international airline. I suppose that's how they conduct business in Texas.

The reception by army drill sergeants in the middle of the night was anything but cordial. We were immediately herded onto buses and transported to the U.S. Army Reception Station at nearby Fort Polk.

Louisiana may be known as a sportsman's paradise, but Fort Polk resembled anything but a paradise. After only a few hours of sleep, we were rudely awakened to the famous and "melodious" *You're in the Army Now* bugle call and the hollering of drill sergeants.

The army wasted little time indoctrinating us into the soldier's life. The process began at the reception station, where we were issued a duffel bag full of uniforms and other equipment. In addition, we listened to lecture after lecture, took another series of tests, underwent more medical and dental examinations, received immunizations, and learned what we would be doing for the rest of our two or (for some) three-year army assignment. Because I had been a welder in civilian life, I was going to be a welder in the army for the next two years.

BASIC TRAINING

After twelve long days at the reception center, we were each assigned to our basic training company. Thankfully, most of the men I had befriended and become acquainted with at the AFEES station, and then at the reception center, were assigned to my company. Packed like sardines in open "cattle cars," we were transported to another part of Fort Polk. We were assigned to Company C, Fourth Battalion, Second Infantry Brigade, which was to become our home for the next eight weeks. I don't know where these vehicle drivers had obtained their licenses, but the trip to our basic training company was no pleasure ride. In fact, I was surprised that no one was seriously injured at the hands of these reckless, crazy drivers.

Basic training at Fort Polk was no picnic. My monthly salary as a recruit or Private E-1 (the letter E designating an enlisted soldier) was only seventy-eight dollars. Like so many of my fellow recruits, I was usually broke by the middle of the month and borrowed money from a few shrewd company loan sharks to get through the rest of the month. I figured that if I was going to make it through basic training and stay out of trouble, I'd better maintain a good attitude and strive to be a good soldier. I confess that I didn't excel at everything, but I did the best I could.

We trained long and hard six and sometimes seven days per week, often in blistering heat. The Louisiana humidity was sometimes unbearable. We learned to drink lots of water and consume plenty of salt tablets to prevent being stricken by heat stroke.

Each morning for breakfast, we ate S.O.S., a thick, brownish, gravy-like substance poured over a biscuit. I never touched the stuff due to its peculiar odor. Instead, I liked to eat grits, toast, and eggs.

We had little time to sleep. As a result, staying awake and alert was hard, especially during the many afternoon classroom sessions.

To my knowledge, every trainee in C Company was from Southern California. Most of our drill sergeants, on the other hand, hailed from the deep South. That difference in region sometimes created quite a stir because those charged with the task of transforming our lives from civilians to soldiers didn't look favorably on young men from Southern California. Sometimes it seemed like we were getting a double portion of harassment. Despite the strenuous training during eight long weeks of boot camp, I had a good time and developed many friendships, but I was glad when basic training was over.

Fort Bliss

During our sixth week, we received orders for our permanent duty assignments. This change meant that after basic training we'd probably never see our friends again. Some were selected for more military schooling, while others received orders assigning them to overseas duty stations.

My next assignment was Fort Bliss in El Paso, Texas. It was to become my home for the remainder of my two-year active duty commitment. After graduating from basic training on June 26, 1965, I flew home for a brief respite before reporting to Fort Bliss on July 13, where I was assigned to Headquarters Company, 31st Engineer Battalion. I was glad to be assigned to a regular army outfit, where life would be a bit less stressful. One month later, on August 20, I was promoted to the rank of Private E-2. The promotion meant a few more dollars in my pocket.

As a low-ranking enlisted soldier, I spent a lot of time in the kitchen and dining hall performing KP (kitchen police) and other trivial duties. Whatever time was left I spent at the company motor pool, a facility were military vehicles were parked, maintained, and secured.

My job, commonly referred to in the army as an MOS (Military Occupational Specialty), was welding. I faced one problem, however:

nothing needed to be welded. One other soldier had the same MOS, and together we sat around the motor pool, doing nothing all day. This routine became pretty boring after a while. Except for KP duty, I volunteered for just about anything to keep me away from the motor pool.

Exactly four months later, I learned that I was being reassigned to the 13th Ordnance Company, also at Fort Bliss, because of a vacancy and the need for a welder. So just as soon as I had made new friends, I was told to pack my belongings and move on. I didn't like being reassigned, but I was determined to be a good soldier and do what I was told.

Open Doors

I quickly discovered that the workload wasn't any different at my new organization. I was assigned to the company motor pool, where little if anything needed to be done. Not long after that, at a morning formation (military assembly), the first sergeant announced an opening for a three-week typing course and wanted to know if anyone was interested. I knew nothing about typing but figured that taking a typing class beat sitting around the motor pool and being bored and unproductive. Thankfully, I was the only one in the company who volunteered. Because my presence at the motor pool wasn't critical, I was selected to attend the course.

When I finished the typing class, I was able to type no more than twenty words per minute. Yet I was soon asked if I was interested in being the clerk for Staff Sgt. Jim Lowery, the company training NCO (noncommissioned officer). Overjoyed, my response was an immediate "Yes, sir!" *Anything to keep me away from the motor pool*, I thought. I was grateful to have been offered a more meaningful job.

Just before Christmas 1965, I was promoted to private first class. I was finally honored to wear a stripe on my uniform—a good reason to be proud.

Staff Sgt. Lowery was a pipe-smoking man in his late forties who had served in Germany immediately after World War II. He and his wife had adopted an orphaned baby girl from Germany. Nearing retirement, Sgt. Lowery loved to gripe about everything: his pay, the army . . . you name it. He always found a reason to complain, but I let his complaints go in one ear and out the other. Despite his constant grumbling, I loved my new job and enjoyed working for him.

I got along great with my new supervisor and the first sergeant, whose office was next door. Being on good terms with the company's "top kick" was always important. A company commander, usually a captain, may be the one in charge, but the first sergeant dished out the orders and ran the company's day-to-day affairs. I was often selected to compete for "Soldier of the Month," or "Soldier of the Quarter." When I won, I was rewarded with a three-day pass, a twenty-five-dollar U.S. savings bond, or both. These winnings enabled me to fly home on military standby for a round-trip airfare costing less than twenty-five dollars. I never had a problem finding a vacant seat on a flight from El Paso to Los Angeles while on military standby.

After one year in the army, I was again promoted, this time to the rank of specialist fourth class (equivalent rank of corporal). I had many friends and got along great with my superiors. At about this time, I was selected to be the company's guide-on bearer. This honor meant that I carried the company's symbolic flag at formal inspections, parades, formations, and other official military functions and ceremonies. I don't wish to brag, but this was a somewhat coveted position; only soldiers who presented a spit-and-polish image and the ability to make precision movements with the flag were selected for the job.

I enjoyed participating in military drills and ceremonies. As a result, I was selected to serve on funeral details. Because of its proximity to Fort Bliss, El Paso attracted many military retirees and their families, many of whom were World War I veterans. Because many of these soldiers died during my tour, I was required to serve on funeral details almost every other week for the remainder of my time at Fort Bliss. Also, the Vietnam War had begun to escalate, and we occasionally buried a casualty of that war.

Considering Vietnam

In January 1967, our company received a new mission—to process soldiers who had finished serving their tours of duty in Vietnam. Most of these men had served with distinction and were ready to return to civilian life. My job was to conduct interviews, assist those soldiers in completing necessary forms, and help them prepare for separation from military service.

With almost every interview came the question, "What was it like over there?" To my surprise, these men said that they hadn't minded serving in Vietnam. Many in fact said that they had enjoyed "being over there" but were glad to be home, safe and sound. Several suggested that I too would enjoy serving a tour in Vietnam. Many commented that someone with my administrative qualifications would probably never see a bullet aimed in my direction.

Actually, there was a good probability that I would be assigned to a big headquarters in the capitol city of Saigon; work in air-conditioned offices; live in a comfortable hotel; eat steak each night; party with my friends; and meet pretty, petite Vietnamese girls. It all sounded very romantic. What made it even more appealing was the fact that those serving in Vietnam were exempt from paying income taxes. Moreover, each soldier serving in the war zone received an additional monthly stipend of sixty-five dollars for combat service.

Scheduled to leave the U.S. Army in less than three months, I had saved very little, if any. I reasoned that serving a tour in Vietnam, which meant extending my enlistment for only one year, would give me an opportunity to save some extra cash after my discharge. Considering the stories I had heard from those returning from the war, volunteering to serve in Vietnam seemed the logical thing to do. More importantly, I viewed service in Vietnam as my opportunity to earn my American citizenship. The situation in the war zone was relatively calm then, and though I never kept up with casualty statistics in the local paper or on the evening news, I reckoned that the odds of being killed in combat were one in one thousand.

On February 27, 1967, I was promoted to the rank of "spec five" or specialist fifth class. I was proud to have attained this rank in less than two years. It wasn't uncommon in those days for soldiers of lesser rank to retire after twenty years of military service. This promotion meant a considerable pay raise. In addition, I no longer needed to sleep in a bunk bed and share my sleeping quarters in an open bay with twenty-three other men. Assigned to a private room, I shared it with Graham Forrester, a soldier of equal rank, with whom I became the best of friends. Graham hailed from Germantown, an historic district in northwest Philadelphia, Pennsylvania.

The following month, I submitted an official request on a Department of the Army (DA) Form 1049 to extend my active duty commitment and to volunteer for duty in Vietnam. (In those days every personnel action in the army was accomplished by means of a DA Form 1049. I sometimes wondered if the army could function without those forms.) I called my aunt and uncle in California and informed them of my decision. I also wrote my mother, telling her of my intentions and carefully explaining that the odds of my becoming a war casualty weren't high enough to be worth considering.

Less than a month after submitting my request, my first sergeant called me into his office to inform me that my request for reassignment to Vietnam had been approved. I learned that I was being assigned to Headquarters, United States Military Assistance Command, Vietnam (MACV), commanded by General William C. Westmoreland. The first sergeant handed me a stack of reassignment orders and instructed me to report to Building 640 at Oakland Army Base in Oakland, California. He told me to "keep my head down" and wished me the very best.

> Many are the plans in a man's heart,
> but it is the Lord's purpose that prevails
> —Proverbs 19:21

My departure from Fort Bliss on May 1, 1967, was bittersweet. If I passionately disliked one thing about army life, it was saying farewell to my friends and making a fresh start elsewhere.

Your friend,
John

Nine

A Shattered Picture

My dear friend,

I can still see myself sitting at my desk in my Fort Bliss office and intently listening to stories from soldiers returning from the war. These guys painted a beautiful picture for me. It was the picture of a young, happy soldier pecking away at his manual Remington typewriter; working in a comfortable, air-conditioned office; oblivious to the rumble of a distant war; and enjoying a peaceful, happy life in Saigon.

Because the U.S. Army is generous in granting soldiers leave before a change of assignment, I asked for and received thirty days' leave before going to Vietnam. Having made so many weekend trips home during my almost-two-year stay in El Paso, I had become very familiar with the Los Angeles International Airport. I will always remember the airport's main terminal crowded with smartly uniformed soldiers, sailors, marines, and airmen during the buildup phase of the Vietnam War. At that time military personnel traveled in uniform. The Los Angeles International Airport was a hub for servicemen and women traveling between duty stations, the majority coming from or going to Vietnam. I was happy to be home for such an extended time, and glad to visit with a friend from basic training whom I hadn't seen in a couple of years. He was surprised to learn that I had volunteered for duty in Vietnam.

When my time came to leave, Uncle Hendrik and Jake drove me to the airport for the short flight to San Francisco. When I said good-bye to Aunt Julie, she handed me a Bible and said I should make a serious effort to read it. Her gift took me by surprise because religion, God, Christianity, church, and the Bible were topics we never discussed. I didn't question my aunt's motives in giving me a Bible or ask how she'd acquired one. In those days, you didn't see Bible bookstores as we see them in shopping centers or strip malls today. I told Aunt Julie that I appreciated her gift and packed the Bible in my duffel bag, not planning to look at it again.

Waiting

Building 640, Oakland Army Base, Oakland, California, was home of the U.S. Army's Overseas Processing Center. Virtually everyone who walked through its doors was destined for Vietnam. Thousands upon thousands of soldiers from all ranks were systematically processed for assignment to a country that was unfamiliar to most of them. I arrived on the morning of May 31, 1967.

While at the processing center, I underwent a series of routine medical and dental examinations, and received more immunizations. I also completed a myriad of administrative and legal formalities. Twice each day, names were called of those soldiers who had finished their processing. They were told to report to a designated location with their luggage for further transport to nearby Travis Air Force Base. Anxious to complete these procedures, I made sure I was ready for my next move at a moment's notice. My duffel bag was neatly packed in anticipation of flying across the Pacific Ocean.

After three long days, my name and those of many others were finally called. You'd think that after a dreadful hurry-up-and-wait hassle, they'd reward you by putting you on a plane and shipping you overseas. But after arriving at Travis Air Force Base, we discovered that we had even more waiting ahead.

We were transported by bus to a large, refurbished aircraft hangar, which had been converted into a holding facility. The poorly ventilated building was packed with wall-to-wall bunk beds, stacked two high. On arrival we were instructed to claim any vacant bunk and to once again wait until our names were called. By best estimates, five to six hundred men were waiting to be shipped overseas. We weren't allowed to leave the premises, and we were instructed to remain inside the building until our departure time. Some soldiers waited three days, while others were shipped out in less than forty-eight hours.

Lines to the public telephones inside the hangar were long. For most soldiers the telephones provided an opportunity to make last-minute phone calls to family and friends back home before stepping on the plane. Observing these men as they patiently awaited their turn, I wondered who would or wouldn't make it back to the United States alive. I instinctively knew that some of these men would hear the sweet voices of their loved ones on these phones for the last time.

Due to both excitement and anxiety, I couldn't sleep the first night I was there. Like most soldiers, I kept mostly to myself, read a few magazines, dozed off, and occasionally out of sheer boredom, wandered aimlessly around the inside perimeter of the building, impatiently waiting to hear my name called over the PA system. Everyone was obviously anxious to leave. I was no exception and desperately wanted to step on the next departing plane.

After two days in this holding pen, I finally heard my name announced for the next flight out. The journey overseas would take us on a chartered commercial Continental Airlines DC-8, first to Honolulu, Hawaii, for a refueling stop, followed by another layover at Andersen Air Force Base on the Island of Guam, before heading to our final destination.

Several hours before my departure, I joined the many soldiers patiently waiting in line to call home. When I reached Aunt Julie on the phone, I told her that I would be on my way soon. An older cousin was also serving with the U.S. Navy in Vietnam. His letters to his family and friends back home didn't worry Aunt Julie about my impending departure. She wished me well, told me to be careful, and said she looked forward to seeing me again when I finished serving my time overseas.

The fragrance of flowers welcomed us when we stepped off the plane and onto the tarmac in Honolulu that night. After a brief stopover at Andersen Air Force Base early the following morning, we touched down at Bien Hoa Air Base outside of Saigon, the capital of South Vietnam. The entire flight to Vietnam, mostly at night, had lasted between fourteen and sixteen hours.

Koelper Compound

Everyone on the plane was instructed to remain seated except those soldiers assigned to United States Military Assistance Command, Vietnam (MACV). Only a handful of us were escorted off the plane ahead of everyone else and driven in military sedans to Koelper Compound in the heart of Saigon.

You wouldn't have known a war was going on. During the ride from the air base to Saigon, I felt like I had stepped into another world. The noisy city streets were crowded with people, cars, trucks, mopeds, carts, bicycles, and stray animals. Every driver seemed to keep one hand on the steering wheel and the other glued to the horn to maneuver his way through congested, chaotic traffic. A peculiar, unpleasant odor hung in the air. It was the smell of dead fish left to dry on the corrugated tin roofs in the hot, humid tropical air.

Koelper Compound was a military processing facility for arriving and departing soldiers assigned to Headquarters MACV. We were immediately assigned to our rooms in what had once been a French hotel and instructed to take the rest of the day off to recuperate after our long flight across the ocean. Someone would wake us up the following morning, said the sergeant who had assigned us to our private rooms.

I found the dining facility and open-air movie theater located on the penthouse floor. That evening I ate my first juicy, one-inch-thick, New York prime-cut steak with French fries at what I thought would be my home for the duration of my time in Vietnam.

No one needed to wake me the following morning. The traffic noise outside the gate of Koelper Compound was my alarm clock. Our day started with a series of lengthy briefings that lasted almost an entire week. We learned such things as the history of the war and how to win the hearts and minds of the Vietnamese people. We also received regular updates on the current military conflict as well as lessons in Vietnamese culture, customs, geography, and many other topics of interest.

I discovered that MACV, in addition to exercising command and control over U.S. and allied forces in Vietnam, also consisted of advisory teams geographically dispersed from the tip of the Mekong Delta in the Deep South to the demilitarized zone (DMZ) in the far North. I was surprised to discover that some of us would be assigned to one of these advisory teams, but I quickly dismissed the thought of being assigned anywhere outside Saigon. A remote jungle outpost that lacked all the comforts of home didn't appeal to me. I felt confident that a clerk wasn't needed on an advisory team and assumed that my skills were needed right here at the comfortable headquarters in Saigon.

DA NANG

At the conclusion of the many briefings and orientations, Sgt. First Class Gerald Haldane handed me a set of orders. I was being assigned to I Corps headquarters, a major subordinate organization of MACV. I couldn't believe my assignment—I assumed it must have been a bureaucratic oversight.

When I asked the personnel sergeant about my reassignment orders, he replied, "It's no mistake. You're going to Da Nang, and you're leaving tomorrow!" Noticing my apprehension, he added, "You needn't worry. You're going to like it up there. It's a nice, quiet place with beautiful beaches and pretty women. Besides, those guys in Da Nang haven't heard a shot fired in anger yet. Trust me. You have no reason to be alarmed!"

Along with my reassignment orders, I was instructed to report to the supply room, where I was in for a few more surprises. I was issued an M-1 jungle carbine with two "banana" ammunition clips, a bulletproof vest, four sets of lightweight tropical jungle fatigues, two pairs of tropical combat boots, a helmet, a year's supply of mosquito repellent, a duffel bag full of other equipment, and many other items of clothing.

This isn't the uniform of an army clerk, I thought. I began to feel apprehensive about my impending future.

Among the many items issued to me was a jar full of pills. When I asked the supply sergeant what they were for, he said, "Oh, those pills will keep you awake at night." With a chuckle he added, "You'll need plenty of them where you're going!"

I didn't like what I was hearing, and I couldn't figure out why I, a clerk, would need to take pills to stay awake at night. I also learned that I would be traveling to my next duty station while wearing my newly issued combat outfit.

The following morning I was transported to Bien Hoa Air Base for a flight on a U.S. Air Force Hercules C-130, a four-engine propeller airplane, to Da Nang. It was an aircraft with a tailgate—in U.S. Air Force terminology, an aft-loading ramp. Much of its cargo was strapped to this tailgate.

I stepped onto the plane with fear and trepidation, not knowing what awaited me or whether I was going to make it out alive. We were seated on long rows of canvas-covered, aluminum-framed, fold-down seats facing each other. The aircraft made a brief stop at Cam Ranh Bay and picked up a few more passengers. A half dozen other soldiers were on the same flight, destined for assignment at I Corps headquarters.

The journey lasted several hours. Soon after our arrival, we traveled to what I thought was going to be my home far away from home. I trusted the personnel sergeant in Saigon and was determined to make the best of my situation.

The office facilities and sleeping quarters in Da Nang, however, were nothing like the comfortable living arrangements in Saigon. This time I shared a room. Foxholes, trenches, and barbed wire protected I Corps headquarters facilities. Sandbagged lookout posts manned by heavily armed soldiers punctuated every corner.

Late that afternoon, Colonel Robert Forbes, the Corps Commander briefed us on the mission and tactical situation in a geographic area that stretched fifty miles—from the Gulf of Tonkin to the Laotian border and from the city of Doc Pho in Quang Ngai Province to the DMZ bordering Communist North Vietnam, a distance of approximately 230 miles.

Hue

The next day was more of the same. Before the day was over, Steve Kowalski, an army clerk, informed me that two other soldiers and I were being assigned to Advisory Team 1, located in the ancient city of Hue (pronounced "way").

"Wait a minute," I protested. "This isn't what I was told by the personnel sergeant in Saigon. My permanent duty assignment is supposed to be Da Nang!"

"Sorry, there's a need for someone with your qualifications in Hue, and you'll be leaving tomorrow by helicopter," the clerk said.

I asked Kowalski exactly where Hue was located. With an ear-to-ear grin and a bit of sarcasm, he replied, "It's *way* up there!" He pointed his finger in the air.

I didn't know what to make of his gesture. I wasn't amused, nor was I happy at the thought of being assigned in close proximity to Communist North Vietnam.

I had never flown on a helicopter before. Except for its incredible noise, however, I enjoyed the almost-forty-five-minute, low-altitude flight that barely cleared the treetops. When we arrived in Hue, a young soldier met and greeted us. We were immediately transported to the office of the commander and senior province advisor, Colonel Jack Winthrop Applegate.

Short and stocky, Colonel Applegate was a hard-charging, swashbuckling, no-nonsense U.S. Army officer. With a loaded .45 caliber pistol always strapped to his shoulder, he was one of those characters we encounter in life and never forget. When Captain Billy Stevens, his administrative officer, paraded us into his office, Colonel Applegate was working at his desk. Out of the corner of my eye, I noticed that he peeked at us over the edge of his gold, wire-rimmed glasses.

With a facial expression that spelled impending doom, he suddenly jumped up from behind his desk, pointed his finger in our direction, and in a harsh tone of voice shouted, "You there!"

Not knowing if he was pointing at me, I heard him repeat himself and say, "Yes, you. Who *are* you!?"

Before I could answer, Captain Stevens interrupted, "Sir, this is Specialist Rozema. He is slated to go to Quang Tri."

I had no idea what Quang Tri was. But the sudden, explosive atmosphere in the colonel's office told me this wasn't an appropriate time to ask questions.

Turning to Captain Stevens, Colonel Applegate loudly said, "Captain, you know better than to bring a soldier who needs a haircut into my office! Take that man to the barbershop right now and bring him back when he's finished!"

I felt bad for the young officer, who escorted me to his jeep and drove me to the barbershop. When we arrived, Captain Stevens ordered the Vietnamese barber, who spoke only broken English, to cut my hair ahead of everyone else. All this took about twenty minutes, and I wasn't looking forward to returning to Colonel Applegate's office.

My two companions were sheepishly sitting on a large sofa in front of an oversized tactical situation map that covered an entire wall. Colonel Applegate was still seated at his desk. As we entered, he calmly got up and invited me to join the rest. Next, we listened to an almost-two-and-a-half-hour-long, uninterrupted lecture on the art of war in the two northern-most provinces of South Vietnam. I fully expected to be severely reprimanded, but Colonel Applegate acted as if nothing had happened. Calm and friendly, he captivated us by adding many personal anecdotes while giving us an overview of the enemy situation.

The colonel proudly told us that he had climbed the army ranks from a buck private to a colonel. He mentioned that General Westmoreland had offered to promote him to the rank of brigadier general, but he had politely turned down the offer because all he'd ever wanted to be was a colonel in the infantry. Nothing else. He boasted that he had never set foot on a college campus. With a look of glee on his face, he told us that during an interview for one of the major television networks, he had personally thrown a popular, nationally known newscaster out of his office. I don't know how many of his stories were true, but he certainly kept us spellbound with his fantastic tales.

At the conclusion of his briefing, Colonel Applegate told me that he was assigning me to Advisory Team 4 in Quang Tri, the northernmost province in South Vietnam. I would be flown there by helicopter the next day to replace a soldier who had died in an accident.

> You will hear of wars and rumors of wars, but see to it that you are not alarmed. Such things must happen, but the end is still to come.
> —Matthew 24:6

I felt betrayed by the soldiers at Fort Bliss who had told me deceptive stories about the wonderful life in Vietnam. The beautiful picture they had painted was now shattered. I had no idea what was in store for me. But whatever it was, I had a sense of foreboding about this place called Quang Tri.

                    Your friend,
                    John

Ten

Life at Kilroy Compound

My dear friend,

It didn't take long for the UH-1 helicopter to fly along the coastal plains from Hue to Quang Tri. During the flight I sat beside the soldier manning the helicopter's M-60 machine gun. I quickly learned that helicopters are easy targets and afford little protection. I wondered why anyone would want to be a pilot or gunner on these fragile, noisy aircraft in time of war.

Specialist Fourth Class Andrew Lockhart from Washington State greeted me upon my arrival at Kilroy Compound and helped me get settled. Kilroy Compound was named in honor and memory of Captain Michael W. Kilroy, the first American soldier killed in combat in Quang Tri on May 19, 1966. You will find his name engraved on the Vietnam War Memorial in Washington, D.C., among the 58,261 men and women who so valiantly lost their lives for the freedom of our nation.

Getting Situated

Lockhart introduced me to the compound commander and first sergeant, who immediately assigned me to my "hootch" (living quarters). I shared my new accommodations, which lacked every comfort and luxury, with Gildardo Escalante, a young navy corpsman (medic) from

Southern California; and Spec Five Michael Frederick McDermott from Maine. One Vietnamese maid was responsible for keeping our hootch clean. For a nominal monthly fee, she washed our dirty laundry, ironed our clothes, made our beds, and daily spit-shined our boots.

Later on the day of my arrival, I was also introduced to the commander of Advisory Team 4 and his deputy. I was assigned the job of administrative NCO. Andy Lockhart was our clerk, and Sgt. Nguyen Quai, a South Vietnamese army soldier and former schoolteacher, functioned as our translator. Captain Michael J. Rhoades, adjutant and administrative officer, was my immediate supervisor.

We worked seven days a week, but like our Vietnamese counterparts, we enjoyed a three-hour siesta from noon to 3 P.M. each day. Our offices were located at the Quang Tri Citadel, an old fortress built in 1824, which was surrounded by a murky, odorous moat littered with trash and debris.

No bigger than a small-sized town back home with twelve thousand inhabitants, Quang Tri was situated on the east bank of the Thach Han River, ten miles inland from the Gulf of Tonkin, nineteen miles south of the demilitarized zone. The bulk of the enemy's forces, including their best regiments and divisions, were stationed in the northern provinces.[1]

We had to be on our guard for North Vietnamese regular army soldiers already firmly entrenched in Quang Tri Province. Equally dangerous were the Vietcong, South Vietnamese Communist guerillas, commonly referred to as "VC" or "Charlie." These were ordinary South Vietnamese citizens who sympathized with the Communist regime in the North. They were the hidden enemy: well armed, trained for battle, and indoctrinated for service in military and paramilitary organizations. Most wore no uniforms, mingled with the crowds, and posed a great danger to the safety of our armed forces.

I was thankful that elements of the U.S. Third Marine Division were stationed in areas that separated us from North Vietnam. I figured that in the event of a large-scale invasion, the enemy would contend with a well-trained, determined, lethal fighting force. Even with the U.S. Marines' presence, Quang Tri wasn't a safe area by any stretch of the imagination.

When I wasn't working at the citadel, I was at Kilroy Compound, my home far away from home. Its main entrance and exit were located west on a road leading into Quang Tri. Wide-open rice paddies to our north separated us from the village of Tri Buu. On its eastern perimeter were other rice paddies and a distant tree line. Our small outpost, not much larger than a one-and-a-half-acre tract of land, was located on the edge of town and consisted of five rows of one-story wooden barracks—two for officers and three for enlisted personnel. In addition, we had the luxury of a recreation room, which also functioned as a makeshift movie theater. The facility also provided two small social clubs (one for officers and the other for enlisted men), a dining facility, and a large kitchen.

Our compound was protected by a four-and-a-half-foot-high perimeter berm, a mound of compacted earth with fortified, six-man bunkers stationed at approximately thirty-foot intervals. An abandoned, one-story, brick school building on the southwestern corner provided additional protection. Machine gun emplacements were also positioned at strategic points on the perimeter. An 81-millimeter mortar was situated close to its northern flank, and a twin 40-millimeter, gun-mounted half-track, known as a "Duster," was located on the northeast corner of the compound. The area immediately surrounding the compound, which included a helicopter pad, was heavily mined and protected by coils of barbed wire. Bright spotlights illuminated the open rice paddies and other potential avenues of approach at night.

Kilroy Compound, home to approximately sixty-five soldiers, sailors, marines, and airmen, was partially bordered on the south by an open field used for a helicopter landing and takeoff pad. Two heavily armed U.S. Air Force HH-3 helicopters, popularly known as "jolly green giants," were stationed at the compound during daylight hours. It wasn't safe for them to remain at the compound overnight since most attacks occurred after sundown. Therefore, these two aircraft flew to their permanent home base in Da Nang late each afternoon and return early the following morning, its crew at high alert.

Because their sole mission was to rescue U.S. fighter pilots shot down over enemy territory, Kilroy Compound's close proximity to North Vietnam made it the ideal location from which to embark on dangerous missions. During an actual rescue operation, one helicopter remained airborne, providing aerial cover, while the other helicopter's crew executed its rescue mission on the ground.

The army contingent primarily consisted of advisors to the military Regional and Popular Forces of Vietnam to include support personnel. The navy element was comprised of medical and dental personnel. These guys worked at a local Vietnamese hospital, providing free medical training and services. The twelve-man Marine Corps detachment was responsible for the security of the compound, and the air force crew operated the communications systems around the clock and provided daily aerial reconnaissance in Quang Tri Province.

The day after my arrival, I wrote to my mom in Holland and my aunt and uncle in California to inform them of my new mailing address. I also told them about my first impressions and calmed any fears they might have had about my new assignment. Within ten days, I received a reply from my mother, which became a prized possession. It was such a joy to receive letters from home during my stay in the war zone.

Guard Duty

Kilroy Compound routinely came under a short but heavy rocket and mortar attack two or three times per month, always under the cover of darkness. These attacks had no set pattern. An attack might occur at 8:00 p.m., midnight, or 5:00 a.m. It appeared that we ruled the day, while the enemy ruled the night.

I was assigned to a bunker and a guard position on the open northern perimeter berm. My instructions were to make my way to my bunker as fast as I could. If I happened to be at my guard post during an attack, however, I was to remain at my post and not leave until the danger had subsided and I was properly relieved.

Except for the advisory team's army commander and his Marine Corps deputy, everyone, regardless of rank, was required to serve as perimeter guard at night, including the navy's medical team personnel who were noncombatants. We were usually scheduled to serve as perimeter guard once a week and occasionally twice a week. In addition, a small contingent of friendly or allied South Vietnamese soldiers was stationed at the compound and assisted our Marine Corps detachment with providing security.

Guard duty meant occupying a designated guard post on the perimeter berm during the hours of darkness for two-hour shifts, staying awake and alert, and being ready to repel a potential ground attack. One soldier was court-martialed and immediately reassigned because he had fallen asleep while on guard duty. Though smoking on guard duty was also prohibited, I broke this rule many times by keeping my cigarettes lit and taking frequent drags under the cover of my poncho.

Shortly after my arrival, a two-and-a-half-ton truck parked in close proximity to our hootch took a direct hit. Pieces of shrapnel penetrated its engine block and decimated the driver's compartment. I had no idea that a rocket or mortar round could inflict so much devastation.

To prepare myself for a potential attack, I arranged my gear each night before going to bed so I was able to quickly jump out of my top bunk, grab my equipment, and run for cover. While I dragged the rest of my gear to my bunker, I must have been a hilarious sight: a six-foot-one, one-hundred-sixty-pound, bony warrior armed with a loaded rifle and dressed only in white boxer shorts, a bulletproof vest, and a helmet. I didn't worry about getting dressed until I had safely arrived at my designated damp, mosquito and bug-infested shelter.

During an attack, it took a while for Spooky to arrive on the scene and give us a display of her awesome power. This modified World War II AC-47 aircraft had to fly from Da Nang, a distance of approximately eighty miles, to reach our beleaguered outpost. Immediately upon its arrival, it circled high above suspected enemy locations and generously dispensed volleys of fire that sounded like the distant roar of a jet engine. She was equipped with three lethal machine guns, each capable of firing six thousand rounds per minute. Every fifth round was a tracer, which created a continuous bright-red, illuminated stream of bullets strafing enemy targets below. Flares lit the night sky, enabling its crew to locate, chase, and destroy the enemy on the ground. It was a spectacle to behold.

Casualty Reports

The province of Quang Tri was divided into several separate districts. At each district headquarters we supported a subordinate three or four-man U.S. advisory team, commanded by a major. Captain Rhoades and I periodically visited these district advisory teams by helicopter. As a precautionary measure, the helicopter dropped us off and picked us up at a prearranged time. These guys never remained on the ground because the aircraft became an easy target for the enemy lurking at every corner.

Enemy fire wasn't our only concern. On one of our visits, we were almost blown up midair by friendly fire. Unbeknownst to the pilot or co-pilot, we were flying through airspace used by U.S. naval gun ships for bombarding suspected enemy locations inland.

Part of my assignment consisted of handling casualty reports for those assigned to the advisory team. Casualty reports were always first transmitted telephonically, followed by a detailed written account of the events. I processed my first casualty report within a few weeks of my arrival.

The Vietcong ambushed one of our district advisory teams on a routine supply run to Kilroy Compound, killing an NCO and critically wounding the district advisor. This was the first time I saw a man die before my eyes, and it was a gruesome sight.

Military service members in Vietnam served a period of one year and had an option to voluntarily extend their tours. The enemy situation in Quang Tri, however, didn't motivate anyone to stay a day longer than necessary. Our commander, his deputy, and my immediate supervisor completed their tours within a few months after my arrival. Our new commander, Lieutenant Colonel Joseph P. Seymoe, a 1948 distinguished West Point graduate from Waco, Texas, took command of Advisory Team 4 in September 1967. Major J. Wallace McClintock arrived as his deputy, and Captain Glen Freeman, our operations officer, was transferred to fill the vacant adjutant and administrative officer position.

Friends

I discovered that Specialist Lockhart, who had greeted me upon my arrival and helped me settle in, was a Christian. He didn't go into much detail, but he and a small group of local Vietnamese were building a small Christian church somewhere on the outskirts of Quang Tri, a project entirely financed by his home church. Andy was twenty-one and had married his high school sweetheart only a few months before his departure to Vietnam.

I remember him as an unassuming, hard-working soldier. I never saw him hanging out at the club or movie theater during evening hours. He didn't overtly share his faith with us, perhaps because neither Captain Freeman nor I showed interest in what he was doing with his free time. In fact, both Captain Freeman and I relished ridiculing and poking fun at Lockhart's faith, but he quietly took the grief in stride.

I also became friends with Specialist Jerry Atkins, who had dropped out of Princeton University during his junior year and joined the army. He told me that he was Jewish and that his grandfather had been an immigrant from Russia. Due to persecution in the New Jersey area where he had grown up, his father had legally changed the family name. I didn't know what being Jewish meant; I only knew that the Nazis had committed brutal atrocities against the Jews in Germany during World War II.

The Pills

One day, Jerry asked me if I had tried one of those pills issued to us at Koelper Compound. I told him that I hadn't because I'd been able to stay awake and alert during guard duty without the help of medication. But at my friend's persistent urging I decided to try one.

The pill's effects were profound. It made me feel good; in fact, I literally became "high." I understood why the military dispensed those pills—sleeping wasn't possible until after its effects wore off. I didn't see anything wrong with taking them. After all, since the U.S. Army had issued the medication, I naturally assumed it was safe to use. No one warned us of its hazards.

It wasn't until a year or so later that I learned of the dangers of becoming addicted to this type of medication, commonly referred to as "uppers." In retrospect, I'm glad that I experimented with the drug no more than four or five times during my tour of duty.

A Friend's Advice

Major William Singleton, a black army officer, was another soldier I befriended during the war. I rarely spilled my guts to others, but one night while serving on guard duty together, I shared my obsession of proving to my stepfather that I was a better man than he was and not the stupid idiot he had made me out to be.

Major Singleton confided that when he was a boy, an older brother, who served in Europe during World War II, had been hailed as a hometown hero upon returning from the war. For no apparent reason, he resented the fact that his brother had received all the accolades, honors, and attention. A highly decorated soldier, his brother had also earned a battlefield commission and was subsequently promoted to the rank of Captain. When Major Singleton was little, he'd determined to someday prove to his older brother and the rest of his family that he could do much better. He endured a lot of pain and agony trying to prove he was a better man than his brother, and he encouraged me in the strongest terms to lay aside my feelings toward my stepfather.

Though Major Singleton's story was touching, taking his advice was easier said than done. When I left home in the spring of 1962, I had been convinced that my stepfather was no longer part of my life. But I had been wrong. Unable to look beyond my past, I still felt shackled to a man who continued to torment me by making me feel that I was no good, that I would never be able to measure up, and that I would always be inferior.

The truth was, his past torments had become a part of my present—a part of who I really was. The feelings of inadequacy and inferiority he had fostered were always prowling in the dark shadows along with my deep anger toward him. Proving him wrong had become the driving force in my life. To be sure, I'd physically left my stepfather in Holland, but in many ways he'd followed me to California, to Louisiana and Texas, and yes, even to Kilroy Compound in Quang Tri, Vietnam.

> May those who seek my life
> be disgraced and put to shame;
> may those who plot my ruin
> be turned back in dismay.
> May they be like chaff before the wind,
> with the angel of the Lord driving them away.
>
> —Psalm 35:4–5

The conflict in Quang Tri Province intensified in November and December 1967. Our district advisory teams became targets of more frequent attacks. For some, such attacks became almost a daily routine. With each new day, I was fully cognizant of the possibility that I might not make it back home alive. This suspicion became more apparent the longer I served in Vietnam.

Your friend,
John

Eleven

The Snare of Death

My dear friend,

Large elements of heavily armed North Vietnamese regular army units were making their way on foot through the dense jungles of Laos and Cambodia on the now infamous Ho Chi Minh Trail, infiltrating the South. Continuous heavy bombing by B-52 aircraft, including chemical defoliation of vast jungle regions, did little to stop the influx of enemy soldiers. History reveals that some of Vietnam's fiercest and bloodiest battles were fought at Khe Sanh in Quang Tri Province. U.S. Marines suffered many casualties.

Kilroy Compound sustained its first daytime hit with a mortar attack on New Year's Day, 1968. Lieutenant Colonel Joe Seymoe, a great American hero at only forty-one, was tragically killed on January 21, 1968, near Khe Sanh. Accompanied by two-dozen allied Vietnamese soldiers flying in three helicopters, he died while trying to reach the besieged district headquarters at Khe Sanh.

Prevented from touching down due to continuous heavy shelling and ferocious fighting, he and his men, who occupied the lead helicopter, chose to land at a clearing on a distant hilltop and proceed on foot to the beleaguered district advisory team. As they came in for a landing, two of the three helicopters were fired upon with handheld, antiaircraft weapons and blown up at virtually point-blank range.

The third helicopter never landed. Though the aircraft was severely damaged, the pilots, crew, and occupants managed to safely return to Quang Tri and gave a full account of that day's tragic events.

Before his departure early that morning, Major McClintock had volunteered to take on the doomed mission, but Colonel Seymoe had instructed him to remain behind and run the affairs of the advisory team in his absence. Sending his deputy would have been easier, but doing so wasn't Colonel Seymoe's nature. Keenly aware of the dangers, Colonel Seymoe chose to go himself and paid the supreme sacrifice.

Hope for the Best

The vicinity of Kilroy Compound was relatively calm on the morning of January 30, 1968, the first day of the Vietnamese lunar new year or Tet. Most had been given an extra day off. Major McClintock, now acting commander, and I were at the headquarters offices inside the citadel. It was a regular workday for us. Across the open quadrangle inside the old fortress, one U.S. Army captain and an NCO, along with two Vietnamese soldiers, manned the Tactical Operations Center (TOC).

Strangely, with each passing hour, the reports of enemy attacks on major cities and strategically important U.S. installations began to increase. This rise was odd since a ceasefire was in effect due to the lunar new year celebrations.

Deciding not to take any chances, Major McClintock ordered the compound commander to immediately initiate defensive preparations. He instructed me to lock all offices and together, return to Kilroy Compound. After leaving instructions with the soldiers at the TOC, we climbed into our jeep and drove toward the main gate. For security reasons, only one citadel gate was used for exit and entry into this old, fortified, South Vietnamese military encampment.

Our jeep's engine idled as we paused at the open wooden gate of the citadel's main entrance. Like all Vietnamese cities, towns, villages, and hamlets, the streets of Quang Tri were always incessantly crowded, noisy, and busy with plenty of activity. On this day, however, the streets were strangely deserted and frightfully silent. Not a dog, cat, chicken, or other stray animal was in sight. Obviously the local population had learned about the surprise enemy attacks throughout their country. (That night their city would prove to be no exception.)

The absence of activity on the city streets made us an easy target. Somewhere hidden behind a tree, a shuttered window, a partially opened door, or other natural or man-made obstacle, I fully expected to see a machine gun barrel or a Soviet-made rocket launcher aimed at our jeep. We didn't know it then, but a platoon-sized sapper unit of the North Vietnamese Regular Army had already infiltrated the city.[1]

We were less than a mile from the citadel's main gate to Kilroy Compound. Carefully surveying Quang Tri's main street, Major McClintock, an unpretentious, soft-spoken man of few words and a great American soldier, told me to push the accelerator to the floor and hope for the best.

We held our breath as we made a dash for relative safety. When we arrived, everyone was busy preparing for the potential onslaught. Reports of fierce fighting continued coming in at an alarming rate.

Silence before the Storm

I was assigned a defensive position on a newly expanded and unprotected northern perimeter berm overlooking the distant village of Tri Buu. Captain Jerry Lafitte, my area commander handed me an antiquated Browning .30 caliber machine gun and several canisters of ammunition. Unlike many who leaned forward on the perimeter berm with whatever weapon they had in their possession, I decided to dig a shallow hole on top of the berm large enough to accommodate the size of my body in an almost-curled-up position. I also built a twelve-inch-high circular wall with sandbags for additional protection and figured I was sufficiently protected from whatever was going to fly in my direction.

After everyone was finished securing his defensive position, all we could do was wait for our enemies to unleash their savagery. Since we had heard so many distressing reports throughout the day, we were braced for a bloodbath with potentially disastrous consequences.

By nightfall our little outpost was blanketed by a low-hanging, drizzling fog and an eerie silence broken only by the noise of buzzing mosquitoes, other flying insects, and the familiar chirping sounds of crickets playing in the minefields encircling Kilroy Compound.

It was the silence before the storm.

Onslaught

At exactly two o'clock the following morning, all hell broke loose. This time Spooky couldn't come to our rescue because fierce fighting had spread to so many parts of the country. In fact, the whole country was engaged in all-out brutal fighting, and South Vietnam was engulfed in flames. Well-planned and carefully coordinated attacks by the Vietcong and large contingents of heavily armed Communist North Vietnamese Regular Army soldiers completely surprised everyone within the U.S. military hierarchy.

Bullets and chunks of shrapnel flew only inches from my head. Hundreds of exploding rockets, mortars, and other incendiary devices rained down in and around our postage stamp-size outpost. Several landed within twenty feet from me. Every exploding piece of ordnance sounded like a bolt of lightning striking the ground. Adding to my misery, I had the misfortune of being positioned close to our 81-millimeter mortar, a high-priority target for the two North Vietnamese infantry battalions that had surrounded us.

Seconds after the initial onslaught, we began taking on casualties. Within arm's reach, a friendly Vietnamese soldier serving as a perimeter guard was cut in two, his hip and lower abdomen blown to pieces.

Disregarding his own personal safety, a medic, Warrant Officer Cecil Hardwick of the Royal Australian Army, dashed across the open field amid a barrage of incoming rockets and mortars and arrived on the scene to administer first aid. But he was too late. The young soldier was dead.

Above the sounds of incredible violence and destruction, I heard men crying and screaming for help. To make matters worse, my World War II vintage machine gun repeatedly jammed. Desperate attempts to fix the obstruction without exposing my head to all the flying debris became an incredibly frustrating experience. Amid the destruction and all the confusion, the situation was hopeless. I became acutely aware that I was staring death right in the face. As this realization sank in, I was overcome with horror.

If there was ever a time in my life when I needed God the most, it was there in my tiny foxhole amid the unrelenting barrage of incoming rockets and mortars. I was convinced that I would never see the light of day again. Terrified and grief stricken, I cried out to God in great anguish.

My Plea

"God, if You're real, please save me!" I begged. "How can You let this happen to me? Separated from my family by thousands of miles, why are You letting me die tonight? I don't think that it's fair that I should die. I'm barely twenty-four-years-old, and I've hardly begun to live. I haven't done much with my life; in fact, I've yet to discover what life is all about, but now it's all coming to an end. What have I done to deserve this? God, I promise, if You'll let me live, I'll do better. I'll do something constructive with my life . . . if only You'll let me live!"

Someone has said that there are no atheists in foxholes. While I may not have been an atheist, I was hopelessly desperate for God to come to my rescue. I didn't think it was fair for me to die at such a young age. There I was, desperately pleading with God to spare my life and making promises, not knowing if I would ever have a chance to keep them.

Though much of the intense firefight subsided by daybreak, widespread enemy attacks in the northernmost provinces continued for several days. In other places, fierce fighting continued for weeks. Miraculously, we lost only two lives; however, the Communists wreaked havoc, death, and destruction on the citadel, many other parts of the city, and surrounding areas, resulting in the death of more than twenty Americans.[2] I'm convinced that we were spared total annihilation because soldiers of the 1st Brigade, 1st U.S. Cavalry Division, and the 1st Battalion, 5th Cavalry, had established their forward headquarters and base camp six miles southwest of Quang Tri City only days earlier in anticipation of a major battle.[3]

The breathtaking magnitude of the enemy's attacks on strategic targets completely surprised the top echelons of the U.S. military command structure and marked the turning point of the Vietnam War. Despite American military superiority on the battlefield, we sustained heavy losses. Reports on the exact number of American casualties conflict; however, it's safe to say that U.S. military deaths lies somewhere between two thousand and twenty-five hundred, perhaps even more.

The figures are more staggering, however, when we consider the casualties sustained by the enemy. The cities of Quang Tri and Hue were primary objectives, second only to Saigon.[4] The Communists would have celebrated a great political victory had they succeeded in capturing those two provincial capitals.

The 1968 Tet Offensive will be remembered as the bloodiest battle of the longest and most unpopular war the United States has ever fought. Despite the size and scope of the enemy's brutal assaults throughout South Vietnam, they failed in their efforts to achieve their objectives. In the end they suffered a crushing defeat.

Going Home

Less than a month before my separation from active service, I was promoted to the rank of staff sergeant. My one-year service extension, which took effect on March 10, 1967, meant that I couldn't complete a normal twelve-month tour in Vietnam. That fact suited me just fine. The only thing on my mind was being separated from the U.S. Army and becoming a happy civilian.

I left Quang Tri on a CIA-owned and operated Air America single-engine propeller airplane. Unlike my departure from Fort Bliss, this time I experienced no mixed emotions. With little delay in Da Nang, I caught a flight to Bien Hoa Air Base and upon arrival was transported to Koelper Compound for processing. I was relieved to learn that I was booked on a flight home the next day. I was thankful beyond words to have survived an ugly war and was looking forward to safely setting foot on familiar soil after a long, bumpy flight across the Pacific Ocean.

Our plane arrived at Travis Air Force Base late in the afternoon on March 10, 1968. I, along with several dozen other soldiers, was transported to Oakland Army Base to be discharged from military service. It was to become the longest day of my life. I hadn't been able to sleep at Koelper Compound or on the long flight home, and I was exhausted.

When we arrived at the processing facility, we learned that we would be discharged from the U.S. Army the following morning. The remainder of that day and the entire night was spent listening to many lectures, completing a myriad of administrative procedures, and undergoing final medical and dental checkups. Each person was issued a brand-new tailored Class A uniform with all the accoutrements for the final leg of our journey home.

Early the following morning on March 11, 1968, armed with my duffle bag, separation orders, a final paycheck, and an airline ticket, I took a taxi to the San Francisco International Airport for a flight to L.A.

Unlike soldiers returning from World War II, no one greeted us at the airport. There was no ticker-tape parade, no army band to welcome us home. No one proclaimed, "You guys did a great job!" No one said, "Thank you for putting your life on the line. We're very proud of you!"

I felt like my country had let me down.

> I call to the Lord, who is worthy of praise,
> and I'm saved from my enemies.
> The cords of death entangled me;
> the torrents of destruction overwhelmed me.
> The cords of the grave coiled around me;
> the snares of death confronted me.
> In my distress I called to the Lord;
> I cried to my God for help.
> From his temple he heard my voice;
> my cry came before him, into his ears.
>
> —Psalm 18:3–6

I'm ashamed to admit it, but when I left Kilroy Compound early on the morning of March 8, 1968, I had already forgotten God. But God in His great mercy didn't forget me!

Your friend,
John

Author's Note:

The story, "The Snare of Death," is dedicated to the brave soldiers, sailors, marines, and airmen, including the men of the Royal Australian Armed Forces Detachment, with whom I served from June 1967 to March 1968 at Kilroy Compound, Quang Tri, Republic of Vietnam.

I also dedicate this story to the heroic pilots and crew of Spooky, including the brave men of the 1st Brigade, 1st U.S. Cavalry Division, and the 1st Battalion, 5th Cavalry, who came to our rescue during the onslaught on the city of Quang Tri in January and February of 1968.

I'm not one to be easily stirred with emotion, but I fought back tears as I began writing the opening lines of this story.

Twelve

A Wrong Turn

My dear friend,

It felt so wonderful to be home again in beautiful, sunny Southern California. It felt even better not to be awakened in the middle of the night by the sounds of rattling gunfire or exploding incoming rocket and mortar rounds.

Though the army had always been good to me, it hadn't offered what I was looking for in life. Frankly, I wasn't sure *what* I was looking for. Trying hard to forget my wartime experiences, I didn't want to talk about them and even avoided those who'd been to Vietnam. Despite some heavy gambling with my friends overseas, I'd still set aside enough money for a down payment on a modest home on a cul-de-sac in a quiet neighborhood in Monrovia.

Three important events took place after my discharge. First, I became a naturalized U.S. citizen on June 20, 1969, almost seven years after setting foot on American soil. Becoming an American citizen was a very proud moment in my life and the culmination of a lifelong dream. A great love for my country—a love that endures to this day—had been instilled in me at a young age. Second, as part of the naturalization process, I legally changed my name from Roel Rozema to John Dennis Rozema, a name I had unofficially adopted when I was drafted in 1965.

Third, like so many of my fellow war veterans, I enrolled at a nearby community college under the GI Bill.

Further Education

A month after my discharge, I returned to my former employer though I didn't plan to spend the rest of my life working as a welder. In fact, I wanted a more rewarding and challenging career. I might have forgotten God, but I didn't forget my promise on that fateful night in my foxhole at Kilroy Compound. I was determined to make something of my life, and that meant I needed to begin by improving my education. Two of my first cousins had attended a community college, and I decided to follow in their footsteps.

Pasadena City College, founded in 1924, is situated in the heart of the beautiful city of Pasadena on Colorado Boulevard, known to many as Route 66 because of the popular sixties hit TV series. When I enrolled, I was assigned to Walter Meredith, an academic counselor who happened to have graduated from the Technical University of Delft in the Netherlands with a graduate degree in engineering.

Walter told me I was a notch above the average American high school graduate because of the high academic standards in the Netherlands. My college entrance examination scores, however, were nothing to be proud of, and Mr. Meredith didn't hide his disappointment. Because of my mediocre scores, I enrolled in summer school, taking day and evening classes to brush up on my academic skills.

I had always enjoyed and excelled in mechanical drafting, one of my favorite subjects, while in vocational school. In fact, after my seafaring fiasco, I had been offered a job as an apprentice mechanical draftsman for a small engineering firm in a neighboring city. But my stepfather had said, "No! There's no need for you to work in another city while there are plenty of jobs for people like you in our own town."

I had worked for minimum wage as a machinist's helper in a factory that manufactured contemporary school and office furniture. No one in my immediate family had protested my stepfather's decisions. We'd all played the subservient role, did what we were told, and dared not question his motives.

Now I thought much about which profession to choose. At one time I'd wanted to be an artist but realized that this vocation wouldn't pay the bills or satisfy my hungry cravings. Seemingly, on every street corner were artists who were far more talented and creative than me. Living the bohemian lifestyle also didn't appeal to me.

One day, after a long discussion and at Mr. Meredith's urging, I decided to major in architecture. After satisfactorily completing my courses during the summer break, I started taking architecture classes in the fall of 1969 and passionately loved every minute of them. Frankly, I loved my studies so much that I felt like I was addicted to a drug. Working on my projects gave me an adrenaline rush.

There were two other Vietnam veterans in my class studying under the GI Bill. In those days, bill recipients received $185 per month. Though it wasn't much, it met my financial needs.

It didn't take me long to make new friends, many of whom were right out of high school. Pasadena City College had a small architecture department. Three instructors, licensed architects, and members of the prestigious American Institute of Architects staffed the department. I was determined to become the best student in my class.

Times of Unrest

The sixties and early seventies were crazy times in our country. In the South and many other parts of America, blacks and whites were fighting for racial justice and equality. I didn't realize the extent of bigotry and racial hatred in our land until I returned to school, where I learned about the Jim Crow laws, gerrymandering, and other shameful tactics of oppression and mistreatment of black people.

Furthermore, America was undergoing a social upheaval that appeared to start in California and spread like wildfire across our nation and even beyond its borders. The American people were fed up with the Vietnam War. Antiwar protest demonstrations dominated the evening news on major TV networks. "Make love not war" became a familiar slogan on the lips of many Americans.

Everywhere, young people were also expressing their disgust with the established order. Rebellion against parental authority was the accepted norm. It was a time for free love, flower power, and flower children, also known as "hippies." "If it feels good, do it!" was the prevailing attitude among many young people of that era. I recall a popular bumper sticker that said, "Remember When the Air Was Clean and Sex Was Dirty?"

Drug use was also on the rise. The Beatles and other rock groups glamorized the use of illicit drugs, and smoking pot became a favorite pastime for many. Dr. Timothy Leary, a Harvard University professor, encouraged experimentation with LSD. In fact, while in prison for drug possession, he became something of a folk hero.

Everything at the time was "hip" and "groovy," and many felt pressured to become enlightened. Young people everywhere flirted with Eastern religions, and our school had its share of barefooted, long-haired Jesus freaks. They approached me numerous times, asking me if I knew Jesus and if I was willing to accept Him into my heart. My immediate response was always a curt, "Not today!" I had heard of Jesus all my life, of course, but I didn't really know who He was. I saw no need for Him. What I wanted—or thought I needed most in life—was money, fame, and fortune. Not Jesus.

Driven to Be the Best

Being the best student became an obsession. I didn't care so much about grades in my electives, but I always made sure I received an A in my architecture classes. I envisioned my name permanently engraved on the cornerstone of every building I would someday design. If my instructor told me and my classmates to design and build a cardboard structure that could support a five-pound brick, I designed one that supported two or three five-pound bricks. If the assignment required making a presentation on two sheets of illustration board, I walked into class on the day the project was due with four or five illustration boards.

I never hinted in class what I was creating for fear that someone would copy my ideas. So instead of joining the rest of the students in the lab, I spent a lot of time lingering and meandering outside on the second-floor balcony, smoking cigarettes, and thinking about and formulating my design concepts.

Someone I used to work with occasionally supplied me with a few "uppers" so I could stay awake at night and feverishly work on my projects. Among my closest friends, I don't think one didn't dream of someday becoming the next Frank Lloyd Wright, the father of American architecture. I was no exception. Driven to submit the best design, I spent an inordinate number of hours working on my projects, determined to prove that I *was* the best.

During my sophomore year, I found a part-time job at a local, prestigious architectural firm. My job was to pour over the blueprints of the Hollywood Presbyterian Hospital, a ten-story building, and submit specific measurements to the project manager. That information, fed into a computer by means of a now-antiquated eighty-column IBM punch card, was used to determine the cost of the building. At the project's completion, I was promoted to an intermediate draftsman.

THE CONTEST

I surprised myself by doing remarkably well in school. I relished the compliments of my teachers and fellow students, and I enjoyed working on my projects with a burning passion. One day, a group of local merchants invited architecture department students to submit a design for the entrance of an annual outdoor arts and crafts show. I was determined to win the contest and spent nights and days creating an exciting, breathtaking entrance. After all entries were submitted and after I examined what my classmates had created, I was convinced that the winning entry was mine.

But to my astonishment, one of my fellow classmates won the contest. The materials he'd used to fabricate his presentation looked as if he'd purchased them at the local flea market. My guess was that he'd spent his lunch hour in the back of his rundown, flower-and-peace-symbol-plastered VW minibus, creating his less-than-mediocre design.

I was completely stunned. The judges, a small group of local businessmen and businesswomen, obviously didn't share my sentiments and had based their selection not on a spectacular design but on what was least costly to build. I was devastated by what I considered to be an absurdly inept decision.

Crowning Achievement

Though some may disagree, I believe Cal Poly, short for California Polytechnic State University, has produced some of our nation's finest architects. The school is situated on beautiful, green rolling terrain outside San Luis Obispo. For many young aspiring architects, Cal Poly was the place to go. Academic standards were high, and because of the large volume of applications received each year, only those who showed the potential to excel were selected to enter the rigorous five-year program.

One day, I received a letter informing me that I had been selected to attend the school of architecture at Cal Poly. I couldn't think of a moment in my life that made me feel more proud. That letter represented a crowning achievement. While others may view such a document as one step in the process of being selected to attend an institute of higher learning, to me that piece of paper was living proof—not only to my stepfather but most notably to myself—that I wasn't the dumb, stupid, ignorant kid he had always made me out to be.

Nothing that I had achieved in life thus far compared to this letter of acceptance. It was such a tremendous comfort and relief knowing that for the rest of my life I didn't need to struggle with believing that I was intellectually inferior. Almost in a state of euphoria, I felt as if I stood on top of the world. After digesting the contents of the letter and recovered from feelings of jubilation, I called my friends to tell them the great news.

Those selected to the school of architecture were subject to a portfolio evaluation by school officials. Based on their evaluation, they decided into which school year the student would be placed. Because I had worked for an architect and was allowed to include copies of my work for consideration, I had an advantage over most other students.

For weeks, I practiced answering potentially difficult questions that might arise during the evaluation. Five lucky students from my class made the long drive to San Luis Obispo and were grilled by school of architecture faculty. I was scared and nervous but glad when the evaluation was over. To my surprise, I breezed through my critique with relative ease and was greatly relieved to learn a few weeks later that I had been accepted as a junior.

I was also nominated for and received an award from the local chapter of the Rotary International for outstanding academic achievement in the field of architecture. I was on Cloud Nine! This may sound absurd, but architecture had become my object of worship. It had gone beyond passion; architecture was now my god. My favorite teacher frequently told me, "John, you need to breathe it, you need to live it, and you need to eat it!"

It didn't bother me then, but during those years at Pasadena City College, I had developed a flair for egotism coupled with arrogance and pride.

The Fall

Transferring to Cal Poly was not like I had envisioned it would be. My dreams of becoming a successful architect and seeing my name engraved on a bronze plaque on the cornerstone of every building I would someday design began to erode.

Almost from the first day, I began to deal with issues that adversely affected my happy outlook on life. Gary Bourchette, my dormitory roommate, made my life miserable from the day I moved in. He kept mostly to himself; for unknown reasons he seemed always angry and never spoke to me. All my attempts to establish a good relationship with Gary were fruitless. Except for the fact that he, too, had majored in architecture, we had nothing in common. By the time I realized my roommate was incompatible, the dorm was already filled to capacity, and changing rooms was too late. My only other option was to move out and find an apartment or condominium, but I couldn't afford to do that. As a result I avoided the dormitory as much as possible and used it only to sleep, brush my teeth, shave, and shower. Also, to minimize contact with my roommate, I virtually "camped out" in the lab of the school of architecture, which was open twenty-four hours a day.

Each Friday after the last class, my good friend, Dan MacDavid, today a successful architect in Southern California, and I jumped into his VW bug and headed home. We traveled on portions of the scenic Pacific Coast Highway and returned to school late Sunday nights.

I continued to do well in my architecture classes, but my grades in subjects not directly related to my major were nothing to write home about. I was placed on academic probation after the first quarter semester. I became depressed and was at a loss as to how to get my life back on track. My friends didn't have the slightest inkling what I was going through.

As at Pasadena City College, a group of Jesus freaks often approached me and used the same lines as the others. "Do you know Jesus? Are you willing to accept Him into your heart?"

My replies continued to be brisk and unfriendly. "Not today!" It seemed like these guys always singled me out as if I had become their target. They looked for me in the dorm and knocked on the door late at night, much to my roommate's irritation. They approached me in the student union or out on the open quad between classes. They must have figured that I was a good prospect for conversion. If I wasn't going to turn to Jesus today, they must have thought, perhaps tomorrow would be the day.

A Visit to Holland

My mother wrote on numerous occasions, asking me, almost pleading, to visit her. I never felt a compelling need to go and always had an excuse. As much as I loved my mother and my siblings, I had no intentions of going back to Holland.

Her invitations went on for several years, and my rejections must have hurt her deeply. When I received yet another request, I decided that a vacation to Europe might do me some good—in fact, it might provide renewed inspiration for my senior year. It was going to be an all-expense-paid holiday. I wrote her back and told her that the summer break was a good time for me to visit.

I made arrangements with two friends from Pasadena City College to rent an apartment in San Luis Obispo during the following school year at Cal Poly. Living in the dorm was no longer an option for me, and I had raised my grade point average enough to be removed from academic probation. While I didn't relish the thought of two more years at Cal Poly, I figured that my attitude would sufficiently change during my long summer break, enabling me to return in the fall and make a fresh start. In a way, I looked forward to seeing my mother and siblings again. My mother had visited me in California in 1963, but ten long years had passed since the last time I saw my siblings.

I was awestruck at the incredible economic growth that had taken place in the Netherlands during my decade-long absence. With the discovery of natural gas, Holland had become an economic powerhouse virtually overnight. Everyone there was reaping its benefits and enjoying a comfortable lifestyle. The Dutch no longer felt a compelling need to perform menial tasks and imported "guest workers," primarily from Turkey and Morocco.

It was great seeing Mother, my brother, and my two sisters after my long hiatus. I can't say that I was overjoyed to see my stepfather, but our relationship was different now. This time I wouldn't let him get away with any sort of abuse directed at me or anyone else in our family. That kind of treatment would not work now because I was no longer the timid, frightened little boy I used to be. At the first sign of abuse, I was ready to go on the offensive.

Thankfully, no abuse occurred. The anger, hatred, and bitterness I had harbored toward my stepfather had mostly dissipated by now. I tried hard to forget the past and get on with my life.

My time in Holland was a wonderful opportunity to get to know my siblings better. We traveled a lot, and during the trips I saw more of Holland than I had ever seen during all the years I lived there. We also vacationed in Belgium and Luxembourg.

During my stay in Europe, I visited several immaculately maintained World War II U.S. cemeteries. An incredibly awesome sight was seeing thousands upon thousands of white marble crosses intermingled with Stars of David, meticulously arranged and contrasting against beautifully manicured lawns on gently rolling green hills. During those moments, I felt proud to be an American citizen. I also visited the grave of General George S. Patton III, buried alongside his soldiers of the U.S. Third Army, and saw his imposing bronze statue in the city of Luxembourg.

After nearly six weeks of vacationing in Europe, it was time to return to California and start making preparations for school. Upon my return, only two weeks remained before the start of the fall semester. My two friends, with whom I had committed to rent an apartment, had already signed a lease and moved in.

But with each passing day, I began to sense great misgivings about returning to Cal Poly. The more I thought about going back to school, the more depressed I became. I made up my mind; I no longer wanted to become an architect.

A Change in Direction

Less than a week before class registration, I notified school officials that I wouldn't be a student during the 1972–1973 school year. I also wrote a letter to Richard Fisher, my prospective roommate, and told him about my decision. He immediately replied and said he was very sorry to hear about my decision. What troubled him most wasn't so much that I wouldn't be sharing an apartment with him, but that I was no longer interested in a career in architecture. Coincidentally, another student from Pasadena City College, who needed a place to stay, agreed to move in with them and divide up what would have been my share of the expenses.

When I made this decision, I felt as if a great burden had been lifted off my shoulders. Although I felt disappointed that I would probably never become a licensed architect, I didn't regret my decision. The energy and excitement I had once experienced for architecture were gone—and so was the passion.

After taking this big step I realized I needed time to think about what to do next. I knew I had to do something. I couldn't just hang around and do nothing, but I wanted to be certain that whatever I pursued next wouldn't turn out to be another dismal failure.

The "Wrong Turn"

After a brief time of chilling out and collecting my thoughts, I began looking for work in the L.A. area. I found plenty of job opportunities, but nothing I saw in the local newspapers excited me. Likewise, employment agencies offered little of interest.

One day while driving around in search of a job, I took a wrong turn. There in front of me stood a large billboard army recruitment poster with a picture of Uncle Sam sternly pointing his finger. Below his face was the familiar slogan "I WANT YOU FOR THE U.S. ARMY." Strange as it may sound, it seemed as if Uncle Sam was looking and pointing his finger directly at me.

Driving home, all I could think about was the time I had spent in the U.S. Army. I couldn't let the thought go away, nor could I dismiss memories of the camaraderie and all the great people I had worked for. I hadn't forgotten that the army had been good to me.

For the rest of the day, all I could think about was the army, and that night I fell asleep dreaming about army life. When I woke up the next morning, the army was still on my mind. Need I say more?

My hometown recruiter promised me a rose garden.

"John, tell me what you want. The only thing I can't promise is your former rank."

The rank issue didn't bother me. I told him I was interested in an administrative job and an assignment anywhere in Germany. Without a moment's hesitation, the sergeant reached for a form in his desk drawer and said, "You got it! All you need to do is sign on the dotted line."

It sounded almost too good to be true. I had always enjoyed working in an administrative capacity. The reason why I chose Germany was to be closer to my family and to continue building the relationships with my brother and my two sisters.

It didn't take the recruiter long to complete all administrative procedures. When he was finished, he instructed me to report three days later to the U.S. Armed Forces Entrance and Examination Station in downtown Los Angeles. I sold my indestructible, maroon 1968 Buick Wildcat; my gun collection; and other items I knew I would never need again.

> There you will worship man-made gods of wood and stone,
> which cannot see or hear or eat or smell.
> But if from there you seek the Lord your God,
> you will find him if you look for him
> with all your heart and with all your soul.
> —Deuteronomy 4:28–29

My "wrong turn" in search of suitable employment marked the beginning of a new life's journey. It led me on a path that would in due time dramatically alter the course of my life.

> Your friend,
> John

Thirteen

On the Run

-∞-

My dear friend,

Traveling north on U.S. Highway 101 toward Fort Ord on central California's coast, three chartered commercial buses carried 180 recruits to the U.S. Army Reception Station. It was October 12, 1972.

As we drove through San Luis Obispo, I thought about Cal Poly, the good friends I'd left behind, and how suddenly the direction of my life had shifted. Though I didn't regret my decision, I was sorry that I probably wouldn't see my friends again.

Fort Ord

The other recruits and I arrived late that night, and a small band of drill sergeants greeted us. These guys didn't appear to be as mean as the ones I'd met seven years earlier at Fort Polk. They marched us to a mess hall, fed us a warm meal, and took us to a classroom to dispense with minor administrative matters before letting us turn in for the night.

Carrying a clipboard, one of the drill sergeants said, "When I call your name, you will give me your religious or denominational affiliation."

Not surprisingly, most men belonged to one of the mainstream Protestant denominations, though quite a few Catholics were among us. Judging from the responses, I surmised that I was the only one who didn't belong to a church. When my turn came, I didn't want to be the oddball. With some degree of relief I said I was Episcopalian. After all, as an immigrant to America, I had been sponsored by the Episcopal Church USA. Based on that fact, I figured that if I owed loyalty to any denomination, it would be to the Episcopal Church.

One all-American, blond-haired, blue-eyed nineteen-year-old reported that he was a Zen Buddhist. The sergeant paused briefly, and many stares shot toward the young man. I thought he had a lot of guts to make that public declaration of his faith in this particular setting.

After a week at the reception station, we were transported to our basic training company—this time not in open cattle trucks driven by a bunch of wild cowboys dressed in army fatigues but in relatively comfortable army buses.

Because of my break in service, I was reduced in rank from staff sergeant to private and treated like any other trainee. I didn't mind the rank reduction because I earned more money as a private than I had while serving as a staff sergeant in Vietnam.

The long war that had caused so much pain and division in our land had finally come to an end. The draft had been abolished, and as a means of enticing young men and women to join the armed forces, salaries for new recruits had nearly quadrupled.

Much had changed during my four-year absence. The army had eased many of its restrictions, one of which was that soldiers were now permitted to grow their hair a little longer and to wear sideburns and mustaches. A standard policy in army mess halls was to feed soldiers steak and eggs for breakfast once a week. In addition, new recruits were virtually guaranteed their choice of military schooling and assignment at the time of their enlistment.

EXPLORATIONS IN ZEN BUDDHISM

Company C, 2nd Battalion, 1st Brigade, was our basic training company. I was assigned to the 4th Platoon along with Greg McAllister, the Zen Buddhist. We quickly became good friends.

Before joining the army, Greg had lived with his family in an upscale neighborhood of beautiful Laguna Beach. He was a typical, ordinary guy with an easy smile. One would never have guessed he was a Buddhist since we never saw him practicing his religion. One day after getting to know him better, I asked him what had attracted him to Zen Buddhism. He replied that Eastern religions and mysticism intrigued him. His aim was to obtain peace of mind and achieve a state of enlightenment through the practice of meditation.

He must have sensed my curiosity and asked if I'd be interested in knowing more about his faith. Not knowing exactly what "being enlightened" meant, I said, "Sure, I could use some peace of mind, and I need all the enlightenment I can get!"

After three weeks of basic training, we received our first weekend pass. Greg took me and a few other friends to a fisherman's wharf not far from the city of Carmel, which overlooked the Pacific Ocean. The city and the surrounding area, known as Big Sur, were famous for their natural beauty and the area residents, many of whom were well-known Hollywood movie stars, artists, and other celebrities.

At a little bookstore, Greg selected three books written by famous Zen masters about the basics of the religion. It wasn't your typical bookstore. Employees were young hippies who burned incense. Mostly they sold books on Eastern religions, mysticism, New Age, and yoga. I told my new friend that living in the barracks probably wouldn't be conducive to practicing meditation, but I promised to study the books when I was settled in my permanent duty assignment.

Steve's Amazing Story

During that time I also became acquainted with Steve Morrison, another member of our platoon. Fresh out of high school, Steve was a new Christian who had grown up in a happy home with a well-to-do family. I noticed that he was always reading his little green Gideon Bible someone had given to us when we stepped on the bus at the AFEES station.

Trainees received a ten-minute break every hour. During that time, most satisfied their nicotine cravings, chatted, or joked around with their buddies. But not Steve. He withdrew to a quiet place to study his pocket-sized Bible. As I did with Greg McAllister, I asked Steve about what caused him to read the Bible all the time. He answered by telling me a most incredible story.

When he was in high school, Steve had dabbled in psychedelic drugs. One night while partying at a friend's home when his parents weren't at home, he had overdosed on LSD. For good reasons, his friends became alarmed and panicked. Driving him home, they helped him to his room.

In his semiconscious state, Steve realized he was dying, and the thought terrified him. With what little physical strength he could muster, he crawled out of his bed toward a bedroom closet. Steve told me convincingly that when he opened that closet door, he saw the face of God! He assured me that in spite of his condition, he wasn't hallucinating. What he saw was very real, and he was immediately convicted of his wretched state. In desperation he cried out to God to save him. And God, by His grace, answered his prayer. Steve said he miraculously recovered and lived to tell the story.

It was an amazing tale. Afterward, Steve severed all friendships and never touched any kind of illicit drug again. He said that he wanted to know God more and that the only way to do so was to study His Word. Steve was a very serious guy and not the type to fabricate stories. I believed every word he said and didn't question what he'd shared with me.

Talking with Greg and observing Steve always reading his Bible made me ponder who was right and what was truth. I had always believed in God; now I became preoccupied with these complex issues, longing to know the truth. My problem was that I didn't have the faintest idea who to believe or where to go to find the answers I was seeking.

New Life in Germany

After eight long weeks of basic training, we each went our separate ways. As always, I hated saying farewell to my new friends. Basic training was followed by six weeks of advanced individual training as an army personnel management clerk, also at Fort Ord, and then ten weeks of basic leadership training at Fort Benjamin Harrison in Indianapolis, Indiana. After graduation, I flew home for a short vacation before leaving for my overseas assignment.

On a warm, sunny spring day in 1973, I arrived in the beautiful city of Stuttgart in what was then West Germany. A smartly dressed soldier in a starched khaki uniform met me at the *bahnhof* (train station). I was surprised when he escorted me to a shiny, big, fancy, black army sedan.

This is no ordinary army assignment, I thought.

I soon learned from my friendly chauffeur that I was being assigned to Headquarters, United States European Command (USEUCOM) at Patch Barracks.

Patch Barracks had been named in honor and memory of Lieutenant General Alexander M. Patch, commander of the U.S. Seventh Army during World War II. Located in the village of Vaihingen on the outskirts of Stuttgart, partially surrounded by beautiful wooded areas with miles of paved walking trails, Patch Barracks was probably the prettiest U.S. military installation in Germany. Many of its streets were paved with cobblestones. I considered myself very fortunate to have been stationed there.

Headquarters USEUCOM comprised military and civilian members from the four branches of the service. I was assigned to the U.S. Army Element as a personnel management clerk. I loved my job, quickly made new friends, and enjoyed the people with whom I worked.

TRAVELS

What was unique about my job was that I had the opportunity to travel to distant countries and visit exotic places. Part of my job was to review and update military personnel records of soldiers stationed at the various U.S. embassies in these countries. I stayed at fancy hotels, wined and dined on the best food, and was treated like royalty by my hosts. Twice I traveled to Ethiopia and visited many other countries along the western and northern regions of Africa. I once enjoyed a safari in an area of Ethiopia that overlooked the distant Blue Nile Valley. I also visited Athens, Greece, and the great cities of Paris and Rome. My travels included tourist sites in Morocco, and I spent a fortune on beautiful wood and ivory carvings in Kinshasa, Zaire, before an international ban on the sale of ivory.

Despite almost being arrested for taking a picture of the airport and being questioned by unfriendly security personnel in Freetown, Sierra Leone, I fell in love with Africa and dreamed of someday being stationed there. I was also able to regularly visit my family in Holland and saw much of the beautiful, impeccably clean German countryside.

ANOTHER LOOK AT THE SPIRITUAL

Within walking distance from our post was Mom's, a German *gasthaus* (hotel and restaurant), a favorite hangout for single soldiers living in the barracks. The proprietor was a kind, elderly German lady who took on the role of a surrogate grandmother. The food was out of this world, and "Mom," as everyone affectionately called her, treated every GI like a member of her own family. My friends and I spent almost every Friday and Saturday evening at Mom's, savoring delicious Bavarian dishes and joining her German guests in consuming inordinate amounts of locally brewed beer unto the wee hours of the morning. Dragging myself out of bed the following morning took much effort. Quite disheveled, I'd make my way to the post's cafeteria for a late morning breakfast.

It just happened that the post chapel was located directly across from the cafeteria. From my vantage point at a window on the second floor, I observed families, neatly attired and carrying their Bibles, going to and from Protestant services.

These people are out of my league, I thought.

The idea of going to church on Sunday mornings and listening to a sermon didn't appeal to me. I had better things on my mind. I wanted to party with my friends and assumed Christians had no fun. I looked at Christians as people who were psychologically deprived of emotional stability; therefore, they needed something to lean on.

I made a conscious effort to read the books on Zen Buddhism but found the material extremely dull and difficult to absorb. Still I bragged to my friends that I was a Zen Buddhist and experimented a few times meditating in the prescribed lotus position. These admittedly feeble attempts were big disasters. Sitting on a hard, wooden floor, I folded one leg over the other, kept my back perfectly straight, and tried to concentrate on absolutely nothing—all the while in that painful position. Attaining a state of enlightenment in this manner was impossible for me.

What a terrible way to seek peace of mind, I thought. *There has to be a better way.*

In short order my interest in Zen Buddhism waned, and my small collection of books on Zen for beginners began accumulating dust.

One day while talking to Brandon Amherst, my best friend from Romeoville, a city near Chicago, I asked him if he was interested in learning about Zen Buddhism. Visibly uncomfortable with my question, he made it clear that he was definitely not interested. He told me in no uncertain terms that he had grown up in church and that as far as he was concerned, "Jesus is the only way—there is no other way!" Not wishing to mar a good friendship, I never discussed the topic again.

Among the many who attended Protestant services at Patch Barracks was my boss, Lieutenant Colonel Howard D. Schulze, his wife, Martha, and their two young sons. Everyone in my office agreed that no soldier could ask for a finer army officer to work for than Lieutenant Colonel Schulze.

One evening at a social function at the officers' club, I told Martha about my involvement in Zen Buddhism. She made it clear from the outset that she was a committed Christian and shared with me how she got "saved." I was puzzled because I didn't know what "being saved" meant. Martha was neither critical nor judgmental. To my surprise, she asked if she could borrow and read one of my books on Zen, and I gladly obliged.

Ten days later she returned the book with a polite note, in which she expressed appreciation for having studied the contents of my book. She concluded that Buddhism leads to nowhere. In spite of hardships we sometimes have to endure, she wrote, Jesus is the only way to true peace and happiness in this life and in the life to come.

I thought a lot about what Martha Schulze had shared with me. I still possessed the Bible Aunt Julie had given me before I left for

Vietnam. Several times I had tried looking for answers by reading it, but no matter how hard I tried, I couldn't understand it. The Bible seemed like a closed book to me.

My friends Dan MacDavid and Richard Fisher from Pasadena City College and Cal Poly were now foreign exchange students in Europe, and I had an opportunity to visit them. Dan was doing his final year at the University of Florence in Italy, and Richard attended the University of Copenhagen in Denmark. It was great seeing my friends again. After lengthy discussions and late-night debates with Richard, I was still inclined neither to return to school nor to pursue a career in architecture.

To me, life in the army was great. I enjoyed it so much that I reenlisted and extended my overseas tour at Patch Barracks for an additional three years. I moved out of the barracks and purchased a late-model Ford Pinto. I also rented a nice, third-floor efficiency apartment at Meisenweg 28 in the village of Leinfelden, which was located on the southern boundary of Stuttgart and overlooked the distant Stuttgart International Airport.

About this time I was also trying to court a young, dazzling, petite army photographer with long blond hair and blue eyes from Bismarck, North Dakota. Unlike my debonair, casanova friend from Romeoville, who seemed to date a different pretty girl every week, I had to work very hard to develop relationships with girls to whom I was attracted. It was the story of my life. Typically, the ones I wanted, I couldn't get, and I wasn't usually interested in the ones who wanted to date me.

THE REPRIMAND

Directly across from our office was the U.S. Air Force Element. Its commander was Colonel Eleanor Skinner. Together with the U.S. Navy and Marine Corps Elements and others, we comprised the Personnel and Administration Directorate headed by an army brigadier general.

One day Colonel Skinner, usually a kindhearted, professional, and friendly officer, stopped me in the hallway. Her facial expression said she was anything but happy with me. I knew instinctively what was about to happen: she was going to rebuke me or, as we say in the army, "chew me out."

"Staff Sgt. Rozema!" she said.

I approached her, stood at attention, and said, "Yes, ma'am."

Uncharacteristically and in an almost harsh tone, which was loud enough for people in adjacent offices to hear her words, Colonel Skinner pointed her finger at my face. "Do you know what you need in your life?" she asked. Without waiting for an answer, she said, "YOU NEED JESUS CHRIST! Do you understand that, Staff Sgt. Rozema?"

Baffled and taken aback, I hadn't the slightest idea what she meant by her statement. Almost angrily, I responded by saying, "Yes, ma'am!" But my heart's immediate, intuitive reply was, "Not today!"

In all my years of military service, I had never heard of anyone receiving such an extraordinary reprimand. I've often wondered whether Colonel Skinner carefully planned this unconventional approach of correction, or had she spontaneously blurted her words without forethought?

I was humiliated and angry. After this embarrassing encounter, I kept my distance from her whenever possible. No one who had overheard the admonishment ever asked me about what might have prompted Colonel Skinner's rebuke.

RADIO EVANGELISM

Each morning, while driving to work from Leinfelden to Patch Barracks, a distance of approximately thirty minutes, I turned on my car radio and listened to the seven o'clock news on the U.S. Armed Forces Network (AFN). Just before the morning news, an army chaplain gave a short, five-minute devotional. I often heard the chaplain say, "Give your heart and your life to Jesus today. Don't wait until tomorrow."

Never interested in what these guys had to say, I usually kept the volume down until the news came on. I also never understood, nor was it ever explained to me, what the chaplain meant when he said to "accept Jesus in your heart" or to "surrender your life to Jesus." As time went by, these messages seemed to come with more urgency and frequency. When I did pick up on them, my immediate, unspoken response was always the same: "Not today!"

Sometimes I became irritated; I wanted to hear the morning news and learn what was going on in the world. I didn't want to listen to an army chaplain. This radio scenario continued for about a year.

One morning early in November 1977, I tuned in to AFN on my way to work as usual. Again, I heard a chaplain say the familiar line. "Surrender your life to Jesus today; stop struggling so much! Don't waste a minute. Do it now!"

This time the chaplain caught my attention. Strange as it may sound, it seemed like he was talking to me personally. But once again my heart's immediate response was the same as always: "Not today, Lord!" But before I had finished uttering "Lord," the chaplain interrupted.

"I know what you're saying. You're saying, 'Not today, Lord!'"

This was the first time in my life God had ever spoken to me personally, and it was through this army chaplain. His words pierced my heart like a sharp, double-edged sword.

How did this guy know how I would respond? I thought. I was filled with awe and wonder. It was the last time someone would invite me, either in person or by a radio or TV broadcast, to surrender my life to God by asking Jesus into my heart.

It may seem paradoxical, but for as long as I could remember, there dwelled inside me a desire and longing to know God and His truth. I suspect that when I was young someone planted a seed in me. Perhaps it was Patrick's mother's comments when I was a boy, or maybe it was the Dutch Reformed Church minister who taught the Christian religious education classes I attended.

I don't know. At the same time I steadfastly refused to accept God's repeated appeals to draw near to Him and know Him.

Hindsight is always twenty-twenty. I didn't know it then, but now I know with absolute certainty that God was relentlessly pursuing me. He wasn't going to let up until I had stopped running and had turned my life over to Him. God used Aunt Julie with her Bible. He used Andy Lockhart, our clerk, and that awful foxhole experience in Vietnam. He used those men handing out pocket-sized Gideon Bibles when I stepped on the bus for boot camp. God used those barefooted, long-haired "Jesus freaks" on the campuses of Pasadena City College and Cal Poly. He used Steve in boot camp and my best friend from

Romeoville. God used Martha Schulze, Colonel Skinner, and the army chaplains on AFN radio.

But because of my apparently incurable stubbornness and hardness of heart, I persistently resisted: "Not today! Not today! Not today!"

I believe God's patience has a limit. I also believe His patience with me was wearing thin. Because I continued to steadfastly refuse Him, God chose to use a different approach. He planned to bring me to the depths of despair and to the very end of my life.

> Answer me, O Lord, out of the goodness of your love;
> in your great mercy turn to me.
> Do not hide your face from your servant;
> answer me quickly, for I am in trouble.
> Come near and rescue me;
> redeem me because of my foes.
>
> —Psalm 69:16–18

It wasn't until death confronted me a second time, when I had no way of escape, that I finally gave up resisting God and surrendered my life to Him.

> Your friend,
> John

Fourteen

Miracle on Meisenweg

My dear friend,

A child who grows up suffering rejection will in all probability look for love in all the wrong places. I borrowed this line from Dr. Erwin W. Lutzer, senior pastor of The Moody Church in Chicago. That statement pretty well sums up how I was unconsciously living many years of my life. This lifestyle reached its peak when I was living in Germany.

For the better part of my early life, I was consumed with the great fear of rejection. I subdued those fears by maintaining good friendships, even if that pursuit meant crossing lines of moral decency. Inside me dwelled a great need to belong, and I was besieged by thoughts that somehow I didn't fit in or wasn't good enough. My stepfather's demeaning words always echoed in the dim, distant recesses of my brain.

I hated myself at the time because I wasn't able to master my speaking of the English language without betraying traces of a foreign accent. Learning how to overcome what I considered a serious communication deficiency was very important to me because I didn't want to be considered an outsider. I also didn't like questions about where I was from. I resented being referred to as a "foreigner" or an "alien" though this reference came up rarely. The latter always sounded like I was a creature from a distant planet. Deep inside, I always wrestled with feelings of insecurity and inferiority.

THE VOID

Why was I unhappy? I loved my job and enjoyed a generous salary. I had an assignment many would envy and couldn't have asked for better people to work with. I lived in a newly built, nicely furnished rented apartment with a spectacular view. I explored much of Western Europe, visited many places on the African continent, and frequently saw my family in Holland. I also had a great time with my friends, but something was missing in my life. I tried to figure out what that was, but I couldn't. This missing ingredient was a constant source of pain and much frustration. I harbored a deep longing, a yearning, a hungering for something more. But whatever it was, it was beyond my reach. There was a great void in my life, and I didn't know how to fill it.

I've heard it said more than once: "Sin is fun. If sin wasn't fun, people wouldn't be doing it!" Living in sin is precisely what I was doing. In fact, I was basking in sin, always looking for something to fill that void in my life. And the more I sinned, the greater the void. Sin and all the world had to offer couldn't satisfy my innermost cravings.

I suspected that my friends, coworkers, and other people with whom I came in contact assessed me as a happy camper. Little did they realize what was brewing inside me. They had no idea that I was such a complex creature who was unable to battle and overcome the punishing giants in my life. Deathly fearful of rejection, I wore a thousand masks. I had become a master at not revealing what was secretly tucked away deep inside.

Concealing my true identity became a natural part of my character until I reached the point that I was tired of pretending to be someone I wasn't. These seemingly insurmountable obstacles had taken on the form of a weighty emotional millstone. The millstone grew exceedingly heavy with each passing day and was slowly dragging me down a slippery slope of destruction. I felt as though I carried the weight and all the problems of the world on my shoulders.

I suppose others in similar circumstances would have made an appointment with a psychiatrist or mental health counselor. During those days, however, just seeing an army psychiatrist could have been potentially detrimental to one's career, especially for someone like me who had a top secret security clearance. I took great pride in serving my country and wearing a soldier's uniform. I wasn't going to let anything happen to destroy that. I was determined to function like any other healthy normal human being and always go the extra mile like a good trooper. Moreover, I resolved to keep these problems to myself and fix them without the help of others. My dilemma was that I didn't know how.

After the Concert

One bitterly cold November night in 1977, several friends and I attended a rock concert near Stuttgart. We frequently traveled from one concert to the next to see all the big names in pop rock culture from the sixties and seventies. As usual, we had a great time. Nothing out of the ordinary took place that evening until one of my friends drove me home afterward. I stepped out of my friend's VW bug and climbed the marble stairs to my apartment on the third floor.

Friends who were with me that evening said they detected nothing about me that might have caused alarm. For no apparent reason, I felt such a heavy load on my shoulders that climbing those five short flights seemed impossible. Suddenly, all my strength was gone. I didn't know what was happening.

When I finally reached the third floor and entered my apartment, I felt as if I had reached the end of my life. I stood on the very threshold of death! Feelings of guilt, shame, loneliness, and pain overwhelmed me. Without warning, my life suddenly became excruciatingly unbearable. Had I been suicidal, I would have probably taken the easy way out—pulled a trigger and prematurely terminated my life. I thank God that I wasn't suicidal, though I'd frequently entertained thoughts of killing myself when I was a teen.

In desperation I threw myself down on my bed—crushed, brokenhearted, and beyond hope. I didn't know what to do except to pray, and that was something I hadn't done since my harrowing experience in that tiny foxhole in Vietnam's killing fields almost ten years earlier.

This time I didn't negotiate with God. Hopeless and totally desperate, I cried out to God to save me because I couldn't live another day, another hour, another minute, or another second under this unbearably heavy burden.

Transformation

Despite my non-Christian upbringing, I had always known in my heart that there was only one God. The Bible makes that fact indisputably clear. To me He was the God who had created the heavens and the earth and all that is in them. He was the God of the Bible, the God of Israel, the God of the Christian religious education classes I had attended as a boy while growing up in Holland. He was the God Steve Morrison had told me about in boot camp, the God of my best friend from Romeoville, and the God to whom I was crying out to save my life.

As I poured out my heart to Him, I sensed His awesome presence in that room. It was as if God Himself reached over and lifted the crushing weight off my shoulders. It was gone in an instant! Physically, I felt as light as a feather, as if I was floating inches above my bed. Yet this wasn't a hallucination; I had a clear and sound mind, but of course describing such an experience is next to impossible.

What followed next was equally incredible. While lying there, I realized I was being bathed in a river of peace and love that defies all human comprehension. This "bath" felt so wonderful that I didn't want it to stop. My guilt, pain, grief, and loneliness were washed away. All the years of deep longing, the yearning for something that had seemed so mystifying, ended that night. That great void I had been desperately seeking to fill was now filled to overflowing. That night God cleansed my perverse mouth, unshackled me from the man who had tormented me most of my life, and set me free from the bondage of sin.

The citizens of Leinfelden were unaware that on this cold November night around midnight a divine visitation occurred in their little village. In a small efficiency apartment on the Meisenweg, overlooking miles of lush, green vineyards and distant mountain ranges, grace and mercy embraced and healed a wounded, broken heart.

> O Lord, do not rebuke me in your anger or discipline me in your wrath.
> For your arrows have pierced me, and your hand has come down upon me.
> Because of your wrath there is no health in my body;
> my bones have no soundness because of my sin.
> My guilt has overwhelmed me like a burden too heavy to bear.

My wounds fester and are loathsome because of my sinful folly.
I'm bowed down and brought very low; all day long I go about mourning.
My back is filled with searing pain; there is no health in my body.
I am feeble and utterly crushed; I groan in anguish of heart.
All my longings lie open before you, O Lord; my sighing is not hidden from you.
My heart pounds, my strength fails me; even the light has gone from my eyes.

—Psalm 38:1–10

Before peacefully falling asleep that night, I asked God to give me a Christian wife. God, who is not ordinarily in any hurry, wasted little time in giving me the desires of my heart.

Your friend,
John

Part Two
In the School of the Most High

Oh, the depth of the riches of the wisdom and knowledge of God!
How unsearchable his judgments, and his paths beyond tracing out!
—Romans 11:33

Fifteen

A Long, Sweet Honeymoon

My dear friend,

I didn't know it then, but on Saturday night, November 19, 1977, I became a Christian. What the Scripture says—that everyone who calls on the name of the Lord will be saved—became a reality for me.[1] I had passed from death to life![2] Being a Christian means being a child of God and receiving the wonderful gift of eternal life and the forgiveness of my sins. I had become a born-again believer. I awoke the following morning a changed person, and I knew my life would never be the same again.

What exactly took place in my little apartment at Meisenweg 28 took a long time for me to digest. It also demanded many more years of study to understand the concepts and grasp the implications of living the Christian life. Like a little toddler holding his father's hand and learning to take those first few feeble steps, I, too, held my Father's hand as I learned the basic tenets of the Christian faith on a journey that took me to many mountain peaks and to deep, dark valleys. The time following my conversion can best be characterized as a long, sweet honeymoon.

Another Unexpected Gift

Early in December 1977 my sister, Hanna, called and invited me to join her, family members, and friends for a traditional New Year's Eve party at her home in Holland. This event would turn out to be another major, life-altering experience. There I saw Janneke, my future bride and love of my life, a gentle-natured, petite, beautiful brunette with deep blue eyes.

I had met Janneke for the first time a few years earlier when she visited my parents' home. I remember the occasion vividly. She swept me off my feet and captured my heart from the moment I saw her sitting on our living room sofa, quietly staring at the floor because of her shy nature. I felt an immediate, irresistible attraction to her, but I never dared to make a move or express my feelings to her because of our age difference. I was thirty-one, and she was sixteen. Asking her out for a date was out of the question. Over time, however, because she was related to my brother through marriage, we developed a casual friendship due to my frequent visits to Holland.

At the New Year's Eve party, Janneke and I sat next to each other and engaged in a long, serious conversation. We were so drawn to one another that it seemed like we were the only two people in the room, oblivious to the festivities taking place around us.

At the stroke of midnight on December 31, 1977, something wonderful took place—we wished each other a happy New Year with a passionate kiss. In a brief intimate moment, I knew deep in my heart that Janneke and I were destined to spend the rest of our lives together. That evening marked the beginning of a courtship that would last almost two years. There was no need to rush outside and watch the traditional Dutch thunderous spectacle of fireworks. Plenty of sparks were flying around inside the living room of my sister's home.

On the night of my salvation, when I asked the Lord to give me a Christian wife, Janneke never crossed my mind. I never mentioned her name in my prayer. I never expressed to the Lord that I specifically wanted *her* to be my future bride. But God, who knows the heart of man and sees what's hidden on the inside, through His kindness was already busy orchestrating what would turn out to be a happy, lifelong union.[3] To my unspeakable joy and great surprise, Janneke was the answer to my prayer!

Background and Engagement

Janneke van de Koot was born on October 23, 1958, in the beautiful, historic city of Woerden in the Netherlands. When she was four, the family moved to Doetinchem, a city located in the "Achterhoek" (far corner) bordering Germany. There her father accepted a teaching position at a local high school. The youngest of four children, she grew up in a happy home. At the age of sixteen, during a downtown street evangelism campaign conducted by a group of teens in her hometown, Janneke surrendered her life, gave her heart to the Lord Jesus Christ, and committed to serve and follow Him all the days of her life.

Seven weeks after the New Year's celebration on the evening of February 19, following traditional custom, I got down on my knees and asked Janneke to be my wife. I promised to love her deeply, to always cherish her, to care for her, and to protect her for the rest of my life. I also promised to be the best husband I could possibly be.

Without any hesitation, her answer was a joyous, resolute "Yes!"

In somewhat unorthodox fashion, I drew a life-size pencil portrait of Janneke and wrote on it a lengthy poem, asking for her parents' permission to marry their beautiful daughter. I presented the framed picture to her parents the next morning. Throughout our courtship they had never expressed reservations or concerns about our relationship because of the difference in our ages. They knew their daughter, the last child to fly out of the nest, was head over heels in love, and they determined to support her decision to marry this American GI.

I was greatly relieved and overjoyed when they gave their immediate and mutual blessing. Thankfully, we were spared any stern lectures or lengthy discussions about our future plans. After her parents gave their approval, we agreed to get married after her graduation from a Christian college, where she was majoring in early childhood education.

Separated by more than three hundred miles, we spent nearly every weekend and holiday together in Holland. When we were unable to be together, we exchanged a poem or love letter each day throughout the length of our courtship. The longer our courtship lasted, the harder it became for us to live so far apart. During our dating period I began regularly attending the Dutch Reformed Church with Janneke, and often accompanied by her mother.

The Wedding

On Friday, August 17, 1979, a beautiful, sunny day, we were married. The civil ceremony at city hall, required by Dutch matrimonial law, was followed by a church wedding. The solemn ceremony at city hall was conducted both in Dutch and English for the benefit of my many friends who traveled to Holland to take part in the festivities.

The church service took place in one of the oldest chapels of the Evangelical Lutheran Church of the Netherlands. Built in AD 1500, it was located in the heart of Doetinchem. Although we were not affiliated with that denomination, we asked the pastor of that church to perform the wedding ceremony because Janneke had attended his Bible studies for teenagers after accepting the Lord.

I remember fighting back tears of joy and amazement throughout much of the hour-long church ceremony. Overcome with emotion, I wasn't able to sing many of the old, traditional Christian hymns known both to English and Dutch-speaking peoples. To be in that idyllic, picturesque church building with a radiant, beautiful, young bride standing at my side, looking like a princess in a fairy tale, was almost too much for me to handle. The warm rays of the August sun, shining through ornate, stained-glass windows, illuminated the interior of this small historically preserved church building.

Joining in the celebration, tightly squeezed together, were more than 150 family members and close friends. To me the events of that day were a demonstration of God's amazing grace, His tender mercies, and His everlasting love. As far as I was concerned, a great miracle took place on this day in the far corner of Holland. I didn't deserve any of this.

Adjusting to a New Life

After a month-long honeymoon in Southern California, I carried Janneke across the threshold of our little apartment in Leinfelden. Though I wanted to, I didn't carry her up the five flights of stairs.

She quickly assimilated into the American military community by volunteering her free time at the newly built Patch Barracks Elementary and High Schools, where she worked in the nurse's station and administered first aid. Soon after settling in her new environment, she registered with the Dutch consulate in Stuttgart, a requirement for Dutch citizens living abroad. While there, we learned to our surprise that a small Reformed Church of the Netherlands (not to be confused with the Dutch Reformed Church) was located in the village of Hedelfingen on the outskirts of Stuttgart. Call it coincidence, but the young Dutch pastor and his family lived within walking distance from our home. We called him the same evening and agreed to meet with them the following day.

Blessed with a German-born wife, Erika, and two young children, Pastor Roel Visser was the designated representative of the Reformed Church of the Netherlands, ministering to Dutch Christian communities in Stuttgart, Munich, and Frankfurt. Everyone was welcome. People from different Protestant denominations, including a few Dutch Catholic families, attended church services held twice each month in the Old Evangelical Church of Hedelfingen, originally built in AD 1317. Many also participated in regular evening Bible studies. One American exchange student, attending the University of Tübingen and majoring in theology with a fairly good command of the Dutch language, regularly attended these services.

We quickly developed a close bond with the Visser family that persists to this day. It was in Pastor Visser's church that I began to drink "spiritual infant formula."

Both Janneke and I eagerly looked forward to attending church services. Each service was followed by a one-hour fellowship time, when we enjoyed freshly brewed coffee, tea, and second-to-none Dutch pastries prepared by the church ladies. We developed new friendships and actively participated in regular Bible studies and other church activities.

Martien

Among those who attended church services in Hedelfingen was a Dutch missionary named Martien Hartman. At the age of twenty-one, while serving as a conscript in the Royal Dutch Air Force, a friend invited him to hear someone speak on God's plan of salvation. It was at this meeting that Martien was introduced to the gospel message. It didn't take long for him to recognize that he was a sinner in desperate need of a Savior. He wasted no time in surrendering his life to Jesus Christ and committing to serve Him all the days of his life.

When he completed his military service obligation, Martien enrolled in the Bible College of Wales in Swansea, Wales. That's where he met his beautiful, British bride-to-be, June James. After their graduation in 1964, they moved to Germany where June worked at a children's home in Siegen near Freudenberg. Martien became affiliated with the missions organization Light in the East with its headquarters in Korntal outside of Stuttgart. The young couple married in 1965.

Martien possessed something I wanted. I wasn't sure what, but whatever it was that motivated this man and his wife, I wanted it badly. They had devoted their lives to sharing the good news of Jesus Christ with people living in countries behind the Iron Curtain, where the mere mention of the name of Jesus could land one in a gulag in the desolate arctic region of Siberia.

The mission of Light in the East was to translate and print Bibles and other Christian literature into the many different languages of the countries behind the Iron Curtain. In cloak-and-dagger fashion, they smuggled these documents across heavily armed border crossings manned by often unfriendly and sometimes aggressive border guards. Smuggling was Martien's job.

A specially rigged VW van allowed him to transport thousands of Bibles and other books to prearranged, clandestine locations in the former Soviet Union and other Communist countries. When I first met Martien, he had been doing this type of work for more than twelve years, sometimes accompanied by June. In spite of extreme dangers and at great risk to their lives, they were relentlessly driven to reach lost souls in countries hostile to the gospel message, trusting their heavenly Father for direction, safety, and protection.

When he wasn't on one of those dangerous mission trips, Martien and June often attended church services in Hedelfingen. When they were there, Martien always singled me out in the crowd during our fellowship times after the services. He habitually pulled up a chair next to me, gently tapped my knee, and said in flawless English, "John, you need to serve the Lord with a flaming heart." I was a brand-new Christian then and didn't quite know what he meant by those words. Without his ever knowing it, Martien would in later years become a strong influence in my life.

Dennis

In November 1979 Janneke and I were overjoyed to learn that she was expecting our first baby. Don't ask me why, but I had always wanted to have three sons. One day during Janneke's pregnancy, I told her convincingly that we would have three boys. To this day I don't know what prompted me to say this to her.

We were both filled with unspeakable joy as we anticipated the birth of our first child. Each day during the ensuing nine months was a new adventure. To see her stomach slowly grow and later to feel the baby move in her womb all added to the excitement in our little household.

At 10:40 A.M., on Saturday, August 2, 1980, on the ninety-ninth anniversary of his great-grandfather's birth, little Dennis Willard Rozema (seven pounds, five and a half ounces, and twenty inches long) was born into this world after a painful, difficult delivery. No words can express the pride and joy we felt when Dennis was born. I was so proud that I didn't even feel the floors of the 5th U.S. Army General Hospital corridors in Stuttgart as Dennis was wheeled to the maternity ward in his clear, plastic bassinet. People in the hallways stopped to admire this newborn baby and comment on his exceptionally beautiful features. Later, friends referred to Dennis as the "Gerber Baby" because of his facial similarities. I felt so unworthy to have received such a beautiful, precious gift from God.[4] I was also proud of Janneke, who had endured so much pain during the long hours of labor and natural childbirth.

On the other hand, I didn't feel gratitude toward the army obstetrician in charge of the delivery; he had seemed uncaring toward this young mother who was about to give birth to her first baby. I found him to be a heartless man who reacted harshly as she was writhing in pain while being sutured, particularly when he kept pushing with great force on her stomach area to expel excessive blood and portions of the placenta from her uterus. This latter procedure was performed repeatedly.

At one point I nearly fainted at seeing Janneke in such terrible pain. She never felt the effects of the locally administered anesthesia and told the doctor so, but he paid little attention to her physical agony.

Because of complications during childbirth, both Janneke and Dennis were required to remain in the hospital for three days. After they came home, I developed the habit of sitting beside our baby's crib for hours each day in awe, quietly gazing at the beauty of what God had created and be filled with an inexpressible joy.[5] I wouldn't have traded this precious child for all the treasures, gold, silver, or money in this world.

Raising Baby

I didn't have even the vaguest notion of how to properly rear a child. I'd had no role model in my life. My biological father had abandoned me before I was born, and by my stepfather's actions, I knew he had despised me. When Dennis was born, I determined *never* to administer the destructive methods my stepfather had employed when he raised me. I was also determined to love my boy no matter what. Unlike my stepfather who had never touched me unless he wanted to slap me around and knock the glasses off my face, I was going to touch my son in a loving way—hold him, hug him, gently squeeze him, and kiss him.

I purposed to be the best dad my newborn son could have. I made a point each day of his life to tell him that I loved him. Seated by his crib while he slept, I softly told him that I loved him. At other times I tenderly cradled him in my arms for hours.

On Dennis's first wellness visit to the doctor, I picked up a bookmark printed with some profound and basic rules about child rearing. I still have a copy of it today. Written by Dorothy Law Nolte, it says the following:

CHILDREN LEARN WHAT THEY LIVE
By Dorothy Law Nolte

If children live with criticism, they learn to condemn.
If children live with hostility, they learn to fight.
If children live with ridicule, they learn to feel shy.
If children live with shame, they learn to feel guilty.
If children live with encouragement, they learn confidence.
If children live with tolerance, they learn patience.
If children live with praise, they learn appreciation.
If children live with acceptance, they learn to love.
If children live with approval, they learn to like themselves.
If children live with honesty, they learn truthfulness.
If children live in security, they learn to have faith in themselves and in those about them.
If children live with friendliness, they learn the world is a nice place in which to live.

Dearly loving my son, keeping him in my constant prayers, relying on the Lord for wisdom, and applying these basic principles, I figured we were off to a very good start.

I conclude by saying something about the kindness of God. I'm not exaggerating when I say that I'm the least deserving of His blessings. Before that fateful New Year's Eve in 1977, at age thirty-four, I had resigned myself to the fact that I would never marry or have a family of my own. The thought of remaining single and growing old, miserable, and lonely seemed like a dreadful proposition. All my valiant efforts to find the perfect mate had been in vain. But God, by His matchless mercies and wonderful grace, displayed His bountiful kindness by giving me a beautiful bride and a beautiful son. The apostle Paul, in his letter to the Ephesian church, writes,

> Now to him who is able to do immeasurably more than all we ask or imagine, according to his power that is at work within us, to him be glory in the church and in Christ Jesus throughout all generations, for ever and ever! Amen.
> —Ephesians 3:20–21

Yes, indeed. God, for whom nothing is impossible, is able to do so much more than we dare to ask, hope, or even imagine, as evident in my personal life. Amazingly, the Lord didn't stop lavishing His kindness on me at this point. No, He did much more than that. He gave me the desires of my heart by giving us two more handsome sons who are equally precious as our firstborn child. (I will tell you more about them in later letters). May the name of the Lord be praised forever!

> Your friend,
> John

Sixteen

A Flower in the Desert

My dear friend,

On Wednesday, December 17, 1980, we said good-bye to our friends at Patch Barracks and our new friends from church with heavy hearts. We flew on a packed Air France Airbus 300 to a country in the Middle East I cannot name for reasons that will become clear.

Sgt. First Class Frank Durell greeted us upon our arrival early the next day after a long, grueling, nonstop flight from Paris, France. Four-month-old Dennis cried from the moment we stepped on the plane until we set foot on dusty Middle Eastern soil. Despite our best efforts, we were unable to calm him down or make him comfortable. Angry, unpleasant stares came from many passengers who were annoyed and impatient because of Dennis's incessant and loud wailing. We felt bad, but our concerns were for our baby's well-being.

Church

Because our home wasn't ready to be occupied, we temporarily lived at the residence of my new boss, who was away spending the Christmas and New Year's holidays with his family in Maryland. One of my first questions was where people went to church. To my astonishment, I learned that the entire country boasted only one Christian church, located at the U.S. embassy compound. Services were held on Fridays, and Sunday was a regular workday for the U.S. embassy staff. Arrangements were made for us to be picked up the following day and transported to church.

The next morning after a restful night, Major Brett Hastings, his wife, and their two young children warmly welcomed us. Then he drove us to the U.S. embassy compound located in the heart of the city. The church met in no ordinary church building by any stretch of the imagination. The plain, windowless, mud-walled structure had once functioned as the embassy's supply and storage facility. Rough-hewn wooden columns supported a corrugated tin roof. Portions of its unfinished, bare concrete floor exposed compacted, yellowish-brown desert dirt.

Major Hastings kindly introduced us to the small congregation, which was comprised of Christians from different denominations and members of the local international community, who were known as "expats," derived from the term *expatriate*. In his introduction, he didn't fail to mention that Janneke was from the Netherlands.

As we took our seats, two young ladies sitting directly behind us leaned forward and warmly greeted us with "*Goede morgen*," a Dutch greeting for "good morning." These two young ladies weren't the only Dutch people in attendance. The man playing the keyboard was from Holland as well as the man who took part in leading the services conducted in English.

This unique church functioned like no other we had attended. It had a casual and warm family atmosphere. Some men wore coats and ties, and some ladies looked their best in Sunday dresses, but others sported sandals; casual, short-sleeve shirts or T-shirts; and jeans, most notably among the young Peace Corps volunteers. The eclectic style suited us just fine.

The church didn't have a designated minister or preacher since the host nation didn't issue entry visas to members of the Christian clergy. Establishing a church or conducting Christian religious meetings outside official U.S. embassy territory was strictly forbidden. This country was closed to the gospel message.

The opening prayer, delivered by the Dutchman who assisted leading the services, had a profound and lasting effect on me. This man didn't pray in the formal fashion I was used to hearing in other churches. He spoke without eloquent words as if he was talking to a friend. His prayer wasn't methodically thought out, carefully composed, or recorded on a piece of paper. No, he spoke from his heart with great sincerity.

The man who delivered the sermon at our first Friday service was a high-ranking State Department official of the U.S. embassy. No seminary-educated, church-ordained minister was present. Services were conducted in an orderly fashion, and exceptionally well-qualified laypersons delivered sermons on a rotating basis. We joyfully and loudly sang famous, traditional Christian hymns from the U.S. Armed Forces Hymnal. These were hymns sung in churches throughout the ages and composed by such notables as Martin Luther, Charles Wesley, Frances Ridley Havergall, even Ludwig van Beethoven, Wolfgang Amadeus Mozart, and many others.

We loved being there so much that we didn't want to leave. Before the day was over, both Janneke and I felt at home in our new, though strange, surroundings. We had met so many wonderful and friendly people, many of whom I was slated to work with.

Everyday Living

Thankfully, we didn't need to wait too long before moving into our large, completely furnished eight-room house with an enormous basement. When our household effects arrived, we stocked the basement with a year's provision of Western nonperishable food items. This included a large supply of Huggies diapers, enough to last us well into the next year.

A donkey-drawn wagon delivered water to our home three times per week. Water needed to be boiled for twenty minutes, cooled, and then slowly filtered before consumption. Our new home, protected by an eight-foot-high brick wall, came with a domestic servant named Ahmed. A courteous, hard-working man in his late thirties, the U.S. embassy paid him to provide security. For an additional small fee, he did all the chores around the house, including washing dirty laundry, ironing our clothes, washing the dishes, cleaning the house, and maintaining our yard. Ahmed also took care of our daily water needs. Depending on him was strange at first, but it freed much of Janneke's time, permitting her to spend endless hours of happy quality time with Dennis.

If this wasn't enough, we were given a Chevrolet Suburban for business and personal use. Dennis quickly became the darling of the American embassy community, and we made new friends in no time. Our neighbors across the street were an American couple not affiliated with the U.S. embassy who made their permanent home in Paris, France. He was an architect on a two-year assignment with a UN international economic development agency. We spent endless hours talking about a topic of mutual interest—architecture.

The local Arab population was friendly toward Westerners. We felt safe living there and explored every part of the city together; however, I never allowed Janneke to venture out by herself. We had plenty of opportunities to get away from the capital city and explore the rest of the country. Its beautiful, breathtaking scenery reminded me of storybook pictures about biblical times.

Tommy

Returning from a trip to Europe, I surprised Janneke, who had grown up with a dog, with a purebred English cocker spaniel. We occasionally took our cute, four-month-old, rambunctious pup for a stroll into town. The Arabian people where we lived didn't keep dogs as household pets, so in no time we were surrounded by dozens of curiosity seekers, both young and old. The scene almost became like a circus. These people had never seen such a peculiar-looking, four-footed animal and thought they were looking at a pig on a leash.

Wild native dogs, resembling a mix of Australian dingos and German shepherds, roamed the desert freely. Once we tried to tame and train a wild pup friends had found near the trash containers of the Sheraton Hotel outside the city. Both Janneke and I did our best taking care of little Tommy, but the disobedient wild animal with razor-sharp teeth didn't appreciate our love, attention, or affection.

Because our little canine friend was mean and vicious, he wasn't permitted to come anywhere near Dennis, and we always kept him outside. Tommy loved to wail loudly hours on end, usually while everyone was asleep. Night after night I angrily chased after the little dog, barefooted, dressed only in Fruit of the Loom white boxer shorts, and armed with a rolled-up section of the *International Herald Tribune*, but with no success. The dog was simply too fast as he ran in circles around the big house. Janneke lay quietly in bed, amused, and listened to all the commotion outside.

After a month or so, I had enough; Tommy needed to find another home. One night after feeding the little dog his sumptuous last supper, we drove him to familiar territory—the trash containers of the Sheraton Hotel. After saying our last farewells with great sighs of relief, we left our little friend to fend for himself under a star-filled Arabian night.

Laying on of Hands

Not long after we settled, Janneke joined a women's Bible study group. Primarily attended by ladies whose husbands were assigned to the U.S. embassy, and by a few from the international community, including two from Holland, this group met weekly. I was happy to see Janneke meet new friends and take part in activities outside the home. She joined a local amateur theater group as well, comprised mostly of people from the U.S. and British embassies.

Whenever we needed to see a doctor or dentist, we flew to Stuttgart, Germany, to be seen at U.S. facilities there. Except in extreme emergencies, medical treatment in the local community was out of the question. Only one registered nurse staffed the embassy's infirmary. She regularly and mercilessly administered the much-dreaded "G" (gamma globulin) shot on bare buttocks, other required vaccinations, and other prescribed medications. After being at our new assignment for a few months, Dennis was due for a regular medical checkup. Janneke also needed to see a doctor for a minor malady.

A few days before her scheduled departure to see the doctor, Janneke came home from her weekly Bible study and said somewhat triumphantly that the ladies in her Bible study group had prayed for her and laid hands on her. I digested her words for a few seconds and became unsettled. I didn't mind these women praying for her, but laying hands on her? That sounded bizarre and even a little scary to me.

When I asked her what laying on of hands was all about, she casually replied, "Oh, it's in the Bible. We do it occasionally, usually when someone's sick. We pray for their healing and lay hands on them."

Though I didn't say so, in my mind I wondered if she was becoming a religious fanatic. "Are you sure what you're doing is the right thing?" I asked.

She tried to calm my fears but was unable to convince me. I wasn't familiar with this practice and had never seen it done. Nor was it something we'd discussed in any of the Bible studies we regularly attended. "Laying on of hands" sounded creepy. Why would anybody lay hands on someone else for healing? Wasn't prayer good enough? These questions occupied my mind.

Janneke enjoyed her time of Bible study, prayer, and fellowship with her newfound friends. I wasn't about to be the one to discourage her from going to these meetings, so I decided to keep quiet about what was troubling me.

As time went by, she sensed that we were slowly growing apart spiritually. Janneke shared these concerns with her friends, and they began to earnestly pray for us, especially for me. Thankfully, over time I overcame my apprehensions. I learned that the practice of laying on of hands during a time of prayer for people in need is biblical and something very special.

Dangerous Mission

Many we befriended in the Middle East were there on a clandestine dual mission. Most held secular jobs but took every opportunity to share the good news of Jesus Christ with the Muslim people. For some, sharing the gospel was their primary purpose for being there. Supporting churches back home had sent them to spread the love of Christ abroad.

But this missions venture was a dangerous pursuit. Being caught proselytizing meant automatic, immediate expulsion from the country or possibly landing in a primitive jail cell or both. Like Martien and June Hartman in Stuttgart, these people had a heart for lost souls among the Arab-speaking peoples. Many spoke the Arabic language fluently, laboring long and hard under the constant threat of getting into serious trouble with local law enforcement officials and religious authorities. God has sent His servants to work in every corner of this globe.

Both Janneke and I enjoyed our new friendships and many hours of sweet fellowship. Many of our friends existed under austere living conditions because of the extremely high cost of living. For example, in 1981 the cost of the annual lease on our home was thirty-one thousand dollars, more than twice what I earned each year.

Like the Hartmans in Germany, there was something about the Christians around us that I wanted, but I couldn't yet put my finger on it. Whatever it was, I wanted it badly. For most of these people, earning a lot of money and living a comfortable lifestyle weren't on their priority list. For instance, one family with three young children ate pancakes for dinner three times per week because pancakes were all they could afford. Their well-cared-for children appeared strong, happy, and healthy; they also loved pancakes. This family always seemed joyful and peaceful despite having virtually nothing in material possessions and always having to carefully manage their meager finances.

As I slowly grew in my relationship with the Lord, I learned from our new friends the importance of accepting the Lord Jesus Christ as my personal Lord and Savior. Accepting Jesus Christ as the propitiation for my sins and placing my faith and trust in His finished work on the cross were very important steps. I knew that God loved me and that He had a purpose and plan for me. I was cognizant of the fact that I was a sinner and realized that all my good works couldn't gain me access to heaven. The only way to heaven was through God's only Son, Jesus Christ. On the night of November 19, 1977, I hadn't known these truths.

Even though I was confident of my eternal salvation, I felt a compelling need to ask Jesus into my heart—for my own peace of mind and to reassure myself. I am convinced that God had sent these new friends across my path to help me understand on a deeper level the riches of Christ and His finished work on the cross.

Our new friends also taught me and Janneke to pray and read the Bible together. This practice was something we'd never done in our marriage. Praying out loud seemed intimidating at first, but after a couple of times, it became easier. It took me a while to muster enough courage to pray out loud, especially in a group setting, and say what was on my heart.

Janneke and I learned a great deal from our new missionary friends. In retrospect, we think this was also why the Lord sent us to this poverty-stricken country in the Middle East. I was originally scheduled to be assigned to the American embassy in Mogadishu, Somalia. But for political reasons, that assignment was revoked, and we ended up in the Middle East instead of the African continent, where I had always wanted to be stationed.

THE REPRIMAND

Near the end of my two-year assignment in the Middle East, I was going through a very dark time in my life. A newly assigned army colonel was surprised to discover that I had been charged with duties and responsibilities that, according to him, should have been given to an officer. He was, in his words, "dumbfounded" to learn that his two predecessors had given me, the only enlisted soldier on staff, so much authority. Though I had received very high marks from a recent inspector general's inspection, he wasted no time in stripping me of many of my functions, dividing them between an army major and a captain on staff. I was crushed and brokenhearted.

Soon after this disgrace, while on a routine visit to the headquarters in Stuttgart, one of the senior officers there approached me and asked how the new colonel was getting along. Without giving my words a second thought, I confided to this man what had recently transpired in regard to my job.

The day after my return, the telephone rang. It was a call from the same officer in Germany; he wished to speak to the new chief. Unable to transfer the call, I asked my boss if he could take the call in my office.

Built like a fullback for the Dallas Cowboys, the colonel calmly took a seat in front of my desk, picked up the receiver, and listened intently to the officer at the other end. While he listened, I could literally see his neck's carotid arteries begin to bulge. The colonel's facial expression told me that he was about to explode any second.

Suddenly, with almost uncontrollable anger he raised his voice and said, "I demand to know the name of the individual who said there was a morale problem down here. And if you're not going to tell me who that individual is, I'll ask for a formal investigation!"

At that moment my heart sank through the two-inch-thick, marble-tiled floor. The colonel wasn't satisfied with the response and loudly repeated himself. When the officer didn't divulge the individual's name, the colonel slammed the receiver down, furiously stormed out of my office, rushed into his office across the hall, and slammed the door with a bang.

I felt deeply hurt and betrayed. I had spoken to that officer in Germany in the strictest confidence. Never for a moment had I considered that my words would go anywhere outside the four walls of his office. Worse, I had never mentioned the term "morale problem" during our conversation.

Things had spiraled out of control and I was mortified. Filled with dread and a paralyzing fear, I was unable to muster enough strength to get up out of my chair. Other staff officers had also made recent trips to Germany. Our new boss was undoubtedly strategizing his next move as he tried to figure out the identity of the disloyal, guilty culprit.

I needed about forty-five minutes to compose myself and regain my strength. After giving the matter careful thought, I decided that the best course of action was to tell my boss the truth. It was best that he heard my account from me rather than hearing a haphazard collection of half-truths from someone else.

With great trepidation but ready to face the consequences, I knocked on his door. To my surprise he seemed calm, composed, and surprised to see me. Perhaps that was because he suspected someone else. He was eager to hear what I had to say.

In detail I recounted my conversation with our liaison officer in Stuttgart. I acknowledged my embarrassment and shame for my actions, and then I apologized for having done something so stupid. I assured him that such behavior would never happen again. I expected him to become unglued, leap across his desk, and go for the jugular, but he remained calm.

Understandably, the colonel wasn't going to let me off unscathed. He gave me an oral reprimand and said he would proceed with an investigation. He also said he wouldn't tolerate any infraction from me, no matter how trivial it may appear, for the brief time remaining on my overseas tour.

For the first time in my thirteen-year army career, I had reached a very low point and had no one to blame but myself.

Hard but Necessary Words

I desperately needed a shoulder to cry on, someone impartial in our small organization who would listen. One evening after work, I privately talked to one of our senior officers on staff, a U.S. Air Force lieutenant colonel, a fighter pilot, and someone I greatly respected.

He had little sympathy for me after listening to my sob story. In addition, what he told me that evening was something I didn't want to hear. To summarize our more-than-two-hour-long discussion, he told me that in his opinion I had abused my authority by treating the local staff too harshly. I was a strict taskmaster, he said.

The colonel was right. Perhaps it had been the culture, but idleness was something I couldn't bear. The five local national employees who worked under my supervision hadn't always exhibited the high standards I demanded of them. Their work ethic had differed vastly from mine.

Sometimes I had felt the need to crack the whip. I had acted harshly and behaved like a drill sergeant. As painful as it was to hear those words from someone I admired and considered a good, trusted friend, I was glad for this conversation. No, it didn't make me feel any better; if anything I felt worse. But for my own good I had needed to hear what he thought. I was now more aware than ever of my professional shortcomings.

Recovering from this painful ordeal took a long time. I learned many valuable lessons and to this day feel ashamed when I remember my stupidity. However, it wasn't the last time I would be entangled in a web of betrayal.

The Bible says that "in all things God works for the good of those who love him, who have been called according to his purpose."[1] I didn't know it then, but God was slowly starting to chip away at the rough edges of my life.

In mid-November 1982, Janneke, Dennis, and Bobby, our English cocker spaniel, permanently left the Middle East and headed to Holland to prepare for the birth of our second child. I followed her in time to celebrate Christmas and New Year's. Our departure wasn't without mixed emotions. What hurt so much was leaving behind the many friends who had become so dear to us. It was also difficult leaving our little church at the U.S. embassy compound, which to us was like a beautiful flower blooming in a dry and thirsty land.

> I will proclaim the name of the Lord.
> Oh, praise the greatness of our God!
> He is the Rock, his works are perfect,
> and all his ways are just.
> A faithful God who does no wrong,
> upright and just is he.
>
> —Deuteronomy 32:3–4

Over a time span of many years, we have visited and attended services in beautiful, ornate houses of worship. Janneke and I have admired and marveled at magnificent church buildings of Europe, including Saint Peter's Basilica in Rome and the Notre Dame cathedral in Paris, which are considered architectural wonders of the world. We have also visited our National Cathedral in Washington, D.C., more than once. Yet in all their splendor and majesty none of these houses of worship can rival that dusty, unadorned, seemingly insignificant, little church in that vast desert region of the Middle East, where our faith took on a new, deeper meaning.

Your friend,
John

Seventeen

End of a Honeymoon

My dear friend,

The ringing of church bells on Sunday mornings is a pleasant memory from growing up in Holland. Most people who live there don't give them a second thought. Neither did I until early on Sunday, January 16, 1983, at exactly seven o'clock A.M., when those bells punctuated the birth of our second son, Kevin Christian. He was delivered at seven and a half pounds and nineteen inches long. Perhaps it was because of the umbilical cord wrapped around his little neck that he loudly exited his mother's birth canal at the last bell chime on that very special Sunday morning.

Except for Janneke's lower back pain throughout much of the final trimester of her pregnancy, Kevin's birth, which I recorded on camera, had come with relative ease. He was born at the St. Josef Hospital in Doetinchem and delivered by a midwife who was assisted by a male registered nurse.

Both mother and son were discharged from the hospital three hours later. Thanks to the excellent social welfare system in Holland, a nurse provided daily postnatal care at home. Once again God, Creator and giver of all life, blessed our little family in ways we cannot express in words.[1] Like his older brother, Kevin is a treasure and a joy beyond measure.

House Hunting in Florida

Only two weeks later, I had to wrestle myself away from my newborn son and fly on a now-defunct Florida Airlines plane to Miami. My next assignment was the Miami District Recruiting Command, not as an army recruiter, but as personnel management NCO. Janneke, Dennis, and Kevin followed a month later. Before their departure, we gave Bobby, our English cocker spaniel, to a local farmer. Transporting a pet on an airplane was costly and too much of a burden. Moreover, we had no guarantee that we would find a home in southern Florida where pets were allowed.

On my first night in Florida, I got down on my knees in my hotel room in South Miami and asked the Lord to provide a home for our family. My preference was that it would not be in Miami, then known as the crime capital of America, but near Homestead Air Force Base, twenty miles south of Miami. Because this would be Janneke's first experience living in the United States, a military installation would be safe and familiar territory for her. Comfortable with shopping at the commissary and Post Exchange, she knew where to find medical, dental, and other needed facilities.

Finding a suitable home for our family was no easy task. New homes were being built in many parts of southern Florida; however, building a home took an average of between five to six months. I couldn't wait that long. Our household goods had arrived from the Middle East and had been placed in a commercial storage facility at a cost of one hundred dollars per day. Janneke and the boys were also scheduled to arrive on February 26, less than a month away. I needed to find a place for us to live as soon as possible.

Because much of southern Florida is known for retirement communities, many rental properties with homeowner's association rules don't allow young children or pets. A week before my family's arrival, after extensively scouting the area and almost exhausting all possibilities, I received a call from Mr. Bill Ryerson, a local builder. He offered us a brand-new, single-garage home that was immediately available in a new subdivision. He would even arrange for us to rent the property until the mortgage was finalized, he said. Because of unforeseen family circumstances, the person who had originally ordered the home was no longer able to proceed with its purchase. The location was perfect. The house was only a paper airplane ride from the main gate of Homestead Air Force Base.

We loved our four-bedroom, two-bathroom home and its location. Practically on the edge of the Florida Everglades, it was less than a fifteen-minute drive from the beautiful Florida Keys. During the hot, humid subtropical summer months, we frequently took the boys swimming at one of the national parks on the Keys. The breathtaking, transparent, turquoise ocean water was like no other we had seen before. I also loved my new job and enjoyed meeting new friends and working with them. We attended weekly Protestant services at the U.S. Air Force Chapel on Homestead Air Force Base, where Janneke joined the church choir during our first Sunday there.

We enjoyed listening to a contemporary Christian radio station and watching a Christian network on cable TV, which operated twenty-four hours a day, seven days a week. As a result of exposure to many programs on Christian TV and radio broadcasts, we developed a deep love for the Jewish people and the nation Israel.

No people on earth have suffered as much as the Jewish people. They continue to suffer greatly through extreme hatred, and other forms of persecution and hostile aggression in many parts of the world and—yes, to our great shame—even here in America. Tragically, history reveals that many of the perpetrators of unspeakable and heinous crimes committed against the Jews have been Christians—Protestants and Catholics alike. It's no wonder that many Jewish people view Christians with great suspicion.

NAME IT AND CLAIM IT

I became intrigued with the teachings of one TV preacher in particular and began watching him almost every week. What aroused my interest was his message that it was okay for me to have all the material possessions I wanted. He didn't specifically use these words, but his messages were clear and convincing. I could acquire anything I wanted; all I needed to do was "name it and claim it."

One day he said, "If I want a brand-new Cadillac, I go to the nearest dealer and pick out the one I want, amen. My next step is to claim it, buy the car, and drive it home. I see nothing wrong with driving around in a brand-new Cadillac, amen."

Wow! This was a new teaching to me, and I liked what I was hearing. It sounded very exciting and almost too good to be true. Bible in hand, this preacher ended almost every sentence with an "amen"; he was someone who obviously knew what he was talking about. It wasn't that I had longed to own a Cadillac, a Jaguar, or a Porsche. But after listening to this man for several weeks, I was inspired to explore greater heights. I had my eyes set on bigger things, like making a killing on the local real estate market.

Real Estate Venture

One day I asked Janneke what she thought of buying a second home. I suggested that we rent the one we lived in and live in another brand-new home in the same neighborhood. Without any hesitation she said she was perfectly happy with where we lived and didn't see the need for our family to move again or maintain a second home.

I tried to make my argument a bit stronger by saying that I wasn't happy with a few of our neighbors. Some of them, for example, didn't see the importance of mowing their lawns every week. Besides, Dennis's little playmate, a girl who lived next door, wasn't always nice to him. She seemed very catty sometimes. Janneke didn't think these minor problems justified buying a second home. I asked her to think about the matter for a few days; perhaps she would change her mind.

After three days or so, I gently approached her and asked if she'd thought about our previous discussion. She said that she had but again reiterated that she was happy with where we lived. Janneke wasn't interested in a second home. Disappointed, I decided to wait a few more days.

One day when I thought the time was right, I explained to her that we would receive generous annual tax breaks on our rental property. Moreover, property values in our neighborhood would most certainly rise, which meant we could potentially earn a lot of money. Buying a second home would be a good decision and a wise investment, I said. Unfortunately, the idea of earning a lot of extra money didn't appeal to Janneke. Her response was the same.

I decided to patiently wait a few more weeks and see if I could get her to change her mind.

During my fourth attempt, using a new strategy and some creative persuasion, I thought I could convince her. Surely she would agree to my wonderful new plan now. I suggested that we buy a new home with a double garage, something we would need when we bought our second car. Like many of our neighbors, we could have a large, screened-in porch; beautiful, imported, Italian terra cotta ceramic tiles on the floors in the dining room, kitchen, and breakfast area; and I could have a studio for future use. The studio was very important to me because I envisioned retiring from the army someday and spending my remaining years painting and drawing to earn a little extra cash to supplement our retirement income.

Janneke listened intently, but after a minute or so she responded with that all-too-familiar line. "I'm very happy where we are. The Lord gave us this home, and I see no need for our family to move to another home."

This time she broke my heart because she didn't see the need to live in a home with all the extra niceties.

I didn't see a problem with what I wanted to do. We owned a home in Southern California, and I wanted to sell that house and use the proceeds to buy a second home in Florida. Convincing Janneke, however, proved to be more than an uphill battle.

After a few more weeks, I introduced her to yet another brilliant plan. If I could convince Mr. Ryerson to sell us a second house at a reduced price, would she relent and allow me the pleasure of going ahead with the idea? By now Janneke was tired of my repeated attempts to convince her that buying a second home was the right thing to do. She replied that if I felt that strongly about buying the house, I should go ahead.

After months of pleading, I was ecstatic!

I wasted no time and rushed off to the sales office before she could change her mind. Once there, I made my proposal and was told that Mr. Ryerson would be contacting me about purchasing a second home at a reduced price. The following day I received a telephone call at work and learned that the builder was more than happy to sell us a home at the price I had proposed.

A contract for a new, four-bedroom, two-bathroom home was prepared, and I paid a nominal nonrefundable deposit the same day. The home included all major appliances, a double garage, a fourteen-foot-by-twenty-four-foot porch, Italian tiles, and a two-hundred-square-foot studio—all on a tract of land just less than one-third of an acre. Land clearing, excavating, and pouring the foundation were scheduled to begin within a month. Each day on my way home from work, I drove by the construction site where my dream home was being built and took pictures of its progress.

The Nightmare

Everything was so exciting until nearly four months later when our beautiful, new dwelling was nearing completion. That's when all the problems started. The sale of our home in California was dragging. Mr. Ryerson demanded his money, and so did everyone else involved in the building and sale of this home—contractors, subcontractors, and others. But I had no money, and these people weren't interested in listening to a sob story about the slow progress of my real estate transaction on the West Coast. They demanded their money now.

As a result, Janneke and I were threatened with extensive litigation. It was only then that my eyes were opened, and I realized the terrible mistake I had made. I had placed my family in a precarious, embarrassing situation that caused much grief and heartache, especially to Janneke.

After several months of delaying creditors' demands for payment and repeatedly postponing the closing on our new home, we received the funds from the sale of our house in Monrovia, California, in early December 1983. Soon we were ready to move into our new home. On the morning of our move, however, our Chevy station wagon, which had run perfectly the day before, refused to start. We needed the station wagon to pull a ten-foot-long U-Haul trailer. Someone came to repair the vehicle, and this delayed our move by several hours. Also, to everyone's surprise, the weather was unseasonably hot and humid. Temperatures in southern Florida during the month of December are supposed to be like springtime in Virginia. That wasn't the case on the day of our move.

As the last item of our household effects arrived at our new home, the electricity unexpectedly stopped working, causing the temperature in our house to reach intolerable levels. The electric company couldn't fix the problem right away. Finally, after two long days, a technician came to do the necessary repairs.

When the electricity was finally restored, we started a load of laundry and went outside to play with Dennis and Kevin. While we were on the porch playing with the boys, hot, dirty water from the full load of laundry came gushing out of the washing machine and into the laundry room, adjacent breakfast area, kitchen, dining room, living room, hallway, and parts of the master bedroom, almost ruining our brand-new, wall-to-wall carpeting.

I wasn't aware of it then, but it wasn't just a workman's error in installing the drainpipe that caused the problem. No, God's anger burned against me because of my stubbornness and ignorance. The Lord had graciously answered our prayers about a home for our family, but buying another home was like telling God that the house He had given us wasn't good enough.

Though Janneke had repeatedly warned me, I insisted on having things my way. I wanted something bigger and better—something my neighbors and I could admire. Yes, that TV preacher had taught error, but I had no one to blame but myself for listening and allowing his teaching to take root in my heart. I was so ashamed of myself for putting our family through so much misery and unnecessary grief. Because of the error of my ways, Janneke and I cried on our knees every day for weeks.

During a particular church service, I remember an air force chaplain telling the congregation that if a Christian's life could be drawn on a graph, it would look like a line with peaks and valleys. We would experience seasons of standing on mountaintops and seasons of going through deep, dark valleys; we would experience times of rejoicing and times of shedding many tears.

When the problems with our second home were finally resolved, I was looking forward to enjoying some extended mountain peak time. Instead I was about to enter the lowest point of my army career.

Betrayal of Confidence

Anyone in the army recruiting business would agree that an assignment to a recruiting organization can be very stressful, especially when recruiting objectives are not achieved. The army cannot accomplish its mission while facing acute manpower shortages, especially during times of war. Pressure is exerted from the top down to the lowest level to recruit qualified young men and women to fill its rank and file.

For some time now, we had not been able to meet our monthly recruitment goals. To remedy this problem, the army handpicked a rising officer to take command of the now-re-designated U.S. Army Miami Recruiting Battalion. He wasted no time in seeking to identify and fix problems he determined had contributed to the organization's failure to meet or exceed its assigned recruiting objectives.

I had a good relationship with our new commander. One day he pulled me aside and shared some of his concerns and frustrations. Although he didn't say it, common sense dictated that our conversation was a matter of strict confidence. Thoughtlessly, I passed some of that information, which was considered sensitive in nature, on to someone else. This time I was the one who had betrayed someone's confidence, and my actions resulted in a snowball effect culminating in dire consequences.

Because of my shameful conduct, I saw my future army career crumbling before my eyes. Dreams of someday retiring at the highest enlisted rank vanished into thin air. Understandably, I no longer enjoyed the confidence of my commander. I received a Letter of Counseling for an unrelated issue and for the first time in my army career a less-than-favorable performance report. My unprofessional behavior brought shame and humiliation, not only on me, but worse, on my commander as well. Wounded and disgraced, I didn't think I would ever be able to recover from this terrible ordeal.

To ease the hurt as I had at my previous assignment, I sought someone to talk to, a shoulder to cry on, someone I could trust. One day an air force chaplain friend suggested that I make an appointment with a psychiatrist. The young, inexperienced chaplain wasn't equipped to deal with my problems.

I remember reluctantly sitting in the psychiatrist's office a week later at Homestead Air Force Base and listening to his words of wisdom. In less than two minutes I realized I was in the wrong place. The doctor, a U.S. Air Force lieutenant colonel, no doubt a learned man, had all the right answers except he had no quick remedy for my stubborn nature, my ignorance, or my stupidity. After our first forty-five-minute "get-acquainted session," I determined that my problems didn't merit being treated by a mental health specialist and decided never to return.

It took a long time for me to recover and the pain to subside.

Release

Thankfully, I'm pleased to relate a happy ending to this story. In the course of time by the grace and mercies of God, my commander had a change of heart. He destroyed the Letter of Counseling and withdrew the less-than-favorable performance report. He even welcomed us into his home and invited me out to lunch while visiting my next duty assignment in El Paso, Texas.

Despite the deep anguish we endured, we experienced many happy times during our three-and-a-half-year stay in Florida. Our boys loved going to the Port of Miami, marveling at the arriving and departing amphibious airplanes, which carried passengers to and from many places in the Caribbean islands. Dennis and Kevin also admired and watched in awe the many cruise ships that docked there. We will always treasure memories of traveling to Key West and exploring beautiful, pristine areas on Florida's west coast. We visited Disney World in Orlando and toured the John F. Kennedy Space Center near Cape Canaveral. Janneke and I consider ourselves very fortunate to have lived in the Sunshine State.

Darren

Just after midnight on December 20, 1984, Janneke and I were blessed with the birth of our third son, Darren Timothy. Like his two brothers, Darren was an adorable, healthy baby weighing seven pounds, fifteen ounces. He was nineteen inches long, and lots of black hair covered his little head.

He was born at the U.S. Air Force Hospital on Homestead Air Force Base and delivered by a doctor who could have been the identical twin of Ben Vereen, a funny and famous African American actor. Had the doctor's name not been different, we would have been convinced that the well-known Hollywood celebrity had delivered our son. This doctor was a comedian in his own right. Perhaps because of his humorous nature and joking gestures in the delivery room, Darren's birth was the quickest and easiest of the three.

> Sing to the Lord, you saints of his;
> praise his holy name.
> For his anger lasts only a moment,
> but his favor lasts a lifetime;
> weeping may remain for a night,
> but rejoicing comes in the morning.
>
> —Psalm 30:4–5

During the time of our misfortunes with our second home and my work troubles, the period I have described as a long, sweet honeymoon was over. Our family was now complete with the birth of Darren. It seemed as if we had finished one phase of an adventurous pilgrimage and were ready to embark on a new one.

Your friend,
John

Eighteen

Not-So-Quiet Time

My dear friend,

Something else we learned from our missionary friends in the Middle East was the importance of observing a set time each day, preferably in the morning, devoted exclusively to the reading and studying of Scripture and prayer. In Christian circles this observance is often referred to as "quiet time." Merely going to church on Sundays, listening to a sermon, or joining a Bible study group is insufficient for personal spiritual development. Also necessary is a personal time of seeking God's heart.[1]

Don't ask me why, but somewhere in the far, distant recesses of my feeble brain, I once thought that my God was the same as gods or deities from other world religions. I tossed that idea out the window early one morning during my prayer and Bible study time while living in Miami.

THE VOICE

In 2 Kings, I came upon the story of Naaman, commander of the king of Aram's army. Scripture records that Naaman was a great man in the sight of his master and highly regarded because through him the

Lord had given victory to Aram. Naaman was a valiant warrior, obviously skilled in battle, but he suffered from the dreaded disease of leprosy.

As the story unfolds, a young, captive, Jewish slave girl, a servant of Naaman's wife, tells about a prophet in Samaria who could cure him of his leprosy. In hopes of being healed from this illness and with the king's approval, Naaman departs for Israel, accompanied by an entourage of servants, horses, and chariots.

When he arrives at the home of the prophet Elisha, he stands at the door, and a messenger tells him to wash himself seven times in the Jordan River, be cleansed of his leprosy, and have his health restored. Being a prideful man, Naaman becomes enraged because the prophet himself doesn't meet with him. He feels greatly humiliated. Instead of meeting the man of God, he is addressed by a mere messenger. What also infuriates him is the fact that he was told to wash in the Jordan River. Weren't the rivers of Damascus good enough? Couldn't he wash in them instead of in the Jordan and be healed?

In a fit of rage, Naaman returns to his homeland. But his servants persuade him to go back and wash in the Jordan seven times. The rest of the story is told as follows:

> So he went down and dipped himself in the Jordan seven times, as the man of God had told him, and his flesh was restored and became clean like that of a young boy. Then Naaman and all his attendants went back to the man of God. He stood before him and said, "Now I know that there is no God in all the world except in Israel."[2]

I thought about these verses for a moment and read Naaman's last statement again, this time slowly and carefully: "Now I know that there is *no* God in *all the world* except in Israel" (emphasis mine).

Reading those words had an electrifying effect on me. It was like being hit by a two-by-four between the eyes except that I didn't feel any pain or ill effects. To be sure, there is only *one* God. God spoke clearly and in an instant showed me that no matter how well-meaning other religions are, there is only *one* God, and He is the God of Israel.[3]

Several weeks later, again early one morning during quiet time, Acts 4:12 came alive. It reads as follows: "Salvation is found in no one else, for there is no other name under heaven given to men by which we must be saved." Unlike the verses in 2 Kings, this verse hit me like a ton of bricks. I read it again slowly, word for word: "Salvation is found in *no one else,* for there is *no other name* under heaven given to men by which we must be saved" (emphasis added).

The obvious name in question here is that of Jesus Christ, Son of the living God. If the effects were profound when I read this Scripture the first time, reading it a second time almost caused me to panic.

"But Lord," I said, "what about the Muslims? What about the Buddhists and the Hindus and all the others?" Again my eyes fell on the Scripture before me: "Salvation is found in *no one else,* for there is *no other name* under heaven given to men by which we must be saved" (emphasis added).

As I read this passage a third time, thoughts of my family raced through my head, thoughts of my mother, my brother, my two sisters, and all the others who were so dear to me. I now found myself in a complete state of panic.

I jumped up from my chair, ran out of the back door, around the house, and into our front yard. I didn't care who drove by, I didn't care what people thought of me, and I wasn't in the least worried about what my neighbors were thinking as I raised my arms to heaven.

With a broken heart and crushed in spirit, I cried out to the Lord. "But Lord," I said, "what about my family?!" I had *not* memorized the Scripture, nor had I carried the Bible with me when I ran outside. But in response to my plea, a voice emerged within me and said very clearly and distinctly, "Salvation is found in *no one else,* for there is *no other name* under heaven given to men by which [they] must be saved" (emphasis added).

I suddenly became acutely aware of the grave and serious implications of this Bible passage. It meant that those who have not accepted God's *free* gift to mankind, who have not trusted in the completed work of Jesus on the cross, who have not placed their faith and trust in Him, are eternally doomed. Contrary to what most believe, those people will *not* receive the gift of eternal life. It meant they were destined to go to hell, a place of everlasting weeping and gnashing of teeth. Their place will forever be in the fiery lake of burning sulfur![4]

I was mortified at the thought of seeing my dear family and friends in this predicament. As far as I was concerned, they didn't deserve this.

Still in my front yard with arms raised to heaven, I cried out to the Lord a second time. I said that I wanted to serve Him. I wanted to reach out to my family. I wanted to reach out to those who were so dear to me and to others who were willing to listen.

This time there was no response.

The Aftermath

It took a while for me to ponder the events of that morning. I sat down with Janneke and told her what had happened. At first we didn't quite know what to make of it. To be sure, we both wanted to reach out to our loved ones, but the question remained—when would we take that big step?

We thought about becoming missionaries. The problem was that we weren't affiliated with a particular Protestant denomination. But we liked it that way because of our experiences with our church in Stuttgart, our little church in the Middle East, and our church at Homestead Air Force Base, where people from different denominations, yet of like mind and spirit, came together to corporately worship the Lord. Membership in a particular denomination didn't appeal to us, nor is it found in Scripture. But becoming missionaries meant that we would need to find other means of financial support.

What happened that morning both Janneke and I treasured in our hearts. We kept the event to ourselves, agreed to pray, and asked the Lord for wisdom and direction. After several weeks we decided that the best course of action was to remain in the army, retire when eligible, and then share the love and good news of Jesus Christ with family and friends abroad.

So it was that early one Saturday morning under a clear blue Florida sky in the front yard of our home outside Homestead Air Force Base, there was born in me a deep desire to reach out to lost family members, friends, and others willing to hear the good news of Jesus Christ. Nothing at that point was more important to me. I didn't care if I had to live in a pup tent and sit on Florida orange crates for the rest of my life; my desire was to rescue people from death and slaughter, to snatch them from the fire.[5] We wanted to do our share in fulfilling the Great Commission and couldn't wait. At times I felt like a thoroughbred racehorse ready to storm out of the gate. Maybe that's what I deeply craved, what Martien and June Hartman and our friends in the Middle East exhibited—a passion to seek after lost souls.

> Enter through the narrow gate.
> For wide is the gate and broad is the road that leads to destruction,
> and many enter through it.
> But small is the gate and narrow the road
> that leads to life, and only a few find it.
> —Matthew 7:13–14

> Multitudes who sleep in the dust of the earth will awake:
> some to everlasting life,
> others to shame and everlasting contempt.
> —Daniel 12:2

Your friend,
John

Nineteen

When Johnny Comes Marching Home

My dear friend,

On the Fourth of July 1986, we departed Miami, driving a rented twenty-two-foot-long, fully loaded, yellow Penske truck, and traveled to El Paso, Texas. We had to leave a lot of furniture behind because there wasn't enough room in the vehicle. Riding shotgun in the truck was a real thrill for Dennis. Janneke, along with Kevin and Darren, followed, driving our packed Chevy station wagon on the almost-two-thousand-mile journey. We combined our leisurely voyage with a two-week vacation, taking in the southern states of Florida, Alabama, Mississippi, Louisiana, and Texas.

After finishing a memorable six-month assignment at Fort Bliss and meeting so many wonderful new friends, we continued our globe-trotting adventures to Southern California, where our car, now a brand-new Ford Tempo, was placed on a boat in Long Beach to be transported to Bremerhaven, Germany.

BACK TO GERMANY

Janneke and I had both been pleasantly surprised to learn that our next assignment would take us back to familiar territory: Stuttgart in southern Germany, a virtual stone's throw from the beautiful Black Forest. This time we would not be at Patch Barracks but across town at Kelley Barracks, home of the legendary "Jayhawk," headquarters of the U.S. Army VII Corps.

Soon after our arrival, our family was assigned to a small but comfortable three-bedroom, apartment-type dwelling at the military family housing complex at Robinson Barracks located north of Stuttgart. We enjoyed a sweet reunion with friends from our little church in Hedelfingen and developed new friendships with people who had joined the church during our six-year absence.

My Baptism

On March 12, 1989, I was baptized, an event long overdue. I would not have mentioned my baptism had it not been for the following: Our church secretary asked me if my extended family from Holland would also attend the services. She needed to know to ensure sufficient coffee, tea, and pastries were on hand for the after-service fellowship. My response was that no one outside my immediate family would understand the meaning or importance of baptism, nor would anyone be willing to drive more than five hours to Stuttgart to witness the event.

The thought that my mother, brother, or sisters wouldn't be there saddened my heart. On any given Sunday, no more than perhaps twenty-five adults plus children were in attendance. Miraculously, on the day of my baptism not one pew was empty in that church, which could seat at least one hundred adults and children. Even the small balcony, normally occupied exclusively by our organist, was filled to capacity.

No special announcements had heralded the event. God saw the condition of my heart and tightly packed our little, beautiful, almost-seven-hundred-year-old church building with new family members. Amazingly, there was no shortage of coffee, tea, or pastries during our fellowship time after the service. What also made this day special was the dedication of both Kevin and Darren to the Lord, an event that is not a tradition in the Reformed Church of the Netherlands. Dennis had been baptized there as an infant.

Dennis and Kevin attended the U.S. Department of Defense Elementary School and kindergarten located at Robinson Barracks within walking distance from our home. They made lasting friendships and enjoyed many opportunities to see much of the beautiful European countryside. To this day

Dennis remembers our excursions to Paris, Rome, Florence, Pisa, Switzerland, the Austrian Alps, and many other sites of great historical significance.

Unprecedented Access

It was very exciting to be in Germany on November 9, 1989, and witness the destruction of the Berlin Wall, which had separated West Germany from East Germany, and see the crumbling of the Iron Curtain. We were glued to the TV during those days. As history unfolded before our eyes, it brought with it eerie feelings of uncertainty. The sudden, unexpected turn of events in the former Soviet Union, coupled with the fact that one country after another were declaring their independence and abolishing their once-staunch Communist ideology, caused many to feel uneasy, not knowing what would happen next.

The collapse of the Soviet Empire allowed unprecedented access for the gospel message to reach people living in areas where the proclamation of the gospel had previously been nonexistent.

Work for Martien Hartman and his fellow laborers at Light in the East went into high gear. In addition to Bibles and other Christian literature, they also participated in a vast distribution of material goods, specifically medical equipment and supplies, blankets, and clothing. They no longer needed to contend with mean, aggressive border guards. Never in its history had Light in the East experienced such a great opportunity to spread the love of Jesus to those who exhibited great spiritual hunger and were ready to accept the truth of the gospel message.

Martien continued to gently remind me to "serve the Lord with a flaming heart." I didn't need to ask him what he meant this time. My passion to reach lost family members, friends, and others willing to hear the good news of Jesus Christ didn't diminish one iota during those three wonderful years in Stuttgart.

Assignment in Virginia

During the winter of 1990, after serving in Stuttgart for three years, we had to leave behind our dear friends, colleagues, and the city that had become our second home. As always, saying good-bye was a sad time.

My next and final assignment was Headquarters, United States Army Training and Doctrine Command (TRADOC), located at historic Fort Monroe in Hampton, Virginia, situated at the tip of the Virginia peninsula. My new boss, an army colonel, conspicuously displayed a Bible on the credenza next to his desk. When I reported for duty on March 3, 1990, I knew I was in the right place.

Our family moved into a nice, two-story, three-bedroom apartment complex on Willow Oaks Boulevard in Hampton, conveniently located across the street from Langley Elementary School, where we soon enrolled all three boys after our arrival in the Old Dominion.

Falling in love with Virginia, particularly the Hampton Roads area, birthplace of colonial America, took no time. As a family, we explored historic sites such as Williamsburg and Jamestown, frequently visited our nation's capital, and spent countless lazy hours "crabbing" and fishing for flounder in the Chesapeake Bay.

As the time drew near for us to say farewell to army life, I began to have cold feet and second thoughts about our long-planned move to the Netherlands. I had always enjoyed our frequent but brief visits to Holland while stationed in Germany; however, for unknown reasons, the country where I had grown up as a boy had become foreign to me. The thought of leaving behind everything dear and familiar to me suddenly became a scary proposition.

War Scare

My retirement date was involuntarily delayed because of Operation Desert Storm, the First Gulf War. On the evening of January 16, 1991, while driving home from a local restaurant after celebrating Kevin's eighth birthday, we heard the announcement on the radio that the United States armed forces had invaded and bombed targets in Baghdad and other places in Iraq and Kuwait.

Our future was now uncertain, and we wondered if my next assignment would be in the Middle East. I had considered that possibility because of the war's buildup, which had begun nearly six months earlier. The U.S. military anticipated many casualties because of the enemy's suspected stockpiles of chemical and biological weapons. The worse case scenario, if called upon to serve in Iraq, was that I, too, could become a casualty of that war.

Talk of their father going off to war sounded frightening to our boys. To calm their fears and anxiety, Janneke delicately explained that there was no need to be alarmed. If something dreadful happened to their dad—in the event that he had to fight a war overseas—he would go to heaven and be with the Lord Jesus. She went on to explain what it takes to go to heaven, to which both Kevin and Darren eagerly responded. Dennis had already accepted the Lord Jesus Christ into his heart a few years earlier when we lived in Germany. Now Kevin and Darren were ready to make that decision. Before going to sleep that night, while kneeling at their bedsides, Janneke led both boys to the Lord in prayer.

Operation Desert Storm lasted forty-three days. Thankfully, the United States and her allies sustained few casualties. Retirement and plans to move to Europe were now certain.

SETBACK

We were determined to make our move to the Netherlands debt-free; this plan only seemed to make sense. For many years we had been faithfully setting money aside each month in preparation for this move.

But in February 1991, our tax preparer abruptly derailed those plans early one evening after work. To my great shock, I learned that we owed the Internal Revenue Service thousands of dollars due to capital gains taxes on the sales of our two homes in Florida. This payment virtually wiped out our savings account. I informed the lady at H&R Block, who prepared our tax returns, that our first home sold without a penny profit and that our second home sold at great financial loss. Showing little sympathy, she calmly replied that our financial setbacks on the sale of these two homes had no bearing on our obligation to pay the IRS.

I was almost in a state of panic. Pacing the corridors of the mall, I cried out to the Lord about our financial dilemma. Moving overseas debt-free was now out of the question and caused a great deal of added anxiety.

Long before our move to the Netherlands, Janneke and I agreed that she would find a job there and work outside the home to supplement our army pension. I didn't speak the Dutch language well enough to feel comfortable in any work environment. I would remain at home and be the homemaker. Almost one year before our scheduled departure, she began to mail neatly prepared job applications, résumés, cover letters, and portrait photographs to many different Christian schools in Holland, hoping to land a job as a kindergarten teacher. A friend in Holland who was a kindergarten teacher supplied the job leads.

Nine months later, after thirty-three painstaking attempts and much prayer, we had received not one favorable response. We took that news to mean that the Lord didn't want Janneke to be a kindergarten teacher. This development was a great disappointment, especially for me, because teachers in Holland receive lucrative salaries with generous benefits. We both needed to learn lessons in trusting the Lord and in remembering that He would care for our family and meet our needs.

Opportunity

In March 1991, Pastor Roel Visser, our faithful friend in Germany, and his young son came to Hampton for a short visit. He brought along a job ad from a Christian magazine seeking a married couple to be managers for a Christian youth center in a city not far from where I had grown up. Neither Janneke nor I thought we would stand a chance, convinced that many couples, eager to serve the Lord, would welcome this opportunity to work with young people.

We decided not to apply. But less than two months before our scheduled departure, Roel Visser called to let us know that even though the job had been advertised for several months, amazingly not one couple had applied for the position. We were now both convinced that this was the job the Lord had in mind for us.

Janneke wasted no time in calling the person whose name was listed on the job ad. She was told to contact the organization immediately upon our arrival in Holland. The salary wasn't great, but the opportunity sounded promising and exciting.

One day I was called to the office of the TRADOC command sergeant major. When I arrived, the command sergeant major insisted on knowing exactly why I was retiring.

"Soldiers your age don't retire from the army," he said, "unless there are problems." He wanted to know if I had a conflict with the adjutant general.

I assured the command sergeant major that I enjoyed an enviable professional relationship with my boss and considered him to be one of the greatest army colonels I had ever worked for. I told him that my primary reason for wanting to retire was to "spend more time with my family and see my boys grow up." While that answer was partially correct, I didn't have the nerve to tell this man that the real reason I wanted to retire was to serve the Lord.

When I left his office, I was overcome with great shame and anger—anger directed at myself. That wasn't the first time. Others wanted to know what my plans were after my retirement. As usual, I was always quick to evade the issue, not wishing to reveal my true motive for leaving the army, afraid that my reputation would be tarnished. Each time it happened, I cursed and hated myself afterward for not being forthright and mustering enough courage to tell people the truth.

Retirement

On July 31, 1991, a pleasantly warm and sunny day, nine officers and two enlisted soldiers retired from the U.S. Army at Fort Monroe. I was one of the two enlisted soldiers. An end had come to my association with great, noble, honorable men and women of all four branches of the service with whom and for whom I had proudly served over a time span of nearly twenty-two years. The army was a big family to me, and it broke my heart to see my service come to an end on that day. I will forever treasure in my heart the many friendships made while serving our great nation. I consider it an extraordinary honor and privilege to have been part of one of the finest, if not *the* greatest, organization America has produced—the United States Army.

The unforgettable event took place on a manicured parade field situated in front of the generals' quarters overlooking the beautiful Chesapeake Bay. The honor guard, dressed in their ceremonial Continental Army uniforms, added to the pomp and circumstance. I'll never forget the scene: a U.S. Navy behemoth aircraft carrier, returning from her mission in the Middle East, slowly sailed by Fort Monroe while her sailors, dressed in sparkling, white uniforms, stood at attention evenly spaced along the edge of its flight deck. While the carrier passed by, the United States Continental Army Band played the national anthem. It was a scene that sent chills up the spines of everyone there.

Soldiers retiring from active service at Fort Monroe are asked which song they would like the band to play at their retirement. I selected "When Johnny Comes Marching Home," the popular marching song from the Civil War era, written by Patrick S. Gilmore, an Irish immigrant to America.

While I never considered Holland to be my home, I thought it was a nice send-off and an appropriate tune to close my army career. For some, the playing of their selected song by the band was probably the most moving aspect of the day's events. As the ceremony drew to a close and as the band struck up the first note, each soldier stepped out of formation and marched in a long, straight line off the parade field. When it was my turn, I couldn't help fighting back tears as I marched to the drumbeat of a song from days gone by.

Less than twenty-four hours after my separation from the U.S. Army, we were on a plane traveling from Norfolk, Virginia, to Atlanta, Georgia. From there we would take a flight to Amsterdam, the Netherlands, with an uncertain future ahead of us.

> Go home to your family and tell them
> how much the Lord has done for you,
> and how he has had mercy on you.
>
> —Mark 5:19

Janneke and I determined not to lean on our own understanding but to trust the Lord that He would direct our paths and provide for our immediate family.[1]

Your friend,
John

Twenty

My Golden Calf

My dear friend,

Before our move overseas, we decided to purchase a smaller, more economical vehicle with a manual transmission. Prior to the unexpected price increase of a barrel of oil in the spring of 2008, few in America knew that the price of gasoline in western Europe was then almost three times more than what we pay here at home. Also, because of computer malfunctions, our 1987 Ford Tempo had repeatedly placed the lives of our family members in great danger on the German autobahns (expressways). The car needed to be replaced.

Buying an American car was a no-brainer. We loved our country and felt that purchasing an American-manufactured automobile was our patriotic duty. Based on the advice of a colleague, who had just purchased a new Ford Escort, I visited a Ford dealership in a neighboring city one evening after work.

Looking for a New Car

A friendly salesman, eager to sell his next car, greeted me warmly. I told the young man that I was interested in buying a new Escort. His enthusiastic response was that I had come to the right place at the right time because the dealership was making room for the 1991 models, which had arrived the previous week. Only two 1990 Ford Escorts were left in their inventory. When I saw the cars, I understood why they had not yet been sold; they didn't suit my taste, nor were they pleasing to the eye. After a few unflattering remarks about these two vehicles, the salesman suggested that I select a 1991 Escort before negotiating a deal. That sounded fair enough. Next, he took me to a long lineup of new Ford Escorts.

As we strolled along the long rows of new vehicles, making a choice was hard. We stopped at one, which stood out from all the others. It was a shining, red, aerodynamic strawberry metallic Ford Escort. It wasn't just an ordinary red car; no, it had a beautiful, deep, strawberry-red metallic finish.

"What do you think about this car, John?" the salesman asked.

Mesmerized by its appearance, I said I really liked the car. If the price was right, I said, I might buy it. I could already see myself cruising down the European highways, getting all the stares and attention I wanted. The sticker price on the new car was a little over twelve thousand dollars.

"Would you like to take it for a test drive?" he asked.

There was no need, I said. The car was brand-new, and obviously nothing was wrong with it.

"I'm certain it'll run just fine," I said.

When he asked how much I wanted for my trade-in, I told him that I had seen the Ford Tempo advertised in local newspapers for forty-five hundred dollars, which is what I wanted. Our Tempo had been well taken care of and was impeccably clean. At only three years old, it had less than fifty-five thousand miles on the odometer.

"Well, John, that sounds like a fair deal to me. Why don't we go inside and start the paperwork."

The salesman escorted me to a cubicle inside the posh, new showroom, where he drew up a preliminary sales contract. I also said that I wanted five hundred dollars off the sticker price. He didn't see a problem with that.

When he completed the paperwork, the salesman excused himself, told me he needed the approval of his boss, and left the cubicle. My eyes followed him to a big man who, resembling a judge, was seated at an oversized, mahogany desk on a raised platform smack dab in the middle of the showroom.

What followed next was like a scene in a courtroom drama as my "lawyer" salesman pleaded with the "judge" on my behalf. However, instead of serious negotiation, both men were laughing as if telling each other dirty jokes. After they stopped laughing, the "judge" slowly got up from his chair with some degree of difficulty, made his way down from his elevated position, followed sheepishly by the salesman, and approached the cubicle where I anxiously awaited the verdict.

With one hand holding a big cup of hot coffee and the other repeatedly pulling at his two-inch-wide, red suspenders, the "judge" told me his name. Then he said, "John, the best I can do for your trade-in is twelve hundred dollars."

I had already felt intimidated by his presence. Now, humiliated and insulted, I felt shocked by his offer. *This is my reward for being a loyal Ford customer for nearly fifteen years*, I thought.

"Sir," I said, "I purchased that vehicle only three years ago at a Ford dealership in El Paso, Texas. I paid twelve thousand dollars for that car. I've taken very good care of it; you could eat off its engine. It has only been driven fifty-five thousand miles, and it's worth a lot more than what you're offering me."

But the "judge" refused to budge. "I'm very sorry, John, but all I can give you is twelve hundred dollars. That's the best I can do."

Keeping my cool, I stood and politely informed him that it was nice to meet him. I told the salesman that I appreciated the time he had spent with me but that I'd do my business elsewhere. The saying that "a sucker is born every minute," which seemed to be their modus operandi, didn't work on me. Without another word, I walked out the door, strode to my car, and drove off the lot in deep disappointment because I loved that strawberry metallic Ford Escort.

A few weeks later, I decided to look for a car at another Ford dealership. Parked on their new car lot was a new strawberry metallic Ford Escort with a manual transmission and matching interior colors. It was available for immediate purchase and delivery.

The situation was a little different here. Yes, a "judge" was sitting at a big desk on a raised platform in the middle of the showroom. But unlike the other Ford dealership, the staff took my Ford Tempo for a test drive and carefully checked it. After driving around for ten to fifteen minutes, they offered me thirty-two hundred dollars for the vehicle. They also agreed to take five hundred dollars off the sticker price. I thought the deal was reasonably fair and accepted the offer.

I left the dealership and proudly drove home in our shiny, new automobile. After taking the family for a long drive (and receiving a traffic ticket for exceeding the speed limit by ten miles), I parked the vehicle in a conspicuous place so my neighbors could drive by and admire our newly acquired, aerodynamic 1991 strawberry metallic Ford Escort.

Problems

Early the next morning I awoke, checked on my new toy, and discovered to my dismay that the vehicle was covered from bumper to bumper with feline paw marks. The tires were also stained by neighborhood dogs who had marked their territory.

My blood was boiling! I wanted to strangle every stray cat and dog in the neighborhood. I don't know why, but these animals had seemingly singled out my car from all others. Perhaps its new car odor had seeped through a microscopic crack in one of the doors, or its appealing appearance had attracted these animals to my proud possession.

After thoroughly washing the vehicle, I drove to the local Kmart and bought a vinyl cover. The problem with the dogs, however, didn't go away because the cover didn't reach all the way to the ground. Before going to bed each night, I meticulously covered our car to protect it from unfriendly, four-footed nighttime predators.

Driver's Training

Teaching Janneke how to drive a car equipped with a stick shift required extreme patience. Usually right after work, we went with the boys to the parking lot of the shopping mall in Hampton and allowed her all the space she needed.

Boy, oh boy, I can still hear those gears grinding each time she got behind the wheel of that car and fumbled with the clutch and the stick shift. After many attempts—and trying not to make her more nervous or frustrated than she already was—I let her drive the vehicle by herself. As I observed her from a distance, I could see our beautiful, little strawberry metallic Ford Escort bouncing up and down and doing the cha-cha at each parking lot stop sign. I was beginning to wonder if any teeth would be left on the gears of the transmission by the time we shipped the car overseas. By her own admission, Janneke wasn't very coordinated in shifting gears and depressing the clutch while simultaneously keeping her eyes focused on the road.

When I felt comfortable that she could safely operate the vehicle without tearing up the transmission, I let her keep the car so she could pick me up after work. I can still hear the boys ecstatically telling me, "Dad, you should have heard Mom grinding those gears at every stop sign and stoplight." Each time this happened, I tried hard to remain calm and not show my frustration.

BAD TO WORSE

One day when Janneke picked me up from work, I noticed a huge dent, measuring approximately twenty-four by twelve inches wide and three inches deep on the right rear fender. When I asked her about the damage, Janneke wasn't even aware of it. She casually responded that it must have happened while she was grocery shopping at the commissary at Langley Air Force Base. She remembered parking next to a big truck.

Unlike me, Janneke didn't appear to be overly concerned. What angered me most wasn't her calm demeanor or her failure to detect the damaged fender but the person responsible for causing the damage and driving away. He or she hadn't had the common courtesy or decency to leave a note with a name and telephone number.

Behind my office building at Fort Monroe was a narrow alley with parking spaces designated exclusively for compact vehicles. On one particular, steaming-hot summer day, I parked close to a three-inch, round, metal handrail. I wanted to ensure that a careless driver didn't clip the rear end of the Escort, so I parked as close to the handrail as possible, leaving no more than an eighth of an inch between the hood of the car and the bottom of the handrail.

Around two o'clock that afternoon, a sergeant, who was smoking a cigarette outside, raced into my office and told me to get outside and look at my car. His body language and the tone of his voice, convinced me that my car was on fire, but no. Because of the heat, the tires had expanded. The hood of the Escort was no longer an eighth of an inch from the rusty, old handrail. It was now firmly wedged under the bottom of it.

This time I was angry and annoyed with myself because of my stupidity—I should have known better. Several men were required to push the front end of the vehicle down while I slowly backed the Escort out of its precarious position. This new strawberry metallic Ford Escort was beginning to cause me much grief.

Soon after this incident, I returned to my car after work one day and discovered that my beautiful, little, red car was coated with tiny droplets of white paint. A painting crew working at Fort Monroe had been spray painting the exterior wood trim on several office buildings. They had worked a good distance from the parking lot but close enough for the wind to carry the spray to my car.

Not wishing to enter into a dispute or possible lengthy litigation with the painting contractor, I decided to fix this problem myself. I purchased a can of rubbing compound, carefully removed every tiny speck of latex paint from my vehicle, and in the process destroyed its paint job. When I was finished, our car no longer resembled the shiny, new strawberry metallic Ford Escort I had driven off the lot a short while ago. It looked more like a vehicle that had seen its better days.

Difficulties in Holland

Upon our arrival in Holland we quickly discovered that the American Ford Escort wasn't like the European model. That meant we couldn't buy parts at any auto parts store. Only one car dealer in the entire country imported American automobiles from the three major U.S. automakers, and imported parts were very expensive. We also discovered that full insurance coverage for our Ford Escort for one year exceeded a month's salary. We elected not to get collision coverage, hoping and praying that we wouldn't get involved in an accident. Finally, we were required to obtain a special exemption to drive the Escort in Holland because it didn't meet strict Dutch vehicular standards.

Driving through a heavy rainstorm one evening in Holland, I asked Janneke if she felt something strange below the dashboard. "Funny that you should ask," she said, "because it feels like my feet are getting wet."

We pulled into the nearest gas station and discovered that our car, then only eighteen months old, was leaking like a sieve. By the time we arrived home late that night, an inch of water filled the floorboard. This problem, added to a long litany of mechanical woes, had caused our strawberry metallic Ford Escort to become a source of much grief.

THE LESSON

The book of Exodus in the Old Testament chronicles the difficult journey of the nation Israel. The Israelites wandered in the desert for forty years after their release from four hundred years of slavery and mistreatment at the hand of the Egyptians. Of all nations on earth, Israel was singled out and privileged to receive the Law from God Himself through His servant Moses on Mount Sinai. God had chosen Moses to lead the Israelites to the land He had promised their forefathers. Moses spent a long time alone with God on the mountain, receiving the Law. As a result, the people became impatient, frustrated, and agitated. The rest of the story is recorded as follows:

> When the people saw that Moses was so long in coming down from the mountain, they gathered around Aaron and said, "Come, make us gods who will go before us. As for this fellow Moses who brought us up out of Egypt, we don't know what has happened to him." Aaron answered them, "Take off the gold earrings that your wives, your sons and your daughters are wearing, and bring them to me." So all the people took off their earrings, and brought them to Aaron. He took what they handed him and made it into an idol cast in the shape of a calf.[1]

My fascination with American cars began as a young boy looking at pictures in *Life* magazine and seeing Hollywood movie stars cruise around in their big, fancy automobiles on the big screen. That fascination gradually evolved into a love affair, beginning when I bought my first car at the age of eighteen through every subsequent car purchased up to the strawberry metallic Ford Escort.

In addition, two events routinely happened in the neighborhood where I lived in Southern California every Saturday: people were busy vacuuming, washing, waxing, and polishing their cars; and they were mowing their lawns. I was no exception. I had always treated our cars with utmost care. I avoided parking our car next to a big truck, a sports utility vehicle, or other oversized car to avoid any potential damages to our vehicle. I panicked at even the thought of finding a dent or scratch on my new car.

I yelled at our boys once when I thought they were treating our car in a careless manner. I relished all the attention each time I cruised around in my latest acquisition. It wasn't until much later that I realized that our family car—not just the Ford Escort—was an idol in my life. I was no better than the people of Israel at Mount Sinai, who had fashioned a golden calf. I too had bowed down to useless idols shaped in the form of a piece of metal mounted on four wheels.

> You shall not make for yourself an idol in the form of anything
> in heaven above or on the earth beneath or in the waters below.
> You shall not bow down to them or worship them;
> for I, the Lord your God, am a jealous God.
> —Exodus 20:4–5

God has peculiar ways of getting our attention. We often must go through difficult, painful trials to learn valuable lessons. The Lord used my disappointments with that Ford Escort to show me the wickedness of my idolatry. The agonizing lessons I learned was to "flee from idolatry" and "purify [myself] from everything that contaminates body and spirit, perfecting holiness out of reverence for God."[2]

Your friend,
John

Twenty-One

An Opportunity Squandered

My dear friend,

Homesickness was a stranger to me. At the age of eighteen, I left my parental home convinced that I would never return. I had traveled to many parts of this world, yet never once up to this point had I experienced the powerful emotion of being homesick. To me homesickness was a sign of weakness; it wasn't something for the strong.

I didn't know what homesickness really was until early one Friday morning on Dennis's eleventh birthday when we stepped off the plane at Schiphol International Airport in Amsterdam. After an almost-eighteen-hour-long journey, we were bone tired. I couldn't understand why this emotion was hitting me at this particular juncture in my life. Struggling to maintain a good attitude while not revealing my true feelings to Janneke or the boys, I remember repeatedly crying out, "Lord, what have I done? I have left behind all that is dear to me."

These thoughts came to me as we walked down the long airport terminal corridors, following other passengers to immigration, baggage claim, and customs. Deep down in my heart I knew our move to Holland wasn't permanent, but how long we were to stay remained a mystery.

Moving overseas had been a traumatic experience for our family, especially for me. There was no guarantee of finding a job. Our boys didn't speak the Dutch language, though both Janneke and I felt confident they would learn it quickly. We had neither a permanent home nor the slightest idea what awaited us in the weeks or months ahead. All we wanted to do was serve the Lord by sharing the good news of Jesus Christ with our family and friends and others who were willing to listen. We arrived in Holland during the summer break, allowing our boys to adjust to their new environment, to meet new friends, and to learn the Dutch language.

The Surprise

We temporarily lived with my mother in Ede in the home where I had grown up. After recovering from jet lag and adjusting to a new time zone, Janneke called the contact person at the Christian Youth Center and scheduled an appointment for a job interview. Several board members were still on vacation. An interview was scheduled for the following week on Tuesday evening, August 13, 1991.

The job ad specifically stated that they were seeking a "Married Couple to Manage a Christian Youth Center." Exactly what that description entailed, we didn't know, but we envisioned a facility under the auspices of a Protestant church or denomination where different activities for youth of all ages took place. We were both under the impression that they were looking for a couple who would be responsible for making certain that youth activities were properly managed and supervised and that the facility was kept safe and clean.

The responsibilities sounded easy enough. We knew nothing about the organization, but when we closely examined the job advertisement, we felt comfortable and qualified to do the job. We eagerly looked forward to meeting the board members, finding a permanent place to live, and touching the lives of many young people.

Janneke and I felt nervous as we drove up to the address that had been given to us. There was no church building in sight. All the members of the governing board warmly welcomed us. They had a vision to reach young people with the truth of the gospel message. What we learned that evening about the position, however, came as a complete surprise to both of us. In fact, it was something we weren't quite prepared for.

Our "Christian Youth Center" was a two-story, brick row house that functioned as a coffeehouse. This was certainly not the organization we had envisioned. While nothing is wrong with managing a coffeehouse, the demands to be placed on me were more than I could handle. Among the board members conducting the interview was one individual who had been serving as the coffeehouse manager. After working there for many years, he felt that it was time for him and his family to move on.

The former manager, a man in his mid-thirties, had obviously done a wonderful job. Expectations were that whoever replaced him would do equally fine if not better. As he carefully described his day-to-day responsibilities, I became very apprehensive. His daily routine consisted of leaving his home very early in the morning and conducting his quiet time in one of the coffeehouse upper rooms, after which he thoroughly cleaned the facility. Next, he went on an extensive shopping spree at the local grocery store since cooking was a major part of his job.

While I intently listened to what he said, it sounded like he cooked an inordinate amount of French fries, croquettes, and other scrumptious delicacies for the evening's activities and fellowship. He spent much of his afternoons precooking and preparing the food. He was also held accountable for all financial transactions, responsible for the sale of food and drinks served at the nonalcoholic bar, and personally supervised all activities in the coffeehouse.

In addition, he was available to provide basic biblical counseling to youngsters who showed a need for counseling or individual mentoring and to conduct regular Bible studies. Then came the clincher: his workday ended after ten o'clock each night on days when the facility was open, which was usually five days per week and included every Saturday.

Nowhere in the conversation did I hear that his wife played any role in managing coffeehouse affairs alongside her husband. Yes, he was frequently assisted by one of the board members on busy evenings, but responsibility for the daily coffeehouse operations apparently rested squarely on his shoulders.

The goal of the coffeehouse was to invite adolescent males to come, hear the gospel message, and experience Christian fellowship. It was an opportunity to keep these young men off the streets and out of trouble. The latter goal sounded exciting; the former was something I wasn't equipped to deal with. We applauded these people for their zeal in reaching out to young men. However, when we asked about Janneke's participation in the day-to-day activities, the response wasn't that she was unwelcome; but most of the kids visiting the coffeehouse were teenage boys who hung around the streets at night. They needed a strong man to maintain order and ensure control of the facility. Janneke was welcome to help when there was a need.

Throughout much of the two-hour interview, I didn't like what I was hearing. Why had they advertised that they were seeking a married couple, when in fact they seemed only interested in me? My biggest objection, which I didn't voice, was being away from my family almost fifteen hours on days when the coffeehouse was open. None of this information had been available to us when we inquired about the job. Janneke shared my sentiments. I also didn't like the idea of Janneke not being a part of this ministry and felt uncomfortable about her not being present at the coffeehouse. Taking an active role during evening activities because she needed to be home with our boys would also have been very difficult for her.

As I carefully listened to all the discussions taking place that evening, a picture formed in my mind of what awaited me at the coffeehouse—and it wasn't very pretty. There I stood in a poorly ventilated, steaming-hot kitchen, dressed in a long, dirty apron reaching down to my ankles, clumsily peeling and cutting up bushels of potatoes by hand. I could see myself bathed in sweat while tripping over dirty, greasy pots and pans stacked in every corner of the kitchen, all the while trying to concentrate on cooking mountains of French fries, chicken, meat balls, and croquettes. An exaggerated picture, yes, but that's how I saw it.

Something else bothered me, and what I'm revealing here shows my very dark side called "pride." The army had trained me to be a leader, not a follower. As a leader I always aspired to be in leadership positions because I wanted to be the man in charge. I relished taking on additional responsibilities and savoring all the accolades and recognition that came with the job. I was used to telling one soldier to do this and another to do that. I expected them to get the job done and get it done right the first time. It wasn't the other way around.

The thought of cooking and cleaning for a bunch of rowdy, wild, rambunctious teenagers from off the city streets was unacceptable and too much to ask of me. I knew I was going to be terribly unhappy and had a hard time accepting the fact that the Lord had sent me halfway around the world only to be disheartened by running a coffeehouse.

At no time during the lengthy discussions did we give these people the impression that we were not interested in the job. Despite our misgivings and apprehensions, we both remained positive and upbeat. At the interview's conclusion, we said we needed time to think and pray about our decision. We promised to give them a definitive answer within twenty-four hours.

We were faced with a big dilemma. On one hand, we both loved the idea of reaching out to young people and sharing with them the love of Christ. On the other hand, the demands of the job would create too much of a hardship on our own family. We had three young sons and felt that my being away from home night after night for so many hours wouldn't have been a healthy situation. After leaving the coffeehouse, I told Janneke how I felt about the situation. We prayed before going to bed that night, but in my heart I had already made up my mind that this wasn't for us.

The following morning we visited the home of a board member to tell her in person that we weren't going to accept the position. Later that afternoon, we returned to the coffeehouse a second time to tell other board members. Regrettably, they didn't receive the news very well.

EMMEN

When we awoke on the morning of August 15, 1991, we prayed together and asked the Lord to provide a home for our family and a job for Janneke. I reminded her of a conversation we'd had several years earlier about someday living in the city of Emmen. The conversation took place after we had camped with our boys near the village of Zevenhuizen (Seven Homes) in northern Holland, where my grandfather was born and raised.

On the drive home to Stuttgart, we had seen the city of Emmen from a distance. The geographic location afforded miles upon miles of mostly wide-open agricultural spaces and hundreds of miles of paved bicycle paths going in every direction, mostly on flat terrain. I had said that if we should ever live in Holland, this was the place where I wanted to live.

After breakfast, Janneke and I traveled to Emmen to explore the city and the surrounding area. Although we had never set foot in the city, we took an immediate liking to everything we saw. We liked its fashionable city center with several historically preserved old buildings, including the old Dutch Reformed Church with its Romanesque church steeple built during the twelfth century. The city was also home to one of Europe's finest zoos.

It took no time for us to find a quasi-government agency where one goes to find a home for rent. Because of its overpopulation and restricted space, rental properties in Holland are somewhat tightly controlled because demand for housing is greater than its supply. People are routinely placed on waiting lists and wait for months for a house to become available.

To our great surprise, the housing agency director informed us that she had a contemporary five-bedroom, one-and-a-half-bath, three-story, brick row house *immediately available* for our family. We couldn't believe what we were hearing. She handed us a stack of forms and instructed us to return the completed documents as soon as possible. Late that afternoon, we drove back exhilarated, believing this move was of the Lord. Though we didn't work at the coffeehouse, we were convinced that God had other plans for us while living in Emmen.

Janneke and I excitedly returned the following Monday, bringing the necessary paperwork and rental deposit. That same day we enrolled our boys in a Christian elementary school located only a five minute's walk from our new home. Though almost everything in Western Europe is on a smaller scale, we loved our new dwelling place. It provided everything for our family's needs. Directly in front of our home was a spacious, landscaped open area featuring a soccer field and a playground.

We made arrangements to have new wall-to-wall carpeting professionally installed, and one day before the start of the new school year, we moved into Rolderbrink 412 in Emmen. Also on this day our household goods were delivered from America. We had picked up our 1991 strawberry metallic Ford Escort at the Port of Rotterdam a few weeks earlier. The following morning Janneke and I escorted our boys to school.

In a matter of days they developed new friendships and to our amazement were comfortably communicating in basic conversational

Dutch within a period of two weeks. All three of our boys were very brave as they adjusted culturally and quickly assimilated into their new world. We were very proud of them.

New Direction

"God moves in mysterious ways." Though this familiar line is found nowhere in the Bible, it is nonetheless true. God very possibly wanted both Janneke and me working at the coffeehouse. That doesn't mean I needed to work the same lengthy hours my predecessor had. Perhaps something could have been worked out to everyone's mutual satisfaction, including Janneke's active participation in the ministry. The fact remains that my primary reason for not working there was the demand for prolonged absences from my family. In retrospect and with much regret, I realize that I may indeed have squandered many opportunities to share the love of Jesus with these young people.

But our God is a merciful God; His mercies are new every day (KJV).[1] He is able to turn something bad into something good, and that's what He did in this particular situation. Despite the many mistakes, even terrible ones, we make in life, God doesn't give up on us. This fact shows His faithfulness and bountiful mercies. "If we are faithless, he will remain faithful, for he cannot disown himself."[2] Elsewhere He says, "Never will I leave you; never will I forsake you."[3] That is not to say that our Christian walk has always been smooth sailing. On the contrary, the Lord used even the job interview with the leadership of that coffeehouse to show me my conceited sense of superiority and my despicable pride.

> Pride goes before destruction,
> a haughty spirit before a fall.
> —Proverbs 16:18

The Lord had brought us to Emmen, and while there I was to undergo a baptism of affliction.

Your friend,
John

Twenty-Two

The Fire of Affliction

My dear friend,

Janneke started her new job as a sales clerk and cashier at V&D (Vroom & Dreesman), a large department store and national retail chain on Monday, November 11, 1991. The store was located in the heart of Emmen, and she was hired to work in the Christmas holiday department. She would work thirty hours per week, but the job would last only during the holidays. The timing couldn't have been more perfect because the value of the dollar against European currencies had steadily declined since our arrival overseas. Money in our bank account was rapidly diminishing, and Janneke's job was an answer to prayer.

God's timing is always perfect. Our army pension was insufficient to pay the bills and to feed and clothe our family. Except for a quarterly children's monetary allowance, which every household with minor children receives, we opted not to take advantage of the many overly generous social welfare programs available in Holland.

Thankfully, our boys seemed happy and content at school, and they had many friends. Their teachers were satisfied with their academic progress, and remarkably it didn't take them long to gain an excellent grasp of the Dutch language. We were pleasantly surprised to see above-average grades on their first report cards. Both Janneke and I were very proud of our sons.

During my daily quiet time, I made it a point to recite a portion of the prayer of King David in Psalm 25. "Show me your ways, O Lord, teach me your paths; guide me in your truth and teach me, for you are God my Savior, and my hope is in you all day long."[1] I echoed those words from the depths of my heart, and God answered my prayers. What followed next was something I never bargained for.

THE PRESENCE

Early one morning while home alone after Janneke had started her new job, I was shaving in front of the bathroom mirror on the second floor with my back facing the partially open bathroom door. Without warning, paralyzing fear overcame me. Goose bumps covered my body, and the hairs on the back of my head stood on end.

An invisible, evil presence had entered the bathroom.

Terror stricken, I cried out to the Lord and begged Him to deliver me from whatever was tormenting me. I thought that I could free myself from this dreadful encounter through prayer, but when that didn't work, I then began to sing—loudly enough for our neighbors to hear—the famous old hymn "There Is Power in the Blood."

> There is power, power, wonder-working power
> In the blood of the Lamb;
> There is power, power, wonder-working power
> In the precious blood of the Lamb.

I repeated those lyrics over and over again. But neither my prayers nor my almost-deafening and not-so-melodious singing drove away what appeared to be an evil, demonic spirit. My fear was so intense that I nearly fainted.

I stopped shaving and without rinsing off or drying my face ran downstairs, where I stayed for the remainder of the day. I felt safe and secure in the kitchen, dining room, and living room, but I didn't have the nerve to go upstairs alone. I continued to cry out to the Lord, but God didn't come to the rescue. As soon as I heard one of our boys touch the door handle of the back door, coming home for lunch, the fear immediately dissipated. However, it returned when they headed back to school after lunch and left me alone.

When Janneke arrived home from work that afternoon, I told her what had transpired in our home that morning. Her reaction was one of bewilderment. She was as perplexed as I was and didn't know what to make of my encounter or what to do about it other than to participate in incessant prayer. Thankfully, the presence didn't affect her or the boys. She joined me in crying out to the Lord, but relief was nowhere in sight.

Except for a brief time when Janneke was unemployed, I dared not venture upstairs alone. Prior to the encounter, I had always enjoyed spending time in my upstairs study, a cozy, little hideaway displaying our collection of books and my vast accumulation of army mementos. But now, whenever I wasn't out shopping for groceries or doing chores, I remained sequestered downstairs. Not a day went by that Janneke or I didn't cry out before the Lord, seeking answers for our predicament.

But things only seemed to get worse.

At about the same time, I began to feel sick and emotionally distraught. I suffered frequent bouts of depression and continued to battle homesickness. One day I experienced an unexpected, terrible, choking chest pain that lasted approximately two or three minutes. I was convinced that my life had come to an end. As far as I knew, death was imminent; it was only a matter of days, if not hours.

I pleaded with the Lord to allow me to live long enough to put my life in order. I knew that if I were to die, a grief-stricken Janneke wouldn't know what to do. She wouldn't even know where to find the documents needed to make final arrangements. Concerned that I would create havoc or unnecessary turmoil in our family, I decided not to tell Janneke what had happened that day.

THE END?

I was once a packrat. The army is notorious for handing out forms and other documents to their soldiers. I had saved every piece of paper the army had ever handed to me. Multiple copies of reassignment orders, every leave request, every pay slip—you name it, it was stored away somewhere in a box. Over a span of nearly twenty-two years I had accumulated a wealth of documents, enough to fill two standard-sized, four-drawer file cabinets. In addition, I had saved every single letter or postcard written to me by my family and friends since arriving in the United States in 1962. Hundreds upon hundreds of photographs were also stored in boxes.

I had a very hard time throwing any of it away. I had always assumed that my retirement from the army would allow me plenty of time to sort through these papers, destroy what was of little or no value, and keep what I determined was important. None of these records were filed in any sort of order. But now with my demise seemingly imminent, I realized I needed not days but several weeks to find and sort the important documents Janneke would need in case of my death.

I experienced several more episodes of chest pains, each lasting no more than two-to-four minutes long. Each recurrence grew progressively worse. Sometimes I felt as if a long, sharp kitchen knife had been jabbed through my heart.

I continued to keep these chest pains a secret from Janneke. With each episode I cried out to the Lord and said I wasn't ready to die yet. Often I had an excuse why I should live longer. I once told the Lord that our boys would soon be teenagers; Janneke needed a strong man around, and our boys needed their dad. For many years I had been zealous about reaching out to people with the truth of the gospel message. Now that the time had finally arrived for us to work in the vineyard of the Lord, it seemed certain that my life was in great jeopardy. I was completely baffled about why this was happening. I protested to the Lord, asking Him why it was that some despots lived to a ripe old age when nearly every day I felt that I was heading for the grave, even though all I wanted to do was serve Him with heart and soul. God never gave me an answer.

What also crushed my heart was the fact that if I died, I wouldn't be buried at Arlington National Cemetery. Since I had been only forty-seven years old at the time of my retirement, and since I had been in excellent physical condition at the time, dying had been the last thing on my mind when we left the United States. In the event of my death, we had no plans for funeral arrangements.

I still considered myself to be a young man with lots of potential to spread the love of Jesus abroad. One day after another painful attack that caused much distress, I called a dear friend, a registered nurse who had served with her husband as missionaries in Africa, Asia, and the Middle East for many years. She told me to hang up the phone immediately and see a doctor.

What the Doctor Said

When Janneke came home from work, I casually told to her that my chest had been feeling a little funny lately and that perhaps a doctor should check it out. I didn't tell her about my telephone conversation with our friend.

Janneke set an appointment for the following day with a doctor at our neighborhood medical clinic. After close examination the doctor, a nice man, said, "Your heart rate and blood pressure are like those of an athlete, and your heart sounds fine!" He couldn't find anything wrong with me and sent me home.

Over time, I scheduled several more appointments with this doctor, always with the same complaint. Each time he told me to go home because he couldn't find anything that was cause for alarm. For someone my age, he said, I was in excellent physical condition. Instead of easing my tensions, however, this news caused even more frustration because I didn't have any answers for my infirmities.

The Dream

For nearly two months beginning in late November 1991, I began having horrible nightmares to the point that I dreaded going to bed at night. Night after night, I woke from a terrible dream, drenched in sweat and terrified to make a move or even to utter a sound. Every night, like a little boy who is afraid of the dark, Janneke had to escort me to the bathroom in the middle of the night.

I don't remember another time in my life when I felt so completely helpless and had to depend on someone else as my source of strength and courage. Almost all the nightmares were about my demise. I have forgotten all those mortifying dreams, except one:

In the middle of a cold, dark November night, I awoke to the sound of our doorbell ringing. Strangely, Janneke was already dressed and standing beside the bed in our dimly lit bedroom. She gently told me to get dressed because it was time for me to go downstairs and die. Crazy as it may sound, I didn't protest, nor did I ask her what she meant by her words.

Feeling totally defeated, I resigned myself to the fact that my time on earth had finally come to an end. I was gripped with an unfathomable fear. In contrast Janneke remained cool, calm, and collected and said I had nothing to worry about. "Someone will meet you downstairs at the front door," she said.

She continued reassuring me that I had no reason to be afraid. After I got dressed, which seemed to take a very long time, she took me by the hand, slowly escorted me past the boys' bedrooms down the two flights of stairs, and led me to the front door. My heart was thumping wildly as we arrived downstairs. Next, Janneke calmly told me to go ahead and open the front door.

We didn't say good-bye to each other. Without asking any questions, I reluctantly reached for the door handle and yanked the door wide open. There, on a cold, dreary, black night stood Satan, disguised as a famous, handsome Hollywood movie star. He was wearing a dark trench coat and a black fedora, and a beautiful, blond-haired, blue-eyed woman stood at his side. With an inviting smile on his face, he motioned for me to come with them. "Please, John, come with us."

With whatever little strength was left in me, I stepped backward, slammed my back against a radiator heater, and shouted, "Depart from me, Satan! I'm a child of the King! I belong to Him! Leave me alone!"

It was at this moment that I awoke, trembling with fear and anxiety and on the verge of a nervous breakdown.

Back to the United States?

In early January 1992, Janneke was laid off from her job at V&D. I enjoyed having her home each day because her presence enabled me to spend more time alone in my study. Moreover, we could do things together again. I didn't really want her to find another job. If necessary,

I was prepared to return to the United States, roll up my sleeves, and go to work. We had enough friends and acquaintances in the U.S. federal government to assist me in a job search.

I had planned in my heart to go by myself. Once settled, Janneke and the boys would follow. I thought the Lord was angry with me for rejecting the job offer at the coffeehouse and believed I was no longer fit to serve Him. I told Janneke that if she wasn't hired by the end of January, I would start contacting our friends and making preparations to return, hopefully to find a job in the Washington, D.C., area. I woke up each morning with excitement at the prospect of going home.

When I woke on the morning of January 31, 1992, my excitement about returning to the United States had completely disappeared. I couldn't figure it out. The lack of excitement also confused Janneke because she was convinced that I would feverishly begin contacting our friends in the D.C. area, send them copies of my résumé, and solicit their help in finding a suitable job. But none of this happened.

After being out of work for nearly two months, Janneke received a call from the state employment agency. The employment counselor instructed her to report to the hospital for a job interview the following day. She had applied for a part-time position at the hospital once before but had been told that she couldn't be hired due to monetary constraints. We had both been disappointed because the position was an opportunity for professional growth.

To make a long story short, the funding for the assistant nurse position in the children's ward of Scheper Hospital in Emmen was approved. Among several candidates, Janneke had been selected for the job, even though she had no experience in this field. Once again we could see God's hand at work here. She was offered the job at just the time when we were in financial need.

From Bad to Worse

On some days I felt like a healthy, strong seventeen-year-old. On days when I felt good, I jogged for miles, sometimes with a young friend, or pedaled my bicycle for several hours, enjoying miles upon miles of wide-open, lush, green pasturelands surrounding the city of Emmen.

On days when I didn't feel so well, however, I usually felt a tingling sensation beginning in my toes, working its way up my legs, and causing me to break out in a cold sweat and lose all strength in my lower extremities. At times I felt so weak that I couldn't stand or walk. Similarly, I felt a tingling sensation starting in my fingertips followed by numbness and pain in my left or right arm. The pain sometimes extended to my shoulders, neck, and lower jaw.

It wasn't uncommon for my heart to race uncontrollably, usually when I was in a resting position and especially when I was lying in bed. I was afraid to lie on my left or right side because I heard the rapid pace of my heart beating into my pillow. Before falling asleep, I pleaded with the Lord not to allow Janneke to wake up early the next morning and find my lifeless, stiff, cold body next to hers. Once my body temperature dropped so low that two sleeping bags and two thick, woolen blankets couldn't keep me warm; I shivered throughout the night. I also frequently suffered debilitating migraines and lost my peripheral vision. These migraines sometimes lasted two to three days. I dreaded going to see a doctor, only to be told that he couldn't find anything wrong with me.

I experienced something else that drove me to the brink of utter despair and hopelessness. For unknown reasons, evil, wicked, and blasphemous thoughts began creeping into my head. I didn't know where these thoughts were coming from or what was causing them. I certainly hadn't invited them in. They often assaulted me during my quiet time while I was reading my Bible. It became so bad that I literally wanted to throw myself down on the floor and refuse to get up. I even thought about asking the Lord to take my life because I had suffered all I could take. All my pleas remained unanswered.

One day when I felt that I needed to cry out to someone other than to the Lord or to Janneke, I called our missionary friend again and told her what had been happening for the past six months. I told her that I had read several accounts of demonic oppression occurring even in the homes of Christian missionaries serving in remote parts of the world. The conversation switched to objects of worship, specifically our vast collection of African artifacts I had purchased years earlier on many of my official travels for the U.S. Army. She told me that her pastor was an expert in identifying these objects. He would gladly examine them to see if they were in fact the cause of all the demonic oppression and spiritual trauma I had experienced. She didn't need to say anything more.

When Janneke arrived home from work, I told her that we would immediately destroy our entire collection of souvenirs: white marble-like statues of Greek gods, ebony wood and ivory carvings purchased in Africa, a thirty-inch-by-seventy-two-inch oil painting acquired in Ethiopia, delicately handwoven prayer rugs, and other expensive items we and others had admired. Much of our exotic art collection had been left in unpacked boxes.

Over the next three or four days, Janneke and I carefully unpacked every box, sorted through everything in our collection, and proceeded to destroy everything we had accumulated during our travels overseas using a saw, hammer, chisel, and Stanley knife. We disposed of them by making multiple trips to the municipal dump. When we were done, we both felt as if a heavy burden had been lifted off our shoulders.

SOMETHING NEW

Springtime in Holland is a marvelously joyous time, especially after a long, wet, dark, and dreary cold winter. Waking up each morning to the sounds of birds singing and smelling the fragrance of flowers in the air bring joy and happiness to anyone's heart. One morning, on a beautiful spring day in early June, new neighbors were moving in next door. They were a young couple in their mid-twenties who were in love and were purchasing their first home. Janneke was at work, and the boys were still in school.

For the first time in seven months, I was able to go upstairs alone, sit in my study, and not be overcome with fear. The windows of my study were partially opened, and I could hear these young people sweet-talking each other as they excitedly unloaded their household effects. It was such a joy to peacefully sit behind my desk, listen to this couple move into their home, and not be afraid. Our "spiritual housecleaning" had worked!

Each day thereafter, while everyone was gone, I was able to conduct my morning quiet time in my study alone. Interestingly, no one who had previously visited our home ever asked what had happened to our display of souvenirs and artifacts.

The Truth

Although I was no longer afraid to go upstairs alone, my physical maladies continued. One Friday evening in late June 1992, I told Janneke I would make an appointment at the medical clinic of the U.S. Air Force base in Soesterberg, an hour-and-a-half drive from Emmen. I had reached the end of my rope and felt that something needed to be done medically—and soon. I was tired of waking each morning and living with the notion that each day was the last day of my life on this earth. I called the clinic the following Monday and briefly described my afflictions. I was told to report the next day.

On Tuesday, June 30, accompanied by Janneke, I learned the truth. An EKG revealed that I had suffered a heart attack. The nurse practitioner couldn't ascertain when the heart attack had occurred, but he did mention damage to the heart muscle. The nurse also thought I had suffered several TIAs (Transient Ischemic Attacks) or ministrokes.

Due to the serious nature of my medical condition and the distance to the U.S. Air Force base, I was referred to the hospital in Emmen to be seen by a cardiologist. When we arrived home, it was the first time Janneke had ever broken down and cried because of my physical condition.

It didn't take very long for me to be seen by a well-known cardiologist at the hospital in Emmen. The doctor, who appeared to be in his mid-fifties, was thoroughly trained in U.S. medical procedures. Because he didn't have my medical history on file, he suggested that I have a complete physical "makeover." He scheduled me for a series of tests and examinations spread over a period of thirty days. A follow-up visit was scheduled for early August. Every major organ in my body, including my heart, would be thoroughly examined. That day I went home while attached to a twenty-four-hour heart monitor.

A month later, after completing a myriad of medical tests and examinations, I returned for a follow-up visit. Janneke came along for moral support. Even still, I was so frightened and nervous that I couldn't sit in a chair in front of the doctor's desk. In fact, I was so fearful that I expected to faint any second. He kindly offered me a seat, but I respectfully declined.

Directly before him on a neatly arranged desk lay a medical archive two inches thick. He carefully opened the folder and slowly began thumbing through the pages of section A. "John, the results of your kidney examination reveal that your kidneys are in excellent condition," he said. I wasn't surprised because I had never complained about kidney problems. "Let's move on to the next section," he said. The doctor took his time and flipped to the following chart in the record. "Well, John, it appears that your liver is functioning properly. We didn't find anything wrong with your liver." And on and on it went.

As he went through each section of the medical archive, his response was the same: he couldn't find anything medically wrong with me. He turned to the results of extensive lab work and said everything looked fine. "There's nothing wrong with your blood or urine," he said. "Everything looks wonderful!"

But wait. He hadn't yet gotten to the most important and final part: the condition of my heart. My heart was throbbing with fear as he slowly and carefully opened the last section of the record. I fully expected the man to tell me that he needed to perform open heart surgery and that I had a great risk of dying on the operating table. He took his time going over the results.

When he was finished, he said, "Let's see, John. We weren't able to detect anything wrong with your heart. In fact, your heart is in excellent shape; it functions like that of a twenty-four-year-old. Why don't you come back in five years, and we'll check you out again."

I felt so euphoric that I didn't feel my feet touching the floor. I wanted to jump across his desk and hug, squeeze, and kiss this man—and not let go! His comments were like an unending, sweet symphony to my ears. It was one of the best gifts anyone could have ever given me. I left the hospital that morning as a new and a changed man.

THE ARTICLE

We subscribed to *Het Zoeklicht* (*The Searchlight*), a Christian magazine wholly devoted to examining current world affairs and studying the signs of the times in light of the second coming of Jesus the Messiah. An article appeared in the August 22, 1992, issue that seemed completely out of place. The article had nothing to do with Bible prophecy or with looking at events that showed the imminent return of Jesus Christ. The two-page article, titled "Dying with Christ," was written by Ivo Sasek. I had never heard of Ivo Sasek, nor had I ever seen a previous article written by this man in the magazine.

I know it may seem odd, but I felt as if this particular feature had been written exclusively for me. The article caught my attention because it described my situation in almost exact detail. I'm ashamed to admit it, but I had always enjoyed all the fun and pleasures this world has to offer. Subconsciously, I chased after bigger and better things in life, never completely satisfied with what I owned. I was very much conditioned by the basic principles of this world: prestige, social status, career, financial security, you name it.

What I learned from the magazine article was that I needed to separate myself from worldly things. "Don't you know that friendship with the world is hatred toward God? Anyone who chooses to be a friend of the world becomes an enemy of God."[2] James wrote these words in the New Testament.

I needed to learn to die to these worldly principles and put this truth into practice. Shamefully, my focus had mostly been on my own selfish desires; I didn't always seek the Kingdom of God first. Instead of cherishing the pleasures of this world, I needed to learn to live my life in complete submission and obedience to Jesus Christ. Going on a vacation with my family or visiting a theme park is no sin. However, I needed to embrace the concept that Christ is the source of my joy, that Christ is the source of living a happy and fulfilled life—not what this world has to offer. I needed to replace the perishable with the imperishable. My chastisement, though severely painful, was intended to bring me to a closer relationship with Him. The discipline was also intended to reject, bit by bit, my love affair with this world.

In his article, Mr. Sasek explained the process of suffering that we, as Christians, sometimes have to endure to loosen our grip on worldly things. Jesus wants to be our "all in all." In this intimate relationship, there is no room for a romance with worldly principles and material goods that are of no lasting value. The magazine article gave me a feeling of spiritual exhilaration and a clear understanding of all the travails I had experienced.

Suffering is a lonely road. Your closest friends will have no idea what you're going through during long periods of trials or pain. "John, your children are healthy; they're happy. You have a roof over your head, and you have food on your table! What more do you want? You have no reason to complain!" I heard these words when I tried to share my hurt with a trusted friend. To a great degree, Janneke suffered alongside me. Together we learned to suffer in silence. Among our close friends, not one was aware of what we were going through during our first year in Holland.

Christians are not immune to suffering. If we are serious about our walk with the Lord, then hardships and painful trials will most assuredly come. The suffering I needed to undergo was intended for my own good to achieve the molding and shaping of my character. This is what I meant when I said that God can "turn something bad into something good." That's not to say that I have arrived. Far be it for me to make that claim. I still have a long way to go.

> For day and night
> your hand was heavy upon me;
> my strength was sapped
> as in the heat of summer.
> Selah
> Then I acknowledged my sin to you
> and didn't cover up my iniquity.
> I said, "I will confess
> my transgressions to the Lord"—
> and you forgave
> the guilt of my sin.
> Selah
>
> —Psalm 32:4–5

> The Lord has chastened me severely,
> but he has not given me over to death.
>
> —Psalm 118:18

After carefully studying the "Dying with Christ" article, it appeared that my tough times had finally come to an end. I remember crying out to the Lord in my quiet time early one morning, asking Him if He wanted to reveal anything else to me. God answered by taking me straight to Psalm 119:71. "It was good for me to be afflicted so that I might learn your decrees."

> Your friend,
> John

Twenty-Three

A Spiritual Transformation

My dear friend,

On a Saturday in March 1992, Janneke and I attended a one-day praise and worship service organized by the Evangelical Radio and Television Broadcasting Company in Holland. Approximately three thousand people from many different protestant denominations attended the all-day event. In addition to praise and worship, we also listened to sound biblical teaching. It was such a joyous occasion as we joined the thousands in singing famous old hymns and beautiful contemporary praise and worship songs.

We were comfortably seated in an area where we had a good view of the speaker's podium. I noticed that the people sitting to our left didn't return after the lunch hour; other visitors now occupied their seats. The president of the broadcasting company, also a nationally known and popular pastor in one of the mainstream protestant churches, was the first speaker after the lunch hour.

Conviction

I remember this man making his way to the elevated platform, where he began his teaching with a brief opening prayer. The speaker then invited everyone to open his or her Bible. Seated to my immediate left was a young lady, perhaps in her late twenties or early thirties, who reached for her Bible in her purse. As she started thumbing through the pages of her Bible, I noticed out of the corner of my eye that she had filled the margins on virtually every page with written notes. In fact, almost every chapter and verse in her Bible had been highlighted and underlined.

This may sound strange, but what I witnessed had an electrifying effect on me. I may not have heard an audible voice, but it seemed as if God was telling me, "John, you have been a Christian for almost fifteen years now, but look what she has done." Almost immediately I was overcome with great shame. Like those of the first-century Berean church, it was evident that this young lady had carefully searched the Scriptures and intently looked into the Word of God. Suffice it to say, I couldn't sing another note that afternoon, nor was I able to concentrate on the speakers' messages.

I was dumbfounded and couldn't understand what had just happened to me. It seemed as if my mind had been transformed into a state of confusion. Almost every day I had read at least a chapter or two out of my Bible during my early morning quiet time. This practice was part of my daily routine. I may not have written notes in its margins or highlighted portions of my Bible, but the fact remains that I had read my Bible almost daily. These shameful feelings, which continued for nearly the remainder of that day, caused me to feel unsettled.

Driving home that afternoon, I was ashamed to tell Janneke what had happened after the lunch hour, but I went ahead. She was as mystified as I was. Despite my inner turmoil, I was neither inspired nor inclined to highlight or underline every chapter or verse in my Bible. I also didn't see the need to fill the margins with handwritten notes. When I woke the following morning, I had forgotten about the incident and went about my daily routine.

THE SPIRIT'S PROMPTING

Three months later on a warm, sunny day, I was busy building a small patio in our backyard. Janneke and the boys were home. It was mid-afternoon when I suddenly and involuntarily stopped working, stood up, and dusted the sand from my hands, worn-out Levi jeans, and old Nike sneakers. Then, as if guided by some mysterious and unseen force, I walked through our kitchen and went up the stairs to my study on the second floor. Next, I sat down in the chair behind my desk and, as was my habit, removed my glasses and opened my Bible.

I surprised myself because reading the Bible in the midst of activities on this busy day was certainly something I hadn't planned. I didn't have my mind concentrated on the things of God. My mind was focused exclusively on meticulously arranging the concrete tiles in a certain pattern on top of compacted, level white sand.

Still sweaty and dirty, I opened my Bible and behold, it opened at the beginning of the gospel of John in the New Testament. I bent over my Bible and began to read slowly, "In the beginning was the Word." I didn't utter a sound, but in my heart I reacted with a loud *Wow!*

"And the Word was with God."

Again, I experienced a loud Wow! reaction.

"And the Word was God. He was with God in the beginning."

Wow!

These words and those that followed flew off the pages and into my heart. I was suddenly reading my Bible in a manner like I had never read the Bible before. I can only conclude that what was happening was the Holy Spirit working in me. In front of me on my desk sat an oversized porcelain coffee mug filled with pens, markers, and colored pencils. I started to read the Scriptures again, this time armed with an orange colored pencil and a small ruler. I began carefully underlining and highlighting everything I read. And there was something else: I couldn't stop reading, nor was I able to stop highlighting and underlining the contents of my Bible. I developed an instant and insatiable hunger and love for the Word of God. With that I started writing notes in the margins and on the blank pages in the back of my Bible.

I don't recall how long I sat there reading my Bible, but for the first time in all my years of Bible reading, I was filled with a joy I cannot express in words. I realized what King David had meant when he penned the following words: "The ordinances of the Lord. . . are sweeter than honey, than honey from the comb."[1] Yes indeed, all I was reading in the Bible was sweeter than honey to me, and I couldn't get enough of it.

The Testimony

During the ensuing weeks and months, I took every opportunity to study or—better yet—devour the Word of God. Janneke often came upstairs, pulled up a chair next to my desk, and said, "Darling, we hardly see you anymore." I had to be very careful not to neglect my family or my housekeeping responsibilities. Doing so wasn't always easy considering that I couldn't seem to leave my Bible alone.

One day our friend, Roel Visser, who was now pastor of another church across the border in Germany, an hour's drive from Emmen, called and invited us to attend a Christian rock concert. He wanted me to meet a Christian missionary from South Africa named Jan Veenstra.

Jan Veenstra was the son of Dutch immigrants. His parents had immigrated to South Africa in the late fifties. He shared his testimony with me, telling me that he was a student at the university in Johannesburg and majoring in public accounting. Jan described how he had meticulously planned his future, determined to always work hard, become exceedingly wealthy in the process, and enjoy life to its fullest. He had been so self-assured that he thought nothing could stop him from reaching his dreams and goals in life.

Those plans had abruptly changed one day when a young lady, a student at the same university, approached him on the college campus and boldly shared with him God's plan of salvation. She went on to say that God loved him and had a wonderful plan for him. However, this young lady made it clear that he was a sinner in desperate need of a Savior. He was in danger of going to hell and needed to be born again.

The prospect of going to hell didn't sound very appealing to him, and it wasn't long before he asked the Lord Jesus to come and live in his heart. Jan's perspective on life, including his future goals and ambitions, now took a new turn. Along with his conversion came a deep desire to reach out to lost souls. After graduating from the university, he continued his studies by attending a Bible college. While a student there, God called Jan to the mission field. He was married by then. God told him and his wife to serve as missionaries in Holland.

Throughout much of the mostly one-sided conversation, Jan kept saying, "God told me this," and "God told me to do that." Moreover, "God said this," and "God said that."

Listening to my new missionary friend, I noticed that he appeared to be having frequent conversations with God and sounded very convincing. I didn't question anything he shared with me, but the longer he talked, the more despondent I became. I must confess that I didn't enjoy my time at the concert that evening after my lengthy discussion with Jan.

I awoke the following morning, feeling as bad as I had the night before. I remember standing in the shower and crying out to the Lord. While I wasn't in the habit of praying during my shower time, this time I did. With a broken heart I asked, "Lord, why is it that You always talk to Jan Veenstra, but You never talk to me?" It was a cry and a plea from the depths of my heart. God didn't waste a second to answer my prayer.

Before continuing, I quote 1 Kings 19:11–12 (KJV):

> A great and strong wind rent the mountains, and brake in pieces the rocks before the Lord; but the Lord was not in the wind: and after the wind an earthquake; but the Lord was not in the earthquake: And after the earthquake a fire; but the Lord was not in the fire: and after the fire a still small voice.

That morning in the shower, weeping before the Lord, I clearly and unmistakably heard the still, small voice say, "John, 'everything in the world—the cravings of sinful man, the lust of his eyes and the boasting of what he has and does—comes not from the Father but from the world.'" God's reply came straight from 1 John 2:16, which I had not memorized.

It pains me to say this, but the verse pictured me. While my behavior may not have always been evident, I loved to boast and brag, especially to my friends. Shamefully, I loved bigger and better things and craved the finer things in life. That's not to say that I purchased everything I laid my eyes on because the money wasn't there.

As new believers, Janneke and I had never been "discipled." Though I don't intend to use that fact as an excuse, I'm certain that my life would have been different had I learned to put what I was reading in the Bible into practice. This is elementary biblical teaching. To my shame, I had failed to do exactly what Jesus had taught in His Sermon on the Mount:

> Why do you call me, "Lord, Lord," and do not do what I say? I will show you what he is like who comes to me and hears my words and

puts them into practice. He is like a man building a house, who dug down deep and laid the foundation on rock. When a flood came, the torrent struck that house but could not shake it, because it was well built. But the one who hears my words and does not put them into practice is like a man who built a house on the ground without a foundation. The moment the torrent struck that house, it collapsed and its destruction was complete.[2]

I began to see the Bible as a mirror, and what I discovered when I looked into that mirror wasn't always a pretty picture. It seemed as if the scales had fallen off my eyes!

> The law of the Lord is perfect, reviving the soul.
> The statutes of the Lord are trustworthy, making wise the simple.
> The precepts of the Lord are right, giving joy to the heart.
> The commands of the Lord are radiant, giving light to the eyes.
> The fear of the Lord is pure, enduring forever.
> The ordinances of the Lord are sure and altogether righteous.
> They are more precious than gold, than much pure gold;
> they are sweeter than honey, than honey from the comb.
> By them is your servant warned; in keeping them there is great reward.
> —Psalm 19:7–11

> For the word of God is living and active.
> Sharper than any double-edged sword,
> it penetrates even to dividing soul and spirit, joints and marrow;
> it judges the thoughts and attitudes of the heart.
> Nothing in all creation is hidden from God's sight.
> Everything is uncovered and laid bare before the eyes of him
> to whom we must give account.
> —Hebrews 4:12–13

The Scriptures I had read so many times before had now come alive, transforming my spiritual journey.

Your friend,
John

Twenty-Four

A Church in Peril

My dear friend,

Soon after we were settled in Emmen, it came time to look for a new home church. We decided to start our search with the seven-hundred-year-old Dutch Reformed Church, which featured a newly renovated interior and was located in the heart of the city. By best estimates, that church was capable of seating seven to eight hundred people, perhaps even more.

On our first Sunday there, we were amazed to discover that no more than twenty people were in attendance. Of those twenty, about twelve were children. In all fairness I should mention that as towns and cities grew and expanded after World War II, people moved to the suburbs, where new churches were being built and most people preferred to worship. Tragically, many beautiful, centuries-old church buildings that housed once-thriving congregations in village centers, towns, and cities have since become empty historic landmarks.

After visiting several Protestant churches of various denominations, we stumbled across an exhibit about the history of the Reformed Church of the Netherlands in Emmen. As we browsed through the vast display of historic photographs and artifacts at city hall, an elderly gentleman who acted as a tour guide warmly welcomed us and answered our questions. I explained to him that we had recently moved to Emmen from the

United States and were in the process of finding a home church for our family. I also told him that I had been baptized in the Reformed Church of the Netherlands while living in Stuttgart, Germany, and shared some fond memories of our time in our church there. The friendly old man informed us that he personally knew the pastor of the Reformed Church of the Netherlands, which was located in the neighborhood where we lived. He said he would gladly contact Pastor Huygens and make plans for us to meet him. We agreed to the arrangement.

Within a day or so, I received a telephone call from Pastor Huygens and agreed to meet him the following afternoon at our home. Janneke had just started her new part-time job and couldn't be present at the meeting.

The Meeting

Promptly at two o'clock the next day, Pastor Johannes Karel Huygens stood on our doorstep; he had arrived on a bicycle. In his mid-fifties, he was easygoing, pleasant, and gentle. As with the tour guide at city hall, I explained that our primary reason for moving to Holland was to share the good news of Jesus Christ with our family and friends living there. I also informed the pastor that we were looking for a church where we could become actively involved and receive spiritual nourishment. Moreover, we wanted to join a Bible study group.

To my surprise, Pastor Huygens replied that there were no Bible study groups in the Reformed Church of the Netherlands; however, several members of the Dutch Reformed Church met on a regular basis for home Bible studies. He agreed to have someone contact us, allowing us to participate in one of the two Bible study groups. For a number of years, he explained, the Reformed Church of the Netherlands and the Dutch Reformed Church, the two mainstream Protestant churches in Holland, were going through a historic phase of merging into one denomination, together with the Evangelical Lutheran Church. Separated for more than a hundred years, coupled with a steady decline in church membership, they were ripe for reconciliation, many felt. His church was now participating in a somewhat trial-and-error unification process with the local Dutch Reformed Church. "Things seemed to be going well," he said.

Before he left, I asked Pastor Huygens if he considered his church to be an orthodox church. With a quizzical look on his face, he wanted to know what I meant by that question. I told him that it was very important for us to know if his church was a Christ-centered church, to which he almost triumphantly replied, "Without question, John, the answer is an absolute yes!"

His enthusiastic response caused me to assume that his church was also a God-fearing, Bible-believing, and Bible-teaching church. I took an immediate liking to Johannes Huygens and looked forward to attending his church with my family that following Sunday. The next day, someone visited our home and invited us to join a home Bible study group. We gladly accepted the invitation.

Although Janneke preferred to join the Baptist church, which was only a stone's throw from our home, I strongly sensed that our place was in the Reformed Church of the Netherlands. Pastor Huygens shared his ministerial responsibilities with the pastor of the Dutch Reformed Church. On paper both churches had a combined membership in excess of two thousand people. Unlike the church in the center of town, few empty seats remained in the church where we would take an active role.

THE REQUEST

Less than a week after attending our first church service, a man rang our doorbell one evening and introduced himself as the chairman of the deacon board. He asked me if I would be willing to serve as a deacon in the church. I was completely taken by surprise; these people didn't know me from Adam. My response to the affable, elderly gentleman, who possessed an enviable abundance of silver hair, was that both Janneke and I were available to take an active part in church affairs. If the deacon board saw fit to have me join, then I would pray about the matter first and let him know my decision within a week. After a week passed, I agreed, with some degree of trepidation, to become a deacon at that church.

Not long after my commitment to serve as a deacon, I was invited to attend a brief meeting with other church members who had also agreed to serve in various capacities. Pastor Huygens chaired the small gathering, which offered a relaxed, friendly atmosphere. At this meeting we were each asked to sign an important creed, promising to strictly adhere to and defend, if necessary, historic church doctrines, articles of faith, and the church traditions.

After a brief opening prayer, he asked those in attendance to introduce themselves. When it was my turn, I told the group of approximately eight or nine people that I had grown up in a non-Christian home and immigrated to the United States at the age of eighteen. I had served as a professional soldier in the United States Army, had become a born-again Christian in November 1977, and was now living with my family in Holland. Pastor Huygens became visibly uncomfortable—*agitated* might be a better word—when I said I was born again. I hadn't heard similar remarks from any of the others in attendance.

At my first deacon's meeting, I learned that I was responsible for an area focusing on worldwide missions and outreach. I was asked to attend a series of evening seminars on this topic to prepare me for my responsibilities. The meeting started with an opening prayer by the chairman of the deacon board, followed by a short devotional, which consisted of the reading of a poem by one of the deacons. Regrettably, we didn't read the Bible at this meeting or the meetings that followed, except when the devotion was given by the chairman or by me.

An Interesting Conversation

Soon after my appointment as deacon, I participated in my first missions and outreach seminar conducted at another church in a neighboring city. Prior to this meeting, I was asked if I was willing to transport two people from other surrounding churches in Emmen to the seminar; I gladly obliged. When I picked up my two passengers, I learned that they, too, were newly appointed deacons with the same assignment.

My two curious companions wanted to know what an American citizen like me was doing in Holland. I told them about our desire to reach out to our family and friends with the good news of Jesus Christ. I added that I couldn't bear the thought that my dear family members were destined for hell because they weren't believers.

My lady passenger replied, "John, you don't really believe that, do you?"

"But it's in the Bible," I said. My other passenger confirmed that I was correct.

"Yes, I know that it's in the Bible," she said, "but you really don't believe all that stuff about hell, fire, the Devil, and demons, do you?" I responded by saying that I believed everything written in the Bible, from the first verse in the book of Genesis to the last verse in the book of Revelation. She said she believed God was love, and she refused to believe what was written in the Bible about hell, Satan, and demons.

THE SEMINAR

The seminar, scheduled to last several hours, took place in a large classroom, and twenty to twenty-five people were in attendance from the two mainline Protestant denominations scattered in the geographic region. Most attendees were elders or deacons in their respective churches.

After brief introductions, the moderator, a friendly woman not much older than I was, placed a small Bible on the floor in the center of the classroom. Next, she asked each group member to take a position in the classroom that accurately described the individual's relationship with the Bible. Afterward, she asked each person to explain the specific reasons why he or she chose that particular spot.

I unhesitatingly marched to the center of the classroom until my toes were touching the Bible, expecting others to follow me. Afraid that someone would be offended or that I might damage her Bible, I chose not to stand on it.

I couldn't believe what I saw. Everyone, including the woman conducting the seminar, had pushed his or her back squarely against the wall. All eyes in the classroom were now focused on me; I had become the center of attention, and everyone was eager to hear what I had to say. Using my brief opportunity to speak, I shared my testimony and explained that as far as I was concerned, the Bible and I were inseparable. I also said that nearly every day I read a portion of the Bible, which gave me comfort, joy, and direction in life. It also provided spiritual growth. Moreover, the Bible revealed the heart of God.

What I heard next in that classroom blew me away. I was surprised to learn that everyone in attendance except me had grown up in the church with the Bible. I heard one tragic commentary after another as my classmates explained the reasons why they had chosen their particular position. I'm convinced that the comments voiced by these people that evening broke God's heart. I'm also convinced that God cried that night when He heard these embarrassingly sad remarks. I have forgotten all of them except one: a woman in the group defiantly exclaimed that it was about time for the entire Bible to be rewritten to accommodate the needs of women.

Several months later, I represented the deacon board at a seminar in the northern part of the country. Again, the main topic of the all-day training session was centered on worldwide missions and outreach, and several hundred people were in attendance. Divided into large groups of thirty to forty people, we were invited to take part in several workshops. At the beginning of one of the one-hour sessions, the female facilitator asked the group the meaning of the term "the good news of Jesus Christ." It was a simple question, and I anticipated that many would excitedly leap to their feet and give the correct answer, hoping to win a prize.

However, only dead silence permeated that room. In fact, it was so quiet that one could have heard a pin drop. My heart began to race uncontrollably. With each passing minute, I moved closer to the edge of my seat until I could wait no longer. After what seemed like ten minutes of complete silence, I raised my hand.

"Yes, John, tell us your definition of the good news of Jesus Christ," she said in a friendly tone of voice.

I replied, "I'll keep it very simple: 'For God so loved the world that he gave his one and only Son, that whoever believes in him shall not perish but have eternal life.'[1] That in a nutshell is the essence of the good news of Jesus Christ, and may I add that we, as a church, have a unique opportunity and responsibility to tell the whole world this wonderful message."

Seated nearby was a man perhaps in his late fifties or early sixties. While I was speaking, I saw his face turning beet red. For a second I thought he was going to explode or keel over and die from a stroke or a massive heart attack.

I had barely finished speaking when he raised his voice across that room. "No, no, no! That is *not* the role of the church! We stopped doing that a hundred years ago. The good news of Jesus Christ today is to help the poor coffee bean farmer in South America who is being economically oppressed by the giant coffee companies!"

Obviously upset, he turned to me, pointing his finger in my direction, and concluded by saying, "*That*, sir, is the good news!"

Sadly, many heads in that room were nodding in firm agreement. Only one other person, a young lady in her mid-twenties, sided with me. I felt greatly outnumbered and dejected.

Almost all of the new friends in our Bible study group were of the Dutch Reformed Church persuasion. Both Janneke and I were glad to have met new friends and glad that we shared a common bond and a love for the Word of God. At these small, regular home gatherings I picked up on what they observed were significant problems in our church.

After carefully listening to comments made by friends in our Bible study group, coupled with what I had encountered at the missions and outreach seminars, I began paying close attention to what was taking place in our church. I must have been in another world or asleep during most church services because what I now discovered caused me to almost fall out of my chair and crash through the floor.

Problems

I heard an unfamiliar term at church, *eigentijds geloven*, best translated as "modern-day-belief." That term intimated that we were not backward or old-fashioned in our beliefs; rather we were progressive, contemporary thinkers and believers who had a fresh, new perspective on the Bible. I frequently heard that term mentioned from the pulpit, most notably by none other than Pastor Huygens.

A group of people in our church enthusiastically read a controversial, new book written by a nationally known professor of theology that questioned the authority and accuracy of the Bible. While reading the book itself may not have been wrong, I asked myself why only two small home Bible study groups existed in a church that enjoyed a combined membership of more than two thousand.

I was also perplexed that everyone was invited to attend a lecture by another well-known and prominent theologian who wrote a book questioning the validity of the Christian faith. Church members were encouraged to participate in discussions on the life and work of Carl G. Jung, a noted Swiss psychologist and alleged dabbler in the occult.[2] I was also concerned because these church members were invited to sign up for a study on interpreting the Bible in a new way. To me, such acceptance implied that the church had misinterpreted the Bible for two thousand years. Apparently the time had finally arrived to explain the Bible in a manner that would appease our modern way of thinking and believing.

Many sermons were preached with an emphasis on all the social problems in the world, while the name of Jesus Christ was barely mentioned. We once sang a modern-day hymn addressing God as "she." I was literally blown away one Sunday when I heard the preacher say, "What did Moses know about the game of soccer, jumbo jets, or summer vacations?" In other words, what Moses had written in the Bible doesn't apply to modern, progressive-thinking people like us today.

Once I heard another astonishing declaration in the form of a question to the congregation: "What are we going to do with that Bible?" The question insinuated that because the Bible is such an outdated document, perhaps we ought to toss it out of the window! Pastor Huygens addressed the congregation one Sunday with the following unsettling question and statement: "Do we really need to take the Bible seriously? This hasn't happened throughout the ages!" A lay preacher once remarked in his sermon, "Jesus performed many miracles. He healed the sick, raised the dead, and drove out demons. But the question remains: was He really capable of doing these things?" One preacher closed the Sunday service by praying, "God our Father and God our mother."

Something else didn't appear to be right. I don't believe I ever heard a minister preach a sermon that included elementary biblical concepts such as sin, redemption, repentance, forgiveness, obedience, grace, regeneration, or sanctification.

For quite some time, Janneke and I struggled with continuing our membership at that church. Several God-fearing, Christ-centered, Bible-believing, and Bible-teaching churches were in Emmen. Because of our itinerant military lifestyle and since we had attended a variety of churches over the years, it wouldn't have been easy for us to leave and join yet another church family. We also didn't want to uproot our boys again or abandon our good Bible study group friends.

Despite all the problems, I sensed that our calling was at that Reformed Church of the Netherlands. After much prayer and soul-searching, I determined that we would stay there. Those who didn't agree with what was taking place left and joined other churches. Still others, particularly those of our home Bible study group, didn't want to break their ties with the local Dutch Reformed Church. They had been part of that denomination for nearly all their lives. They understandably wanted to remain loyal, hoping that change would come someday.

After serving on the deacon board less than a year, I resigned out of protest for obvious reasons. Other than the chairman of the deacon board, I didn't think I had hurt anyone's feelings.

The Letter

After praying much and talking extensively with many of our friends, including those in our Bible study group, I decided in my heart that I needed to write a letter to the church board, expressing my deep concerns about all that I had heard and observed at the church. Before undertaking such a delicate task, I made an appointment with Johannes Huygens to let him know my plans.

I had a surprisingly cordial visit with our pastor in his study. He caught me off guard when he began the conversation by saying, "John, I too am a born-again Christian."

I didn't quite know what to make of his statement or understand what had prompted him to say it. I shared my frustrations about the lamentable problems at our church. His reply was that I hadn't been around to see the developments in the church during the previous thirty years. The people didn't want to go back to the way the church had been forty or fifty years ago, Pastor Huygens said. I explained that for several months I had felt compelled to write a letter of concern to the church leadership. To my surprise, he didn't have a problem with my decision, nor was he overly concerned about my letter. I told him that I had attended his church for almost two years and had yet to hear a sermon on Romans 8, which is probably the most important chapter in the whole Bible for the Christian.

Pastor Huygens replied, "John, if you want to listen to a sermon on Romans 8, you need to join the Pentecostal church."

His reply was only confirmation that our church was in deep trouble. I concluded that I needed to proceed with writing the letter.

THE VISION

Apart from speaking to me through His Word, I can count on only one hand all the times God has unmistakably spoken to me. One of those rare occasions occurred one Sunday at church before the start of the morning service. I stood in the church vestibule and looked into a packed sanctuary. Emotionally distraught because of the deplorable spiritual condition of our church, I cried out to the Lord, "God, why is it that You allow these people [speaking of false teachers] to speak Sunday after Sunday?"

Once again, the reply came to me in a still, small voice: "But John, what about all those people?"

That was all God said to me—"What about all those people?" It seemed as if God was saying, "Yes, I hear what you're saying, but Sunday after Sunday these people faithfully come and listen to what is preached from the pulpit. They all seem to like and approve of what is being proclaimed. There is no one who sounds the alarm; there is no one who protests!"

This wasn't the only time that God spoke to me about the distressing situation in our church.

The second time occurred not long hereafter. It happened one morning when I had finished my twice-weekly shopping spree at the Edah, a large national grocery chain located close to the center of town.

I was on the brink of despondency and in a crisis at the time concerning the state of affairs in our church. As I so often did during those days, I cried out to the Lord in utter desperation. As I strolled across the large parking lot to our car, which was parked across the street, a considerable distance from the store, carrying bags of groceries, I repeated my usual prayer, probably for the hundredth time: "Lord what is the problem with your church?" The Lord immediately answered my plea but in a most unusual fashion.

I suddenly found myself standing alone on the deck of a large ship in the midst of a raging storm. I was lost at sea under frighteningly dark and fast moving clouds. This was no ordinary vessel. Fabricated entirely out of wood, it tossed against the high waves in a desperate fight to stay afloat. The ship appeared to be doomed.

To my consternation, I discovered no handrail or any other objects on which I could support myself or hold onto except a tall, wooden mast located in the center of the ship's deck. With great difficulty I struggled to maintain my balance and covered my face with my hands, protecting it from the fierce wind and billowing ocean water sweeping across the bow. I needed to reach the mast to avoid being tossed overboard by the wind's force.

With what seemed like my last ounce of strength, I finally made my way to the center of the ship. At the exact moment that I tightly wrapped both arms around the twenty-four-inch-diameter mast, the violence of the storm subsided. Miraculously, the ship now sailed on a straight course under clear blue skies on an ocean as calm and smooth as a mirror.

I don't know how long I held onto the mast, but at a certain point I let go. Immediately, the sky turned almost black. Hurricane-force winds suddenly caused the ship to bounce up and down violently on the churning waters. High waves beat against its hull with extreme force, threatening to tear the ship into a thousand pieces. This time I lacked the physical stamina to fight my way back to the mast. Seasick, sapped of every bit of strength, and in danger of being thrown overboard, I cried out to the Lord in great fear, begging Him to save me from perishing in the angry waves.

When the vision ended, I realized that I had safely reached our car. I was thankful to see that no groceries had been strewn across the street or parking lot.

The Bible says that God "will respond to the prayer of the destitute; he will not despise their plea."[3] Being emotionally destitute about the sordid state of affairs at our church pretty well sums up my mental state at this time. The Lord answered my cry by revealing the true condition of His church.

The Printing

I didn't share the vision God had given to me that morning with anyone except Janneke, but perhaps I should have. Maybe I hesitated because I didn't fully comprehend the vision. It took a long time for me to determine that the mast symbolized Jesus Christ. The raging storm and roaring seas depicting God's anger frightens me to think about, even to this day!

By placing my signature on an important creed when I agreed to serve as a deacon, I had made a commitment before God and men to defend, at any cost, the truth of the gospel message. I was determined to accomplish exactly what I had agreed to do. To my astonishment, the church leadership largely ignored age-old, historic church doctrines, the articles of faith, and church traditions. No question about it—the people of this church, leadership included, were being led astray by false teaching.

Writing a letter about problems I had observed at church wasn't going to be easy. I had left school at the age of sixteen, and my command of the Dutch language was limited to basic conversation. Yet the urge to express my pain and agony on paper was irresistible. It was like the time when the workshop facilitator had asked about the definition of "the good news of Jesus Christ." My heart had pounded uncontrollably as I moved closer to the edge of my seat.

Once again I was on the edge of my seat, and something needed to be said. I spent several weeks prayerfully composing a lengthy letter and communicating issues of grave concern. I purposely avoided naming names but focused on problems that severely impeded the spiritual health and welfare of our church. A dear friend, who led our Bible studies and shared our pain and frustration, acted as a coach and edited and proofread my letter.

A Church in Peril 213

When the document was finished, I was scared to death and apprehensive about taking the next step. I spent many sleepless nights considering its potential consequences. The last thing I wanted was to cause division in the church.

> There are six things the Lord hates, seven that are detestable to him: . . . a man who stirs up dissension among the brothers.[4]

After completing my seventeen-page, double-spaced, painstaking project and being satisfied with its contents, I was deathly fearful that my letter would create much dissension. Soon after its completion, my family and I spent a weekend with my mother in Ede. On those occasions when we visited the town where I had grown up, we traditionally attended Sunday services at the local Baptist church.

Seated in the front row of the balcony of this small, contemporary, brick church building, I remember the young minister sternly looking straight at me and beginning his sermon on the prophet Daniel with the following words: "We don't have enough Daniels in the church today! We don't have enough men in the church with fortitude and courage, willing to stand up for what is right!"

Wow!

Other than saying, "Good morning" or "How are you?" to each other during the few times we visited this church each year, the Baptist preacher and I didn't know each other. But as he began his sermon, what struck me most was that he avoided looking at everyone in his congregation; instead, he kept staring at me with those piercing eyes.

One thing was certain: God used the occasion to convict me. The minister's opening statement was the inspiration I needed to march to the local print shop the next day and publish enough copies for each church board member.

Early on Monday morning, while my knees knocked in fear, I placed the order with the print shop clerk. He told me to come back at three o'clock that afternoon to pick up my copies. From the time when I delivered the original document until I returned in the afternoon, I felt unsettled and didn't have one moment of peace. Prayer didn't even calm my nerves.

I felt like a big coward when I returned to pick up my order. After paying the clerk, I marched out of the print shop, armed with forty copies of my letter. At the exact moment my right hand touched the brass door handle as I exited the building, I was overcome with a peace and a calmness that cannot be explained.

Before distributing copies of the letter to the board members, I determined out of fairness to our pastor to give him the first copy, allowing him an opportunity to rebut what I had written. When I delivered the letter to Pastor Huygens, I told him I was available to discuss its contents with him. I also told him that I would give him one week to examine the letter before giving copies to board members. I was prepared to destroy every copy if Johannes Karel Huygens saw the error of his ways, changed course, and decided to teach God's Word in a manner pleasing to the Lord.

THE MEETING

Pastor Huygens called two days later and wanted to see me about the letter. We agreed to meet the following morning at ten o'clock.

After the boys left for school and Janneke departed for work, I jumped on my bike and raced three-and-a-half miles to town. At our favorite bakery, I purchased a half-dozen freshly baked pastries and raced back home in time to meet our pastor.

When Pastor Huygens arrived, I could tell by his facial expression that he was anything but amused. I invited him to get comfortable, offered him a cup of freshly brewed coffee and a delicious pastry, a typical Dutch mid-morning household tradition. He angrily responded by saying that he didn't want a cup of coffee, nor was he interested in a pastry.

He began the discussion by saying that if the church board adopted my recommendations, he would immediately resign. I told my guest that my intentions in writing the letter were not for him to resign or leave the church but to preach the Word in a manner honoring to the Lord while simultaneously nurturing spiritual growth in the church.

"There is no room for compromise!" I said. That meant he must stop undermining and questioning the Bible's authority. It also meant he must stop misleading the congregation Sunday after Sunday with doubts and half-truths. He must also cease the creative use of Scripture designed to accommodate his modern, progressive way of thinking. I reminded Pastor Huygens of his pastoral role. As shepherd of his flock, he was responsible for the spiritual health and welfare of his church.

He angrily responded with a question. "You mean to say that I'm the sheepdog?" He was insinuating that I was treating him like a dog.

I also reminded him of a previous conversation in which he had assured me that our church was a "Christ-centered church." When I said that his sermons hardly mentioned the name of Jesus Christ, his face suddenly and strangely contorted.

Seated to my left on our L-shaped sectional sofa, he became very angry with me and pointed his right index finger at my face. Suddenly, while he was bordering on rage, a frighteningly unfamiliar voice spoke from his mouth. This wasn't the voice I was used to hearing on Sundays from the pulpit.

In a high-pitched voice, sounding strangely like an angry woman, he said, "I know what you are trying to do! You are trying to wake us up!"

I wasn't prepared for this. Not knowing how to respond, I sat on our couch, completely dumbfounded.

Pastor Huygens slowly lowered his right arm and calmed down. In the next breath, another voice came out of his mouth, this time that of a young boy. Almost crying softly, he said, "I hate it when people undermine the Word of God."

Feeling sorry for this man, I wanted to move closer and put an arm around him, but I didn't.

Completely astounded by what was taking place in the living room of our home, I didn't know what to say or how to react. Soon Pastor Huygens returned to his normal self and didn't appear to be angry anymore. There was little more to say. Like everyone in our congregation, I genuinely liked Johannes Huygens. He was a soft-spoken and kind man, but as a minister of the gospel, I considered him to be a dismal failure.

After a meeting that lasted more than an hour, I told him that I would proceed with my plan by distributing copies of the letter to the board. To my surprise he left in a somewhat happy mood and didn't seem alarmed about my intentions.

The Delivery

At the recommendation of my friend who had closely supported me in my efforts, I personally hand delivered a copy of the letter to each board member of the governing church body, going from one address in Emmen to the next. All I could do now was patiently wait.

Rumors quickly spread that John Rozema had written a less-than-favorable letter to the church leadership. A deacon with whom I had served, a retired high school teacher, refused to greet me when we met before or after church services. I once ran into him while grocery shopping at the Edah. As soon as he saw me, he angrily turned his shopping cart around and stormed away in the opposite direction.

It was a painful time not only for me but also for Janneke.

Six months later, on a beautiful spring day in April 1994, a one-page letter, signed by the chairman of the church board, arrived in the mail. It was the official board response to my letter. Though the tone was friendly, the letter failed to address my specific areas of deep concern. I'll refrain from a long discussion about the reply's contents; the bottom line was that everyone, regardless of personal beliefs or opinions, was welcome in our church. No change was deemed appropriate.

> For the time will come when men will not put up with sound doctrine. Instead, to suit their own desires, they will gather around them a great number of teachers to say what their itching ears want to hear. They will turn their ears away from the truth and turn aside to myths.
> —2 Timothy 4:3–4

Those who supported my sending of the letter to our church board were greatly disappointed with the board's decision. Knowing that our time in Holland was soon drawing to a close, we decided not to join another church but to remain loyal to the end.

Your friend,
John

Twenty-Five

No Place Like Home

My dear friend,

Janneke and I witnessed to our family and friends by means of short personal testimonies printed in *Rozemagram*, a double-column, four-page newsletter about what the Lord had done in our lives. We published the newsletter three or four times per year and ended each story with the gospel invitation. Not everyone was happy with the *Rozemagram*. We received a few stinging and scathing letters from people dear to us, warning us not to continue sending that "trash."

After living in Holland for nearly two and a half years, we felt that we had accomplished what we had set out to do. Most with whom we talked privately found the stories in our newsletter intriguing and interesting; to our knowledge, however, of the seventy or so recipients in Holland, not one person had accepted the Lord Jesus Christ as his or her personal Lord and Savior. Also, not one person had contacted us, wanting more information about a personal relationship with the Lord. We also published an English version of the newsletter, which we sent to family and friends in the United States. Our mission was to plant seeds—God would do the rest.

We had another move to consider—returning to the United States. Kevin and Darren were slowly beginning to lose their command of the English language after living overseas more than two years.

One evening after dinner in early January 1994, we casually asked our boys what they thought of returning to the United States. There was no hesitation. In unison and with great excitement in their voices and joyful expressions on their faces, their unanimous vote was a loud yes.

We explained that they would first need to finish the school year. Then, if the Lord willed, we would move during the summer school break. Also, if it pleased the Lord, we would return to Virginia. Our boys seemed content with the proposal and understood that they probably wouldn't see their friends again after our departure.

Moving back to the United States would turn out to be another major adventure with unexpected surprises.

A New Burden

Janneke and I prayed and began thinking about what to do next. One afternoon while Janneke was at work, I watched an American daytime talk show program on TV, hosted by an internationally famous TV personality. The discussion topic was child abuse and neglect in America. As I watched the program, I became excited about the thought of working for a Christian ministry in the United States whose mission was caring for abused and neglected children. Surely an organization must exist that could use our abilities.

When Janneke arrived home that afternoon, I told her about what I had seen on TV and asked if she was interested in working with abused and neglected children. My question caused her face to immediately light up. She enthusiastically exclaimed that she would eagerly welcome such a wonderful opportunity. In fact, she appeared so excited that one would think she had won the national lottery. (That's not to say that we played the lottery.) I told Janneke that together and individually we should seek the Lord about this matter. If we were both still excited about the idea thirty days from now, we would proceed with plans to reach out to abused and neglected children. We figured that God would work out the details.

Financing our move across the ocean meant selling or giving away virtually everything we owned. Our desire to return to Virginia was so great that parting with our material possessions was of little concern to us. Because of the prohibitive costs of shipping our household effects, we planned to ship only items of emotional value, including those possessions our boys treasured.

After the thirty days were over and after much prayer, our excitement and enthusiasm for working with abused and neglected children had not dampened. Our next step was to find a Christian ministry dedicated to caring for abused and neglected children. Among our collection of books was a catalog of Christian ministries in the United States. The catalog listed several organizations under the heading "Abused and Neglected Children."

We were elated when we found a ministry located in the Hampton Roads area. Its address was listed under a post office box with the Christian Broadcasting Network (CBN) in Virginia Beach. The next order of business was to write a letter of introduction to the organization's president and inform him that we eagerly wanted to work for the ministry in any capacity they saw fit. We also informed him that we were prepared to work for no salary. While our pension from the army was hardly sufficient to financially support a family of three, much less a family of five, we trusted that the Lord would supply our needs. When I dispatched the letter in early March, we were convinced that our next assignment was somewhere on the eastern shores of the commonwealth of Virginia.

LIMBO

Six weeks passed without a reply. One day Janneke suggested that I contact the ministry, but I recommended that we wait awhile. "Let's not be anxious about anything,"[1] I said. "Let the Lord work this out." By the end of April, we began to advertise among friends and family that our household possessions were for sale. To our surprise, we sold our personal effects like clockwork. We were amazed when two or more people never wanted the same item. It was as if God was sending these people our way. Not everything was sold. We gave many items away, and still others weren't fit to be sold. Those that weren't of use to others we took to the municipal dump.

More than three months passed by, and still we received no response from the ministry in Virginia. This time Janneke strongly urged me to contact them. Perhaps it was my stubborn nature, but once again I told her to be patient and wait; maybe the Lord was testing us.

By early June we still had heard nothing, prompting me to contact CBN by telephone. I spoke with a lady about our situation, and she said there was no record of that ministry listing its address with CBN. She double-checked the information on her computer and confirmed that they didn't know about the organization. She told me to call back in about ten days because her supervisor was on vacation.

Exactly ten days later, I was on the phone again, this time speaking with the supervisor. She confirmed that the ministry wasn't affiliated with the Christian Broadcasting Network. The supervisor understood our dilemma and promised to mail a current listing of organizations they regularly used to make referrals. She recommended that I select an organization or ministry from that list.

By this time I began to carefully examine our true motives. What did we really want to do? Did we want to serve the Lord by reaching out to abused and neglected children, or did we want to move to Virginia? The answer was clear. While we desired to return to Virginia, we felt a greater need to reach out to abused and neglected children. We were prepared to work wherever the Lord wanted to send us next.

Toward the end of June, a referral listing of Christian ministries that dealt with child abuse and neglect arrived in the mail. Within two days, I mailed ten letters of introduction and copies of our résumés to several Christian organizations scattered throughout the United States.

In less than two weeks, we received two replies. One came from an address in Chesapeake, Virginia; the other came from a ministry somewhere in the hinterlands of Texas. The reply from the ministry in Virginia included a beautiful brochure and a welcome letter stating that a three-bedroom, one-bath cottage was immediately available for our family. To make a long story short, our next assignment was to work for a children's home—not in Chesapeake, however, but somewhere else in Virginia.

Our car also needed to be sold. Janneke and I had prayed and asked the Lord to send someone willing to pay fifteen thousand Dutch guilders (the approximate equivalent of seventy-five hundred dollars) for our car. We needed this money to defray the cost of our move overseas and make a fresh start. Someone told us that no one would pay such a steep price for our car, but we weren't discouraged. What's impossible with man is possible with God![2] We felt that the amount was a fair price. Despite its many mechanical woes, the car had been well maintained and totaled only fifty thousand miles on the odometer.

One day when I was speaking to our neighbor, he asked how much we wanted for the Escort; a friend at work was looking for a car. I told him the asking price. Promptly the next day a young man showed up at our home, was interested in buying the Escort, and asked if he could take it for a test drive. After driving around for about twenty minutes, he said he needed to confer with his wife and would let us know of their decision soon. He called that evening and agreed to buy the car at our asking price. The buyer showed up the next day with fifteen thousand Dutch guilders in his hand and drove away a happy, proud, new owner of an American 1991 strawberry metallic Ford Escort. Janneke and I prayed that he and his family would enjoy driving that vehicle for many years to come.

Shock

In mid-July we said farewell to our dear friends in Emmen and lived with my mother until our scheduled departure in early August. Our boys were very excited when we finally stepped on the plane at Schiphol International Airport in Amsterdam to make the nine-hour-long flight across the Atlantic Ocean. However, a rather unpleasant surprise awaited us when we touched down in New York.

When we stepped off the plane at John F. Kennedy International Airport, we joined the hundreds patiently waiting in line at the immigration checkpoint. When it was our turn, the immigration official asked us a routine question: how long had we had been living overseas? "Three years," we replied.

To our shock the official said that Janneke wasn't permitted to enter the United States. Her legal status as a resident alien was no longer valid. This meant she would need to return to Holland on the next flight out!

Unknown to us, in order to maintain legal status, U.S. immigration law requires resident aliens living abroad to physically return to the United States once each year to have their passports stamped. The immigration officer wanted to know what we had been doing in Holland during those three years. This wasn't the time or place to enter into a dispute with the immigration official. I apologized to the lady for being unaware of the law and explained to her that we had lived in Holland and served as freelance Christian missionaries after my retirement from the U.S. Army. I was determined that the boys and I were not going to enter the United States without Janneke. There was only one thing left to do: we said a quick prayer.

The immigration official carefully examined Janneke's Dutch passport again. Then, looking at Janneke, she said reluctantly, "Okay, I'll make an exception this time by allowing you to enter into the United States; however, I'm doing so with the stipulation that you apply for U.S. citizenship at the earliest opportunity. Welcome home!"

This was God's answer to our prayers! We heaved great sighs of relief as the official stamped Janneke's passport and called for the next traveler in line. We thanked the Lord, thanked the immigration official, and quickly proceeded to baggage claim and U.S. customs. Thankfully, we found no other unexpected hurdles to overcome at JFK. Being home again after a three-year-long hiatus was sweet and felt wonderful.

NEXT STEP

After a considerable hike on a hot summer day, we picked up our Hertz rental car and traveled in the direction of the children's home. We took this opportunity to drive through busy traffic in downtown Manhattan and admire New York City's world famous, imposing skyscrapers. From a distance the city's skyline was a sight we wouldn't soon forget.

We drove at a leisurely pace along the East Coast, arriving three days later in a town located approximately twenty-five miles from the children's home. Our plans were to take a week's vacation before reporting for duty. To our disappointment, all hotels were fully booked except for one, a cheap motel that was ripe for an extreme makeover.

After breakfast in town the following morning, we decided to satisfy our curiosity by making a reconnaissance of the children's home and exploring the geographic area before doing anything else. What we discovered wasn't what we had in mind or what we had seen in the information packet sent to us.

The hundred-year-old, three-story Victorian home accompanied by a few adjacent, timeworn buildings appeared to be deserted. We saw no sign of life. We didn't see a parked car or observe a single person on its property. One small, vacant, grayish-colored, one-story home on its premises was badly in need of some tender loving care.

On our drive back to the motel Janneke started to cry. Throughout much of that day she continued to sob almost uncontrollably and couldn't be consoled despite our best efforts. Her incessant crying marked the beginning of a time in our lives characterized by many disappointments and heartaches.

> Never be lacking in zeal, but keep your spiritual fervor, serving the Lord.
> Be joyful in hope, patient in affliction, faithful in prayer.
> —Romans 12:11–12

Shedding many tears has been the price we've paid for wanting to serve the Lord.

Your friend,
John

Twenty-Six

A Time to Cry

My dear friend,

"How good and pleasant it is when brothers live together in unity!"[1] King David wrote these words three thousand years ago.

In the summer of 1988, our friend Martien Hartman had escorted me on a tour of the ministry Light in the East. Jakob Kroeker, a Mennonite pastor, and Walter Jack, a pastor of the Reformed Church, had founded the ministry in 1920. These two great men of God had seen a need to care for Polish and Russian refugees after World War I. Over the years, the mission of Light in the East has changed somewhat, but after ninety years in existence, it continues to thrive and flourish to this day, spreading the love of Jesus abroad and reaching out to tens of thousands with the truth of the gospel message in many far eastern European countries and beyond.

As we toured the ministry, I remember thinking how wonderful it would be to see Christians living and working together in unity. There would be only perfect love and harmony, as evident in the organization Martien worked for. It was then that I deeply longed to be part of a Christian ministry. I had waited a long time for that to happen.

Now, on August 17, 1994, the evening of our fifteenth wedding anniversary, we moved into our new dwelling. The house was furnished only with a double bed and a donated, worn-out La-Z-Boy recliner.

While Dennis volunteered to sleep in the recliner, Kevin and Darren chose the carpeted floor in the living room, using their backpacks as pillows. The temperature inside the house was unbearably hot since the house hadn't come equipped with an air conditioner. We had been invited to temporarily stay at the residence of the children's home president, but we had politely declined, not wishing to be a burden.

During our initial interview over dinner the previous evening at a local restaurant, we had learned that we would become part of a small, seven-man team with the mission to care for abused and neglected children. Three staff members were ordained ministers. Janneke and I would function as relief house parents. In addition, I would be responsible for the maintenance of the facilities, assist with grounds keeping, and help with remodeling a small, one-bedroom house. I knew nothing about maintenance or carpentry, but I was excited and eager to learn.

To our surprise, the children's home was still in its infant stages and not yet licensed. A sixteen-year-old girl, waiting to be admitted, temporarily lived at the home of a staff member. She would remain there until the organization was able to meet strict Virginia license requirements. At present, there were no other children.

Car Trouble

A disturbing incident took place only a couple of days after our arrival that unsettled both Janneke and me, causing us to believe that we may have made a tragic mistake. A senior staff member chastised a child (who was not a resident of the home) over a trivial issue. The boy did not deserve this treatment. Not wishing to cause confusion in our family, we kept the matter to ourselves. We were determined to overlook the incident and to give it our best shot.

Before arriving at the children's home, we had purchased a used Ford Taurus at the same Ford dealership where we had purchased our strawberry metallic Ford Escort four years earlier. Since this was our second car from the same dealership, we had hoped that the salesman would be kind enough to sell us a reliable used automobile. However, our desire was only wishful thinking.

Buying the 1988 Taurus at a cash price of twenty-five hundred dollars would turn out to be another headache of major proportions. The maroon-colored vehicle came with a thirty-day limited warranty. On exactly the thirty-first day after we purchased the Ford Taurus, the car broke down. We could no longer request our money back or return the vehicle to the dealer, a two-hour drive, for necessary repairs.

No one seemed to know what was wrong with the car. Even an automotive maintenance instructor at the local high school was puzzled. He couldn't determine the exact cause of the car's malfunction. Also, we couldn't afford to take it to a reputable garage to have it repaired, if in fact it could be repairable. We had already spent approximately $750 on repairs that were not covered by the warranty in the brief period of time we had owned the vehicle. I felt that the used car salesman had cheated me and vowed never, ever to buy another Ford product again.

One of the staff members, who quickly became a good friend, graciously allowed us to use her Honda whenever we needed to. We were very grateful for her kindness.

We spent the first couple of weeks purchasing necessary major appliances and much-needed furniture at discount furniture stores. Our household effects arrived at the Port of Norfolk soon after our arrival. All our personal belongings had been packed in a single crate large enough to fit on the back of a pickup truck.

Soon after we were settled, Janneke was asked to babysit the two-year-old daughter of one of the senior staff members. This request took us by surprise since we had agreed to help care for abused and neglected children, not to babysit three days per week. We were told to look at the opportunity from the standpoint that babysitting is also a ministry. Being new to the organization and wanting to develop a good relationship with everyone, we reluctantly agreed but were unhappy with the arrangement. Thankfully after nearly six weeks the need for babysitting ended.

Strike One, Two, and Three

Janneke and I were required to obtain child protective services and criminal background investigations as part of our new responsibilities.

After a month or so, the children's home obtained its license, and the Virginia State Department of Social Services granted approval to begin operations for a home not to exceed ten children. Almost immediately, Justin, a six-year-old boy with a history of abuse and neglect, was admitted.

A painful incident took place on the very first evening after we had assumed our duties as relief house parents.

Justin slipped out the backdoor and went into the yard, where he should not have been. Another child was being physically restrained outside, and Justin was just curious and wanted to see what was happening. Janneke saw Justin open the door and immediately went after him, but he was too quick. When Janneke stepped outside to fetch Justin, Tom Garrison, the vice president of this ministry, lost control and loudly scolded her, ordering her to get Justin back inside right away!

This behavior was uncalled for. Tom's yelling was very unprofessional and humiliating. To me it bordered on verbal abuse. Janneke didn't deserve this treatment.

The incident was of such a nature that we had very good reason to immediately abandon the children's home after having been there only a little over a month. We had a huge problem, however; our Ford Taurus wasn't going anywhere. In my heart I wanted to quickly run away from that place with my family. If our car had been in good operation, we would have rented a U-Haul trailer, backed it up to the front door, collected our personal belongings, and left this ministry in our rearview mirror, not knowing where to go or what to do next. Much to my anguish, we were stuck.

Another problem was that our boys had just started classes for the new school year. We didn't like the idea of taking them out of school and enrolling them in yet another one. The children's home was located in a rural and economically depressed area where job opportunities were severely restricted. We didn't realize it at that time, but God had good reasons to keep us at the children's home.

By January 1995, four teenage girls and the six-year-old boy were living at the home. Janneke spent all her time at the children's home from late Friday afternoon until early Sunday evening. I helped her with various household chores throughout the weekend but spent the evenings with our boys at our home.

Dennis, Kevin, and Darren had a difficult time making the transition to the Virginia public school system, brushing up on the English language, and tediously laboring over what we considered inordinate and unnecessary amounts of homework night after night. Thankfully, the boys adjusted well academically.

We faced other problems as well. Our boys often came home from school complaining that all the kids at school were poking fun at them because, unlike their classmates, they weren't wearing designer clothing and shoes. Our limited income prohibited us from purchasing these expensive items. Heartbroken for our sons, we learned that children can be very cruel at times.

Another bombshell hit sometime in mid-February 1995. This one hit like lightning under a clear, blue sky. Every weekday morning, after the children had left for school and before the start of the daily activities, the staff met for a brief time of devotions and prayer. On one particular Monday morning, Janneke and I were confronted and falsely accused of not following home rules while the regular house parents were away during the weekend.

We were completely taken by surprise. The confrontational tone of the mostly one-sided conversation hurt us deeply. We both felt that we had been deliberately and unfairly attacked at the wrong place and at the wrong time. This unexpected blow was so severe that I was simply unable to think straight. When it happened, I was in no frame of mind to respond to the trumped-up accusations. I told everyone in attendance that we would immediately retreat to our home, think carefully about these fabricated charges, and let them know our response the following day.

Feeling betrayed, Janneke and I stayed home for the rest of the day. After much prayer and lengthy discussion, we pondered our next move. Once again the desire to run away from the children's home was almost overwhelming. We considered this incident of such a serious nature that our immediate departure was clearly warranted; however, the old Ford Taurus remained parked in the gravel driveway and was going nowhere.

I determined then that this inexcusable incident was strike two; at the third strike, we would leave with or without the Taurus.

When we returned the following day, Jack Montgomery, one of the two house parents, informed us that charges leveled against us (by the four teenage girls) had indeed been false. Jack and his wife, Margaret, apologized for what had happened. We immediately forgave them for their actions.

We decided not to leave but to continue our day-to-day activities. Despite our best efforts, however, this latest episode had adversely affected our ability to do our work with much enthusiasm for and devotion to this ministry. I couldn't help thinking that in only a matter of time yet another major disappointment would confront us.

My assumptions proved to be correct. Strike three occurred two and a half months later. To the casual observer, this particular incident might have appeared to be minor, one we could have easily resolved, but to me it was the icing on the cake. I had all I could take!

The incident happened at the close of a morning staff meeting in early May 1995.

Tom Garrison, who chaired the meeting, asked, "John, what are your plans for today?"

"Janneke and I plan to visit the army commissary," I said, "and go grocery shopping."

I was surprised to see the vice president become visibly upset with my remark. He immediately terminated the meeting, dismissed the staff, and asked me to stay.

After everyone left, Tom said that I had undermined his authority by *telling* him we were going to the commissary. Furthermore, the children's home policy was that in order for a staff member to take time off, he or she needed to submit a formal leave request in advance.

After more than eight months at this ministry, this was the first time I was made aware of such a policy. My schedule required me to be available to work seven days per week (without pay), including our weekend house parenting duties. Because of these hours, this organization's president had clearly stated in an earlier staff meeting that we could take time off when we had a need. Submission of a leave request was never discussed.

While I didn't have a problem with submitting such a document for an extended absence, submitting a formal written request in advance to go grocery shopping seemed ludicrous to me.

After my discussion with Tom, I made up my mind. Our time at this organization had come to an end. A long list of other seemingly innocent but painful incidents (not mentioned here) also contributed to our decision to flee from this place.

What to Do Now

We wasted little time informing the chain of command of our decision to leave. The leadership asked us to please reconsider, but I had justifiably reached a boiling point whereby we could no longer be part of this ministry. Our decision to leave was irrevocable. Although our Ford Taurus continued to be in a perpetually and mechanically dysfunctional state, we trusted the Lord to provide a way out.

We were allowed to remain in our home until the end of May, giving us approximately three weeks to contemplate what to do next. We took time to examine ourselves and seriously ask ourselves the question, "Where did *we* fall short?" To begin with, we had complained a lot. In his letter to the Philippians the apostle Paul exhorts us to "do everything without complaining."[2]

This was an area in our lives where we needed much improvement. We had complained about the babysitting arrangement. We had grumbled about not having water or electricity at our home several days at a time—a rather frequent occurrence. We had lamented about the public school system, our car, and a myriad of other little things.

For these failures we are truly very sorry. We have asked the Lord to forgive us and have repented of these sins. Then there is something else for which I'm deeply ashamed and remorseful: I once raised my voice almost uncontrollably at the six-year-old boy, something out of character for me and something I never should have done. I had miserably failed at keeping my emotions in check and feel ashamed thinking about my failure today.

I considered our time at the children's home a bad dream and a painful memory for our whole family, particularly for Janneke, who cried nearly every day and suffered frequent, debilitating, and chronic migraines throughout our nine months serving this organization. By and large, working together at the children's home in perfect love, unity, and harmony was only an elusive dream.

> Record my lament;
> list my tears on your scroll—
> are they not in your record?
>
> —Psalm 56:8

Despite the pain, hardships, and disappointments we endured, our desire to serve the Lord had not diminished. After leaving the children's home, we became part of another Christian ministry located within a ten-minute drive from our home.

Your friend,
John

Twenty-Seven

"This Thing is from Me"

My dear friend,

On Tuesday, May 30, 1995, we pulled up stakes and moved into an old, one-bedroom, wood-frame house with a screened-in porch located on a 277-acre farm. A former tenant farmhouse, this one-story clapboard dwelling with a tin roof measured no more than eight hundred square feet. From a distance the home looked like a matchbox sitting under two giant oak trees.

The major renovations this house needed were my responsibility. Remodeling primarily consisted of building a two-bedroom, two-bathroom addition with the help of a few other men.

The thirteen-foot-by-thirteen-foot living room became temporary sleeping quarters for our boys until the bedrooms were completed. The existing small kitchen required a few modifications as well so it could also function as our living and dining room. Except for a toilet and sink, our little abode lacked a bathroom. We took daily showers at the "big house," which was located about a hundred yards away.

Though we felt like we were camping out, we didn't mind our temporary Spartan living accommodations. Janneke and I were happy that we at least had hot and cold running water. The situation reminded me of the austere living conditions of our Middle East missionary friends. After our struggles at the children's home, life on the farm was a breath of fresh air. Despite crammed living quarters, our boys seemed content and happy.

Why were we here? Based on the recommendation of a friend, we had joined a ministry that housed Christian men battling drug or alcohol addiction or both. At any given time, no more than three men were admitted to the farm for rehabilitation, spiritual guidance, and biblical counseling. These men were required to perform a variety of chores on the farm, which was owned by Carl and Evelyn Gibbons, a retired couple who headed the ministry.

Armed with an *Ortho's Home Improvement Encyclopedia*, a portable electric cement mixer, a truckload of cinder blocks, and an array of other tools and building materials, we enthusiastically commenced work on a 270-square-foot addition. Working six days per week was the norm, and as their schedules permitted, Dennis, Kevin, and Darren voluntarily helped with the renovations. Our workday normally began after a brief prayer and devotional time at the big house.

Renovations proceeded at a slow but steady pace. One of our first priorities was the construction of a bathroom, a project phase that thankfully didn't take long. When this remodeling stage was completed, we were happy because we no longer needed to shower at the big house.

Home Church

While living on the farm, we were introduced to a home church. One other family joined us each Sunday, and occasionally other families took part in the service as well. Traditionally, we met around noon with a hot meal followed by an informal gathering, which included the singing of hymns and contemporary worship songs followed by the celebration of Holy Communion. Our first experience with a home church was very exciting because it reminded us of the first-century church when people met in homes.

During the nearly six months that passed by, I enjoyed what I was doing for the most part. What I passionately loathed, however, was sanding sheetrock. Doing that type of work with precision requires a skilled person with upper body strength. I wasn't that person. I felt like my talents were being wasted and hoped to become more involved in the ministry by using my God-given talents, skills, and abilities. But that didn't happen. For a long time I had longed to do a great work for God, but now I only felt relegated to sanding sheetrock hour after hour, day after day.

As time went by, I often asked myself why I was never consulted. No one ever asked me for my opinions, ideas, or recommendations. I also felt like I wasn't understood and was always being placed in the background. It was a hurtful, frustrating experience. For example, Carl Gibbons never once asked me to help serve communion at the close of our Sunday gatherings. That in itself may not have been a problem had it not been for the fact that *someone* in the group was asked to help serve Communion each Sunday—but that someone was never me. Being overlooked cut me to the heart. I didn't share my pain or frustrations with anyone, not even Janneke. But bit by bit, little by little, I was becoming unhappy and disillusioned.

DISCONTENTMENT

The Coming Revival, a book by Dr. Bill Bright, founder of Campus Crusade for Christ, inspired me to go on a fast. On January 16, 1996, Kevin's thirteenth birthday, I ate my last solid meal and savored an extra large piece of birthday cake along with a generous slice of cherry pie. During my fast, I daily expressed to the Lord my deepest desire to be made a humble person. Strangely, when I completed the fast, almost immediately I felt that our honeymoon on the farm was over.

Janneke's dad arrived in late February for a four-week visit, his first visit since our move back to Virginia. I wondered what went through his mind when he saw our not-so-desirable living arrangements. Surely he remembered our beautiful, spacious homes in Florida years earlier.

Although he never questioned our motives for living on the farm, he frequently told us we needed to move away. Yes, the temptation was great to move elsewhere and find a decent-paying secular job; however, what he didn't realize—what we couldn't discuss with him—was the fact that we were on a mission: we were here to serve the Lord.

Moreover, moving away wouldn't have been so simple. Our car had been in the shop for repairs for several months and still wasn't working. In addition, we had virtually no money in the bank to defray the cost of another move. We had learned to carefully manage every penny, and making both ends meet was difficult, especially with two teenagers and an eleven-year-old. Besides, where would we go and what would we do in a rural region where good jobs were hard to find and the unemployment rate exceeded statewide and national averages?

In April 1996, I was hospitalized at the Southside Regional Medical Center in Petersburg, Virginia, because of an apparent heart attack after frequent episodes of excruciating chest pain, often accompanied by nausea and cold sweats. During the forty-five-minute ride to the hospital, I reasoned that the next heart attack, which could occur at any moment, would probably rob me of my life. I despaired of life and envisioned only Janneke and the boys at the grave site on the occasion of my sudden demise.

After spending much of the day in the ER, I was transferred to a regular room and told that I would remain at the hospital for further treatment and observation. Being a hospital patient was no fun. Except for Janneke, I received no other visitors since Dennis, Kevin, and Darren weren't allowed to see me. When Janneke wasn't present, I felt very lonely and longed to see and hug my boys. Thankfully, after three days at the hospital, I was discharged without further treatment or medication.

I had become so frustrated by what I had experienced on the farm that the anxiety affected me emotionally—even to the point that I had difficulty functioning properly. I struggled to imagine anyone being more discouraged than I was. I told an army buddy that I wanted to climb the highest mountaintop, on my hands and knees if necessary, and scrape the skin down to my bones, if that's what it took. When I reached the top, I wanted to scream so loudly that every living creature on the face of the earth would hear me.

I don't know why, but at one point I felt like I was teetering on the brink of insanity. One Saturday morning in May 1996, after returning from a men's meeting in town, I told Janneke, "If I don't see God in all this, you'll have to take me to Central State [a state-operated mental health facility] and have me admitted!"

Streams in the Desert

Allow me to shift gears at this point and tie the story together near the end.

Almost twelve years earlier in September 1984, a drunk driver tragically killed Todd Milan Schulze, beloved son of Howard and Martha Schulze, dear friends of ours. Todd had just returned from visiting his parents in Naples, Italy. In the spring of 1984, he had graduated from the University of Texas in Austin and had a bright and promising future ahead of him. Only twenty-four years old and employed by a commercial real estate company servicing all of Texas, Todd's young life was needlessly and ruthlessly cut short. Nothing in life could be more devastating and painful than the sudden loss of a spouse or a child, especially at the hands of a drunk driver.

I discussed the horrible event with friends and colleagues at the Miami Recruiting Battalion, asking for their advice of what to say to the devastated father and mother. Someone suggested that we purchase *Streams in the Desert*, a two-volume devotional written and compiled by Mrs. Charles E. Cowman, who had served with her husband as a missionary in China and Japan from 1901 to 1917. *Streams in the Desert* would bring comfort to the grieving parents, I was told.

Janneke and I were unfamiliar with this devotional, but we found it at a nearby Christian bookstore. For reasons known only to the Lord, these two little books never left our home. Twice traveling halfway around the world and back, they ended up being unread and sitting on our bookshelf, collecting dust. We had unintentionally kept them in the small collection of books we had shipped to Virginia the year before. They had not been part of the hundreds of other books we had sold or given away.

I didn't know it at the time, but in April 1996 Janneke began reading volume one of *Streams in the Desert* for the first time, beginning with the devotional for January 1. She read one devotional in sequence every day thereafter. A month later, on the day I reached the end of my rope and made the statement to her about "seeing God in all this" or being committed to an insane asylum, she showed me the devotional for February 1. "This may blow your mind," she said, "but read this!"

Below I partially quote the text of that day's devotional, written by Laura A. Barter Snow. The accompanying "This thing is from Me" section is based on 1 Kings 12:24 in the Old Testament:

I would have you learn when temptations assail you, and the "enemy comes in like a flood," that *this thing is from Me*, that your weakness needs My might, and your safety lies in letting Me fight for you.

Are you in difficult circumstances, surrounded by people who do not understand you, who never consult your taste, who put you in the background? *This thing is from Me.* I'm the God of circumstances. Thou camest not to thy place by accident, it is the very place God meant for thee.

Have you not asked to be made humble? See then, I have placed you in the very school where this lesson is taught; your surroundings and companions are only working out My will.

Are you in money difficulties? Is it hard to make both ends meet? *This thing is from Me,* for I'm your purse bearer and would have you draw from and depend upon Me. My supplies are limitless (Phil. 4:19). I would have you prove my promises. Let it not be said of you, "In this thing you didn't believe the Lord your God" (Deut. 1:32).

Are you passing through a night of sorrow? *This thing is from Me.* I'm the Man of Sorrows and acquainted with grief. I have let earthly comforters fail you, that by turning to Me you may obtain everlasting consolation (2 Thess. 2:16, 17). Have you longed to do some great work for Me, and instead have been laid on a bed of pain and weakness? *This thing is from Me.* I couldn't get your attention in your busy days and I want to teach you some of My deepest lessons. "They also serve who only stand and wait." Some of My greatest workers are those shut out from active service that they may learn to wield the weapon of all-prayer.

This day I place in your hand this pot of holy oil. Make use of it freely, my child. Let every circumstance that arises, every word that pains you, every interruption that would make you impatient, every revelation of your weakness be anointed with it. The sting will go as you learn to see Me in all things.[1] (emphasis added)

As Janneke pointed out, this devotional entry certainly did blow my mind. This wasn't just an ordinary piece of paper with typeset on it; no, these words instantaneously and miraculously affected my spiritual life in a most powerful way. Suddenly, everything became clear to me; God was very much in control of events and intimately involved with what was taking place in my life. Now I could breathe a big sigh of relief.

After reading this devotional and digesting what had just transpired, I was determined to henceforth see God in all things. And yes, coping was easier. That's not to say that things on the farm got better, but they didn't get any worse. Deep in my heart I sensed that our time on the farm was nearing an end.

Unlike the children's home, I was determined not to quit this time, no matter how difficult our situation. A few weeks later early on a beautiful June morning, I walked Kevin and Darren to the school bus about a mile away, as was my habit. During my trek back to the big house, I cried out to the Lord in desperation and said I couldn't handle another day on the farm.

Call it coincidence if you like, but when Janneke and I arrived at the big house, before the start of our usual morning prayer and devotional time, we were politely told that the time had come for our family to "move on."

We have a natural tendency to rationalize everything and expect God to meet us on our terms. The Lord, however, doesn't operate that way.

> "For my thoughts are not your thoughts,
> neither are your ways my ways,"
> declares the Lord.
> "As the heavens are higher than the earth,
> so are my ways higher than your ways
> and my thoughts than your thoughts."
>
> —Isaiah 55:8–9

Your friend,
John

Twenty-Eight

Jehovah Jireh

My dear friend,

One of the most interesting Bible stories is that of Abraham when God told him to sacrifice his son, Isaac, as a test of his faith. One day the Lord said to Abraham, "Take your son, your only son, Isaac, whom you love, and go to the region of Moriah. Sacrifice him there as a burnt offering on one of the mountains I will tell you about."[1]

So Abraham took Isaac, accompanied by two of his servants, and traveled in the direction God had told him. After three days, seeing in the distance the place where he knew he must go, Abraham separated himself from his two servants and instructed them to remain there while he went on ahead with his son. Isaac carried the pile of wood for the burnt offering, and Abraham carried the fire and the knife. As they walked, Isaac turned to his father and asked,

"Father?"
"Yes, my son?" Abraham replied.
"The fire and the wood are here," Isaac said, "but where is the lamb for the burnt offering?"
Abraham answered, "God Himself will provide the lamb for the burnt offering, my son." And the two of them went on together.

When they reached the place God had told him about, Abraham built an altar there and arranged the wood on it. He bound his son Isaac and laid him on the altar, on top of the wood. Then he reached out his hand and took the knife to slay his son. But the angel of the Lord called out to him from heaven, "Abraham! Abraham!"

"Here I am," he replied.

"Do not lay a hand on the boy," he said. "Do not do anything to him. Now I know that you fear God, because you have not withheld from me your son, your only son."

Abraham looked up and there in a thicket he saw a ram caught by its horns. He went over and took the ram and sacrificed it as a burnt offering instead of his son. So Abraham called that place The Lord Will Provide. And to this day it is said, "On the mountain of the Lord it will be provided."[2]

Both the King James Version and the American Standard Version of the Bible use Jehovah Jireh, the original Hebrew name of God, which means "the Lord will provide." The following story illustrates how the Lord provided for our family in a time of need.

Late in the afternoon on the day when the farm leadership told us to "move on," we were told that we didn't need to move after all. We could stay on the farm as long as we wanted.

Taken by surprise, I responded, "No thank you. We have appreciated our time on the farm. It has been a tremendous learning experience. This move will be an opportunity for our family to put our faith into practice. I'm 100 percent certain that God will provide us with a reliable car, a good job for me, and a home for our family—not necessarily in that order."

We were grateful that no one was pressuring us to leave the farm immediately. About the time we started making preparations to look for work and another place to live, we ran into someone we hardly knew who "coincidentally" had an extra vehicle. We didn't have to ask. He'd learned of our plight, handed us the keys to his van, and told us to make free use of his vehicle for as long as we needed it.

Life in the country is not as idyllic as some may think. We had great difficulty finding a home for rent. Unlike the big city where one can find "For Rent" signs in abundance, we saw none within a fifteen-mile radius of the farm.

Looking for a New Home

Since we had physically moved nine times since our oldest son was born, we thought it best to keep our boys in the same school system. When we arrived in Virginia two years earlier, Dennis had attended seven different schools in three countries since kindergarten. We needed to find some stability in our family and a place where our boys could grow roots.

Unable to find a rental, I resigned myself to the fact that buying a home was probably the better option but wondered where the money was going to come from. We had very little savings in the bank, certainly not enough for a down payment. For several months, unknown to me, Janneke had been praying that the Lord would provide for our family a home of our own. Our financial situation dictated that we take a giant leap of faith, which is exactly what we did.

Finding a home for sale was easy. Thankfully, within a couple of weeks we found an affordable home we both liked: an older, one-and-a-half-story, two-bedroom Cape Cod on nine-tenths of an acre, located on the outskirts of a small town in southside Virginia. The unfinished attic provided sufficient space to build three additional small bedrooms and a second bathroom. I had learned enough about carpentry, plumbing, and electrical work at the children's home and the farm to feel comfortable building the extra rooms myself.

Our next move was to find a mortgage lender. I remember walking with Janneke into a local bank one Friday morning in July 1996, my knees knocking in fear, thinking they would laugh us out of the building. During the interview with the loan officer, we were asked how much money we were able to put down on this house. I was ashamed to tell this man that we didn't have money for a down payment. I responded by saying that I wanted to keep the little bit of money we had and would like his bank to finance the entire mortgage. The loan officer, a friendly man in his thirties, looked a bit confused. He scratched the back of his head and somewhat reluctantly reached for his desk drawer.

He handed me a thick folder containing a stack of forms. "John, take these home," he said, "and bring the completed forms back when you're finished."

We spent our entire Saturday and much of Sunday diligently and accurately filling out a myriad of forms. When we arrived at the bank the following Monday, we learned that the loan officer was out of the office and left the paperwork with his secretary. Around 7:00 P.M. the same evening, we received wonderful news from the real estate agent that the bank had approved our mortgage loan. This development was quite remarkable and unheard off, considering that processing and approving a mortgage loan application normally takes days if not weeks. Surely the bank hadn't approved our application based solely on our small army pension. Moreover, without so much as dropping a hint, Janneke received a little money from her Dad, enough to take care of the closing costs on the home and help us until I could find a job.

On August 2, 1996, we said good-bye to the people on the farm and thanked them for allowing us to be part of their ministry. It was also Dennis's sixteenth birthday. Moving into our own new home after the difficult and painful two years at the children's home and the farm was a tremendous relief and joy. Not wishing to share a big bedroom with his two younger brothers, Dennis volunteered to sleep on the sofa in the living room until we were able to build a third bedroom in the attic. Purchasing our home without a down payment (and while I was unemployed) and having our mortgage loan application approved within a matter of hours were nothing short of a miracle. God was at work!

SEEKING A JOB

I applied at several places as a human resources officer but with little success. I chose human resources because it closely resembled what I had done in the U.S. Army for almost twenty years. In my heart, however, I wanted to work for a government agency in any capacity for which I was qualified. Having worked for the federal government for many years of my adult life, I reckoned that I would be most comfortable and competent in this type of environment. In fact, in my prayers

I had expressed to the Lord that I really wanted to work for a local government agency.

In July I discovered a job ad in the "help wanted" section of the local newspaper for an eligibility worker at the Department of Social Services (DSS) in a neighboring county. After carefully examining the job requirements, I concluded that I could become very proficient in this job. Interpreting, understanding, and ensuring compliance with federal laws, regulations, policies, and procedures resembled the task I had performed throughout most of my army career. I immediately submitted a Virginia state job application, a copy of my résumé, and a cover letter.

That same day I rushed to the DSS office in the county where we lived, spoke to the eligibility supervisor, and asked her to give me everything I needed to know about government cash assistance programs, food stamps, and Medicaid. My next move was to feverishly study all the materials she'd given to me so I could ace the interview.

I overcame the first hurdle by receiving an invitation for a job interview. When I arrived, I was surprised to learn that none of the questions asked were specifically related to the job. Leaving the director's office at the interview's conclusion, I was confident that I would be working for this organization. But to my amazement, I received a letter a few days later that said I wasn't selected for the position and thanked me for my interest in the job.

I was devastated by this news.

Several weeks passed, and I saw another job announcement for an eligibility worker with the same agency. Puzzled, I called the director about the new job vacancy announcement. She said that the person hired had abruptly resigned. She remembered me well and encouraged me to reapply but reiterated that she couldn't make any promises. After my second attempt, I was astonished to receive a letter from the State Department of Social Services, headquartered in Richmond, Virginia. It said I didn't meet the knowledge, skills, and ability requirements for the job. This time I wasn't invited to a job interview.

During this time we became acquainted with a Jewish lady well into her eighties who many years earlier had encountered Jesus the Messiah. I shared my job-seeking adventures with her, and she responded, perhaps a bit prophetically, "John, don't you worry. The Lord has got something better for you!"

In November 1996, I applied for an employment services worker position, my third try with the same agency. Perhaps our elderly Jewish lady friend was right because this job paid two thousand dollars more per year than an eligibility worker. I interviewed for the position sometime in early December.

By mid-December I had not heard anything about the job at DSS, and our money supply was nearing depletion. Something needed to happen—and soon. In addition to supporting a family, I now also had a monthly mortgage payment to think about.

During this time I saw a job ad in the local newspaper for a street maintenance supervisor. Except for picking up a broom and sweeping the street, I knew absolutely nothing about maintaining a street but figured that applying for the job was worth the effort. I visited the town office and spoke with a clerk at the main counter, inquiring about the job.

The town manager happened to walk by and overheard part of our conversation. After he invited me into his office, I explained that I was a retired soldier with an extensive background in personnel management and administration but without any type of street maintenance experience. He encouraged me to apply anyway, handed me a job application, and asked me to return the completed application as soon as possible. A few days later, I received a telephone call and an invitation to a job interview on Tuesday, December 17, 1996.

When I arrived at the town office, I learned that the director of public works, who was running a bit late, was the person who would conduct the interview. After about a twenty-minute wait, someone who looked a little rough around the edges walked into the office. The director of public works said he didn't really need a street maintenance supervisor; instead, he wanted someone to work in his water treatment facility. The town would pay for any necessary training and prepare me for the job.

The idea of working with chemicals made me apprehensive. What did I know about chemistry? The thought entered my mind during the interview that I would mistakenly mix the wrong chemicals, poison every citizen of this town, and be dragged off to jail.

I told the town manager and the director of public works about my recent job interview as an employment services worker. I told them that that job paid six thousand dollars more than what they were offering me. However, I promised that if I didn't hear back from the department of social services by noon on Friday, December 20, 1996, I would accept the job at the water treatment facility and be ready to start work the following Monday. They understood the predicament I was in and seemed satisfied with my proposal.

When I awoke on the morning of December 20, I still had not heard back from the department of social services. Frankly, I had little confidence that I would hear from this agency and gave up hope of becoming an employment services worker. I reluctantly considered the probability of working at the water treatment facility on Monday.

Around ten o'clock that morning, I drove to our bank and withdrew the last few dollars out of our savings account to purchase necessary groceries for the weekend and our Christmas dinner, leaving just enough money to keep the account open.

Virtually next door to the bank was a little glass shop owned and operated by George Daulton. I didn't know George very well, and he really didn't know me. I knew he was a Christian, however, because no one left his shop without first listening to a five or ten-minute sermon. I had previously visited his little store two or three times to purchase a glass pane for the children's home.

Before heading home that morning, after withdrawing the funds from the bank, intuition told me to stick my head in the door of the glass shop and wish George and his family a wonderful Christmas and a happy New Year. Nothing more. I didn't have time to listen to a sermon that morning because it was Darren's twelfth birthday, and I wanted to be home with my family.

As I entered the shop and conveyed to George my holiday greetings, he interrupted by saying, "John, come here. The Lord just told me to write you a check for two hundred dollars."

I couldn't believe my ears. I was totally floored! There in front of me at the counter, he wrote a check from an account that happened to be from the same bank I had just come from. Well, you guessed it; I gladly hung around and listened to a ten-minute sermon. George Daulton didn't have the slightest inkling what was taking place in my family at that time.

When I arrived home, a huge package had been delivered by UPS. It was filled with Christmas goodies from Ronny Bodine, an old army friend from Stuttgart, Germany, whom we hadn't heard from in several years.

At exactly 11:58 A.M., the telephone rang. I picked up the receiver and said, "Hello?"

The lady at the other end asked, "Is this John Rozema?"

I answered, "Yes, ma'am."

"This is Sandra Wentz, director of the department of social services. I'm calling to offer you the job as employment services worker. Are you still interested in the position?"

"Yes, ma'am," I said. "I most certainly am!"

What Mrs. Wentz didn't know was that my reply to her job offer was an understatement of stupendous proportions. I felt like dancing the Macarena while I still had Mrs. Wentz on the telephone. This job offer was the best Christmas gift anyone could have given our family that year! Thirty-two applicants had applied for the job, but the Lord had given the job to me. Our faith had been tested to the limit, but in this situation, as in all the others, we could clearly see God at work.

We now had the assurance of a good-paying job thirty-three miles away, but we had no vehicle. We couldn't continue borrowing our friend's car forever, so early on the evening of Friday, December 27, 1996, I got down on my knees by our bed and prayed, "Lord, with Your kind permission, I would like to travel to Richmond tomorrow with my family. I would like to purchase a brand-new car I need in order to go to work unless You have another plan. In Jesus' name, amen." I had just finished saying "amen" and was getting up off my knees when the telephone rang.

It was a friend. "John, what are your plans for tomorrow?"

I told him we were planning to buy a car in Richmond and would most likely be gone the entire day.

He said, "John, don't do that. I have a friend in North Carolina who's a good Christian man who also owns a car auction company. We can go there and buy a car from him. It will save you thousands upon thousands of dollars."

Need I say more? The following week, after I had started my new job, Janneke traveled to North Carolina with our friend and his wife. Of all cars on the auction block, she came home with a 1990 silver metallic Ford Taurus station wagon!

> And my God will meet all your needs
> according to His glorious riches in Christ Jesus.
> —Philippians 4:19

Our little castle is situated on the southeast corner of scenic highways 46 and 58. Above the front door, inscribed in bold letters for all who drive by and see, is the name "Jehovah Jireh" as a testimony of God's faithfulness, kindness, and generous heart.

Your friend,
John

Part Three
Graduation

But you have come to Mount Zion,
to the heavenly Jerusalem, the city of the living God.
You have come to thousands upon thousands of angels in joyful assembly,
to the church of the firstborn, whose names are written in heaven.
You have come to God, the judge of all men,
to the spirits of righteous men made perfect,
to Jesus the mediator of a new covenant,
and to the sprinkled blood that speaks a better word
than the blood of Abel.

—Hebrews 12:22–24

Twenty-Nine

No Fear of Death

My dear friend,

Nearly every morning soon after I wake up, I thank the Lord for the gift of life. I can truly think of no greater gift than to be alive and well and to be surrounded by my family, whom I love dearly. Early on the evening of Friday, February 24, 2006, I was convinced that all that was dear to me had come to an abrupt end.

Returning from a day at the office, I picked up our mail at the mailbox across the street, strolled to our car, which was parked at a nearby gas station, and drove the short distance to our home. While walking about one hundred yards to our car, I felt an unexplainable and uncomfortable heaviness in my chest. Three to four minutes later the sensation disappeared.

SOMETHING SERIOUS

I had eaten a not-so-light lunch that day at a local Italian restaurant and reasoned that I must be suffering a case of indigestion. Fifteen minutes later the heaviness returned, but this time the discomfort was more intense and lasted longer. At no time did it occur to me that something dreadfully serious was taking place.

At around 6:15 P.M., as I made myself comfortable on our living room sofa and waited for the 6:30 P.M. *ABC Evening News* to start, I experienced a sudden, excruciatingly burning pain centered in my chest that wouldn't go away. I was able to breathe comfortably; however, when I felt no pulse in my left or right wrist and sensed numbness and pain in my left arm, I knew I was in serious trouble.

Without thinking, I called Darren, who was upstairs in his room, and told him to take me to the hospital right away. I should have known better and dialed 911 to request the local emergency rescue squad to transport me to the hospital; the pain in my chest was getting worse with each passing second.

As I slowly walked to our car, I remember nearly passing out. Before driving me, Darren left a note for Janneke, who was at work, to let her know we were on our way to the emergency room.

On the way to the hospital, which was about eighteen miles away, I repeatedly warned my son to slow down and not exceed the speed limit. This was certainly no time to be pulled over by a traffic cop and be cited for speeding.

The pain was so severe that my mind was preoccupied with thoughts that my life on this earth could end at any time, that death was fast approaching. Unlike other times when I was confronted with death and stricken with great fear, I strangely felt an unexplainable inner peace. This may sound absurd, but I became curious to see what life was like on "the other side." The intense pain prompted me to repeatedly cry out to God, "Lord, have mercy on me. Lord, have mercy on me."

About twenty-five minutes later, we arrived at the front entrance of the emergency room at the Community Memorial Health Center in South Hill. Almost immediately, I was rushed into the building in a wheelchair. After a nurse took my blood pressure and listened to my heart, she told me to remove my clothes, to pull on a hospital gown, and to take four, low-dose Bayer aspirin.

I told the nurse that I couldn't tolerate aspirin because it gave me severe stomach cramps. The look on her face told me to be a "good boy" and do exactly what she had said. Showing little sympathy, she firmly told me to take the medicine anyway, adding that it could save my life.

I felt very proud of Darren, who had maintained his cool under great pressure. He took care of all insurance formalities and called Janneke, who was home by now, to let her know what was taking place.

The News

Seconds after an EKG confirmed my heart attack, my small room was transformed into a scene resembling a TV soap opera. It quickly filled with nurses, an attending physician, x-ray technicians, and other medical personnel.

"John, you are having a heart attack as we speak," the doctor said. "We are currently administering powerful drugs that are designed to open the blockage in your heart."

The doctor wasn't the only one talking to me. One nurse armed with a clipboard bombarded me with questions about my medical history. There were documents to sign and important decisions to make.

By the time Janneke arrived at the hospital, the pain had subsided to a tolerable level, thanks to generous doses of morphine. I was also glad that I felt no ill effects from the safety-coated Bayer low-dose aspirin. We were informed that a helicopter was on its way to transport me to the Medical College of Virginia in downtown Richmond that very evening.

Despite the critical nature of my medical condition, I surprised myself by my lack of concern for my physical well being and for what might happen next. I think being anxious, apprehensive, or scared, especially under these trying circumstances, is perfectly normal, even for a Christian. But strangely, I continued to experience peace that evening amid the hectic and confusing situation in the emergency room. After I was stabilized, the medical evacuation helicopter arrived, and I was airlifted to Richmond, a flight I was told would take about thirty-five minutes.

The aircraft provided very little space. One male nurse, a member of the medical helicopter crew, kept reassuring me that all would be well and that I would soon be in good hands. This was the first time in more than thirty years that I had flown on a helicopter, this time as a very sick patient. Janneke and Darren followed us to Richmond by car.

The Medical College of Virginia, an integral part of the Virginia Commonwealth University, is situated on the corner of East Broad Street, the busy main thoroughfare of Richmond and Interstate 95. The weather was exceedingly cold and windy on the landing pad at the top of the eleven-story building. I was immediately rushed inside and examined by a team of medical experts.

Blockage

"John, we are going to take good care of you," the doctor said. "You have nothing to be concerned about."

That was wonderful news. After necessary but lengthy medical procedures while connected to a monitor and an array of other equipment, I was transferred to a private room in the cardiac intensive care unit on the tenth floor, where I had an excellent view of I-95, one of America's busiest freeways.

Early the next morning the chief cardiologist, who by her mere presence commanded a lot of respect, paid me a visit. I immediately detected that this lady was in a position of great authority. An entourage of young fellows and residents, whom I suspected were in training to become America's future doctors and cardiologists, accompanied her. My bedside became the stage for a lecture hall. Everything the chief cardiologist said as she addressed her students went far over my head, but then she addressed me. She said that I had a blockage in my right coronary artery and that I would become a recipient of a stent the following Monday.

The next day another cardiologist came to visit me. This doctor began the conversation by saying that this was his day off but that he'd been asked to come to work so he could examine the blockage in my heart by means of an echocardiogram. As he carefully observed my heart on the monitor, he kept saying, "Boy, oh boy, you're lucky. Boy, you are so lucky. Boy, you are lucky!"

I wanted to set the record straight and tell this man that my survival wasn't a matter of luck; rather, it was due to God's grace at work in my life. Regrettably, I had no opportunity to speak up. Several others were in the room, and he was in a hurry, rushing to see more patients before returning home.

The procedure to insert a stent in my blocked artery was completed in less than thirty minutes and was virtually painless because of a mild sedative. Thankfully, I was one of the first patients to be treated. I was amazed to learn that a long line of patients were awaiting the same procedure. Among those waiting to be treated were two patients accompanied by armed guards. The scene reminded me of a factory assembly line.

After the procedure was over, the doctor told Janneke that all had gone well and that my artery had suffered 90 percent blockage. I was glad the procedure was over and elated when I heard I could go home the next day if there were no complications. Thankfully, there were none. On Tuesday around noon, I was discharged and felt like a new person.

No Despair

I thank God for all the advances in the modern medicine field and for all those who have so unselfishly dedicated their lives to care for the sick and the disabled. They deserve our utmost respect. I believe it's very important for those who have chosen a medical career to become proficient in what they do and to be compassionate, sympathetic, and caring. The emergency room staff at the Community Memorial Health Center, the crew of the medical evacuation helicopter, and the doctors and staff in the cardiac intensive care unit at the Virginia Commonwealth University Medical Center exemplified these fine attributes in more ways than one.

I attribute the fact that I wasn't afraid for a single moment to the grace, mercy, and kindness of God. Despite my critical medical condition, not once did I despair of life. As I shared with many friends afterward, I was prepared to meet my Savior. Fear is one of my worst enemies. The Bible teaches us that Jesus has taken away the fear of death for believers.[1] This fact was clearly evident in my life on the evening of February 24 and the days that followed. Elsewhere in the Bible we learn that by His death on the cross, Jesus destroyed the power of death.[2] Moreover, for the Christian, death has been swallowed up in victory.[3]

> Where, O death, is your victory?
> Where, O death, is your sting?
>
> —1 Corinthians 15:55

I'm thankful that as a Christian, death no longer has its grip on me.

Your friend,
John

Thirty

A Rude Awakening

My dear friend,

To escape from our daily grind and life in the country, Janneke and I observe a biannual tradition. We spend a long weekend together in Washington, D.C., once in the spring and once in the fall. We enjoy visiting the museums on the National Mall, joining other visitors at our nation's capital, and exploring famous landmarks, memorials, and other sites of national and historic significance. We usually devote our fall outing to early Christmas shopping. When we make our journey to northern Virginia, we normally stay at our favorite and reasonably priced Hampton Inn near the Washington-Dulles International Airport.

THE WALL

Despite countless trips to our favorite town over the years, I'm still unable to visit the Vietnam Veterans Memorial. Even a glimpse in the direction of that distant Wall often causes me to choke up with tears.

During the summer of 1990, we decided to visit the memorial for the first time with our boys. As we casually strolled down the asphalt walkway in the direction of the monument, the familiar bronze statue of three infantry soldiers came into partial view. At that moment I hit an invisible, impenetrable wall and nearly collapsed, overcome with immense grief. I told my family to go on without me and to take their time, but I was unable to move so much as an inch.

I have made repeated attempts to visit this memorial, but my powerful emotions always prohibit me. I'm unable to go anywhere near the location where America remembers those who served so honorably and valiantly in that long, terrible war. Even after more than forty years since my war experience, I sometimes wonder if I'll ever recover from the effects of this conflict. Will I ever visit this hallowed site and see the names of my comrades permanently chiseled on its polished, black, granite Wall?

Change of Plans

In early November 2006, Janneke and I made our customary excursion and planned to visit the newly renovated Smithsonian's National Portrait Gallery. But early Sunday morning, I woke with mild stomach discomfort accompanied by profuse rectal bleeding. My first conclusion was that I was suffering a bleeding stomach ulcer. Not wishing to cause alarm at this early hour of the morning, I decided not to wake Janneke and hoped my situation would improve.

When the situation worsened, however, I had no choice but to wake her. Janneke insisted that we see a doctor immediately. With the help of a hotel desk clerk who gave us directions, we arrived at the emergency room of the Inova Loudoun Hospital near the hotel. Thankfully, our wait to see a doctor took no more than ten minutes. After an initial examination, a doctor told me that I needed to remain at the hospital until he found the cause of this potentially serious symptom. I asked the doctor if he thought I could go home and be treated at a medical facility nearby, but he replied that doing so would be too risky.

"You could bleed to death," he said.

I was admitted as a patient and transferred to a private room that afternoon. Hemorrhaging continued throughout much of the day and night. Early in the evening of the following day, I underwent a colonoscopy. At the conclusion of this procedure, the gastroenterologist told us that he had removed one polyp and discovered an abnormal growth inside my colon. He seemed reluctant to say more other than to mention that getting the results of the biopsy would take several days.

I received a copy of the color photograph that clearly depicted portions of my colon and this strange-looking, dark-colored mass of tissue. The next day, after an abdominal ultrasound showed no further abnormalities, I was discharged and told to contact my primary care physician as soon as possible.

Janneke and I discussed the possibility that I may have cancer, but neither she nor I was overly concerned. Only three or four years earlier, part of my colon had been examined by means of a flexible sigmoidoscope. The results had shown that everything looked perfectly normal and healthy. Needless to say, we never made it to the National Portrait Gallery during this trip.

Upon our return home, I called our friend, Dr. John Wine, a family practitioner from Burkeville, Virginia. I told him what had happened and asked him to recommend the best gastroenterologist in the Richmond area. Without hesitation, John advised me to make an appointment with Dr. Giles Robertson Jr. of the Richmond Gastroenterology Associates, Inc.

Unexpected News

Two days later, Janneke and I were sitting in Dr. Robertson's office. He was on the phone with his colleague in northern Virginia, the doctor who had performed my colonoscopy three days earlier.

"He is sitting by my desk," Dr. Robertson said into the phone. "Why don't you tell him yourself?"

The doctor, a friendly man who looked to be in his early to mid-sixties, handed me the receiver. The doctor in northern Virginia said, "I'm very sorry to tell you this, John, but the results of the biopsy show that the abnormal growth in your colon is a cancerous tumor."

I thanked the doctor for the information and added that I appreciated the superior medical treatment and care I had received from him and others at the Inova Loudoun Hospital during my three-day stay.

I must admit that if someone had asked me, "How much is two plus two?" at the same moment I had been told that I had a cancerous tumor in my abdomen, I wouldn't have been able to give the correct answer. Never for a single moment, however, was I frightened or alarmed. I also didn't think this news was a death sentence, even though my dear sister, Hanna, had died from colon cancer just five years earlier on Ascension Day in 2001 at the young age of fifty-two.

Dr. Robertson scheduled me for a CT scan, a gastrointestinal endoscopy, and a second colonoscopy. He said he would refer me to Dr. Amy Rose, the best-skilled surgeon in the field of laparoscopic surgery. This was priceless information because prior to my heart attack nine months earlier—and for as long as I could remember—I had had a strong dislike of doctors, dentists, nurses, and hospitals. This aversion was primarily due to the medieval medical practices the Butcher of Ede had performed during my youth.

Driving home after our visit with Dr. Robertson, Janneke and I decided to take a detour and go to our church, New Covenant Fellowship. I remembered that the church elders would be holding their bimonthly meeting. This occasion provided an opportune time to do what the book of James prescribes:

> Is any one of you sick? He should call the elders of the church to pray over him and anoint him with oil in the name of the Lord. And the prayer offered in faith will make the sick person well; the Lord will raise him up.[1]

While a patient in northern Virginia, I had called our pastor, Paul Montanye, to let him know what was taking place. Having a definitive diagnosis of colon cancer would be news to the leadership of our small, close-knit, nondenominational church nestled in rural southside Virginia. During our drive to the church that afternoon, I could think of nothing else but that I wanted God to be glorified no matter what my outcome. I felt no compelling need to cry out to the Lord, begging Him to heal me from this potentially catastrophic affliction. When we arrived, our pastor, the elders, and our youth pastor prayed for me. I also prayed that God would give me the grace to bear this calamity.

When Janneke and I arrived home that evening, we told our boys what the doctors had discovered and encouraged them not to be alarmed.

Though they didn't take the news very well, they were thankfully not devastated.

Surgery

Within a week after Dr. Robertson successfully performed the scheduled medical procedures, we met with Dr. Amy Rose of the Surgical Associates of Richmond. I discovered that my surgeon had a long list of impressive medical credentials on the medical clinic's website and knew I would be in very good hands. Both Janneke and I immediately felt at ease as Dr. Rose carefully explained, in a language we could both understand, that she was going to remove approximately thirteen inches of my colon through a one-inch incision in my belly button.

She said the surgery was minimally invasive. If all proceeded as planned without complications, I could be home in four or five days. That news was certainly encouraging. I never liked being away from my family for whatever reason or whatever length of time. Surgery was scheduled at Chippenham Medical Center in Richmond early on Friday, December 15, 2006.

The pre-op procedures on the morning of my surgery proceeded like clockwork. Everyone who took care of me treated me in a most courteous, professional, and gentle manner. Dr. Rose was there too, available to answer last-minute questions, but I didn't have any. In fact, I didn't know what to ask. Next, I was wheeled into the operating room. I don't remember whatever occurred afterward.

"John, wake up! John, you need to wake up!" I heard the nurse repeatedly say. That was easier said than done. When I finally did "wake up" in the recovery area, I was transferred to a regular room. I remember little else of what took place that day.

Dr. Robertson was right. Dr. Rose was probably the most proficient and talented surgeon in the field of laparoscopic surgery. I'm so grateful for her expertise. With great precision she removed the cancerous portion of my colon, including my appendix, through the small incision. I'm reassured to know that I'll never need to be concerned about appendicitis.

The pain following my surgery was tolerable; I had no need to use the morphine pump. To my surprise, I was able to comfortably but slowly walk the hospital hallways less than twenty-four hours after my operation. Four days later, I was discharged and felt wonderful. Before returning home that evening, Janneke and I made a beeline for Starbucks, where I savored my favorite nonfat decaf grande latté with four spoonfuls of Sugar in the Raw.

After a brief period of recovery at home, we met with Dr. Rose again around Christmastime. She informed us that the pathology report revealed a cancerous tumor that was the size of a quarter, classified as stage III-B. Of the forty-four lymph nodes she had meticulously removed, only two were cancerous. Because the tumor had partially protruded through the colon wall, Dr. Rose strongly recommended that I follow the standard protocol for treatment of patients with my diagnosis. A follow-up appointment was scheduled for the insertion of a "porta-cath," a device not much bigger than a silver dollar that is used to administer chemotherapy. The stage was set for a rocky and treacherous road ahead.

> He will have no fear of bad news:
> his heart is steadfast, trusting in the Lord.
> —Psalm 112:7

Your friend,
John

Thirty-One

The Miracle Boy

My dear friend,

This is a story about the power of God.

I first met Dr. Nicole Whitlatch, an oncologist from Duke University Medical Center, in Durham, North Carolina, on January 18, 2007. Dr. Whitlatch and a team of oncologists from the same prestigious medical institution treat patients at the oncology and hematology clinic at the nearby Community Memorial Health Center.

At my initial visit, Dr. Whitlatch scheduled my first round of chemotherapy to begin on Monday, February 5, 2007. My treatment would consist of twelve separate sessions spread over a period of six months. Each session consisted of reporting to the clinic early on Monday morning to receive the chemotherapy until one or two o'clock in the afternoon and then being connected to a portable, battery-operated chemotherapy pump. I would then go home and return to the clinic the following morning. The routine would be repeated the next day and end on Wednesdays around noon. In preparation for the next session, I would report to the clinic on Fridays to have blood drawn. I was also told that I should expect to be sick from the chemotherapy (Fluorouracil [5-FU] and Oxaliplatin).

On the first day, I was surprised when I saw the nurses who administered chemotherapy wearing disposable, protective gowns that reached almost to the floor, thick, latex gloves, and sometimes facial protection. After my treatment I was sent home with an oversized paper shopping bag loaded with decontamination materials to protect me in case the chemotherapy pump leaked.

Chemotherapy

Except for the aggravation of continually carrying the portable pump, which wasn't very comfortable, particularly when I tried to sleep at night or took a shower in the morning, I breezed through my first round of treatment with relative ease. A few hours after waking on Thursday morning, however, I crawled back into bed and remained there until Saturday afternoon. I felt pretty good on Sunday and attended church services. During the week between sessions, I regained my strength and was ready to battle the next round of chemotherapy.

The aftermath of my second round of chemotherapy wasn't like the first. This time I felt a lot worse and had to force myself to get up on Sunday morning to go to church. A friend recommended that I chew on ginger candy to lessen the nausea, but it didn't help. I developed ugly, white sores in my mouth, became sensitive to cold temperatures, and frequented the bathroom more than I care to remember. Something else I found utterly repugnant: the chemo caused me to expel frequent bursts of gas that would have caused even a skunk to hightail it in the opposite direction.

I kept a safe distance from anyone I suspected of having seasonal sniffles, coughs, and other maladies.

Sick and Sicker

When I showed up at the clinic to start my third round, I was told that my red blood cell count was too low, a fact that meant my next cycle of chemo needed to be postponed for an additional week. I was placed on an iron regimen, but the problem repeated itself again before the start of my fourth round. Each successive session of chemotherapy only increased the nausea and a host of other maladies.

When I awoke early on Thursday, April 5, following completion of my fourth round, I knew my customary "stay in bed and double time to the bathroom" routine was going to be even worse than the previous ones. The nausea was unbearable as were the stomach cramps, which were accompanied by diarrhea, vomiting, and fever. The remedies we had available to battle the excessive diarrhea and vomiting were no help. I felt bad about disturbing Dr. Whitlatch and her family on the weekend, and sitting in the hospital's emergency room waiting area for hours with only one men's restroom available wasn't a good idea. I was determined to fight even harder and make it through as in past weeks, but by late Sunday evening, barely able to walk and nearly crippled, I thought I had lost the battle.

We called the oncology clinic first thing on Monday morning and were advised to come right away. Told that I was dehydrated, I received several pints of intravenous fluid. By two thirty that afternoon I was sent home.

"John, you'll feel a lot better tomorrow," the nurse assured me.

But early the following morning on April 10, I felt even worse. We contacted Dr. Whitlatch in Durham. She immediately made arrangements for me to be admitted at the hospital. I could choose between Duke University Medical Center or nearby Community Memorial Health Center. Because of the traveling distance, I chose the latter. I received a call from the clinic and was told to report to the emergency room at twelve o'clock.

"They are expecting you, John," the nurse told me. "You won't have to wait."

Janneke drove me to the ER, where I remained until a private room became available that evening.

After my arrival at the ER, I remember very little except that I was very sick. Never in my life had I even been so incredibly thirsty. At that moment a glass of water was worth more to me than a pile of gold stashed away in a bank safety deposit box. Despite my condition, I tried my best to maintain a good attitude and keep a sense of humor during times when I was alert.

Over the next couple of days, my situation didn't improve. If anything, it became progressively worse. I remember the attending physician telling us that my illness was the result of chemotherapy. My immune system wasn't functioning properly, resulting in a massive bacterial infection, the primary cause of my diarrhea. In addition, I suffered from a severe case of colitis, inflammation of the colon, and sepsis, an infection of the bloodstream caused by toxin-producing bacteria. I also had difficulty breathing.

From Bad to Worse

On Thursday morning around seven o'clock, mustering what little physical strength I could find, I called Janneke. Barely able to talk, I begged her to come to the hospital right away. I needed her now more than ever and was convinced that my life on this earth was hanging by a thin thread.

I vaguely remember Janneke's arrival at my bedside. The doctor seemed totally befuddled because my body wasn't responding to conventional treatments. That day they transferred me to the intensive care unit.

What follows next is an account of events described to me by Janneke, attending physicians and nurses, and our pastor, who kept our church family informed of my condition via e-mail almost daily. Despite being heavily sedated for many of the twenty-six days I spent in the ICU, I remember certain events, which I also have recorded here.

Within twenty-four hours after being admitted to the ICU, I was connected to a respirator while suffering from Acute Respiratory Distress Syndrome (ARDS), a life-threatening disease. My kidneys had also ceased to function (Acute Renal Failure), requiring me to be placed on dialysis. The doctor responsible for inserting the breathing tube became rightfully irritated with me since I unconsciously struggled to remove the breathing apparatus from my mouth. For my own benefit, he ordered the nurses to tie my wrists to the bed frame. How long I remained in this position, I don't know. Days later, fluid accumulated in my now-partially-collapsed lungs, requiring the insertion of drainage tubes on the left and right sides of my rib cage.

Despite being heavily sedated, I continued to be extremely uncomfortable. I can best describe my condition by saying that it felt like a sumo wrestler had made himself comfortable sitting on my chest and had no intention of moving anytime soon. This is no exaggeration;

I was pumped with gallons of Gatorade and other fluids, causing every part of my body to become excessively bloated. I wasn't a pretty sight.

What I Heard

I was often aware of things happening around me, and I occasionally heard people carrying on conversations. I'll never forget hearing Barbara Wine and her daughter, Christina, sing at my bedside. They sang a song they had learned in Spanish while on a missions trip to Mexico a year earlier. I also remember Barbara's son, Robbie, then fifteen-years-old, praying at my bedside and repeatedly telling me in a loud voice, "Don't give up! Don't give up!"

One day, someone sat by my bed and discussed the probability of removing my entire colon. I didn't want that to happen, but I was in no state to convey how I felt about this idea. Besides, if anyone was going to remove my colon, it would be Dr. Rose and no one else! However, I knew I was in no condition to undergo another operation.

When I heard people speaking, I desperately wanted to communicate, especially with Janneke. I tried to make gestures with my hands, a finger, or an arm, but I was unable to do so. Because of the buildup of fluids and the fact that I lacked physical strength, both arms felt like they weighed one hundred pounds each. I wanted to cry out to a doctor or a nurse, letting them know how incredibly uncomfortable I felt due to the enormous pressure on my chest. Unable to communicate and feeling ignored, I wanted to scream to get their attention. This period was indescribably frustrating, causing me to suffer severe depression.

I sensed a distinct separation from my body. At times, I even felt as if I were a prisoner in my own body. I could think and reason. I was conscious of the fact that I was in terrible physical shape while the "real me" seemed perfectly normal.

Due to massive doses of antibiotics, I lost hearing in my left ear. The doctor warned Janneke that I could possibly remain permanently deaf in that ear. For much of my time in the ICU, I was unable to open my eyes because of a serious eye infection.

The effects of many medications caused me to experience a series of inordinately long, extraordinary dreams. I usually forget a dream the instant I wake up, but I vividly remember these dreams—many bordering on the bizarre—to this day.

Funeral Plans

My condition was not going in the direction doctors had hoped. With my life in the balance, they had little hope that my situation would improve. One day the doctor in charge of my treatment told Janneke that he would attempt one final procedure as a last-ditch effort. If it didn't work, he said, he had basically exhausted every known remedy and had little hope of my recovery. What he was really saying was that there was a good possibility I could die that very day.

I'm very proud of Janneke, who remained strong and brave throughout this distressing time in our lives. Though she was grief-stricken at the thought of losing me, she was strong enough to discuss with Pastor Montanye how I would have liked my funeral service. Though we had never given this topic serious thought, Janneke had always known that I didn't want my funeral service to be a sad occasion. She also knew that I wanted to be buried at Arlington National Cemetery.

Worse

Just when it seemed that things couldn't possibly get any worse, they did. On April 24, two weeks after being admitted to the hospital, two technicians arrived to take an x-ray. They were doing their best to prop up my bloated, heavy body and maneuver it so they could take a picture at just the right angle. Because virtually every muscle in my body had atrophied, the technicians had a very difficult time placing my totally limp body in an upright position.

During the process my head suddenly and violently swung backward, causing the ventilator to become dislodged from my windpipe. The monitor alarm immediately wailed, and my heart began beating at a dangerously slow pace. Though heavily sedated, I knew something was horribly wrong.

Other medical staff rushed to the scene and immediately implemented code blue procedures. Close by, Janneke observed what appeared to be total confusion. Overcome with emotion and on the verge of panic, she quickly exited the room, certain the end had come.

Christopher Ackerman, the doctor on duty, was making his rounds in another part of the hospital when he heard the code blue announcement on the hospital intercom. He quickly arrived, administered CPR, and corrected the dislocated ventilator. I didn't feel any pain or the effects from the electric shocks, but I have scars to prove the experience wasn't just a bad dream.

Since my cancer diagnosis, and particularly while I was a critical-care patient, a small army of friends from Southern California, Virginia, North Carolina, and places in between were feverishly praying for me. Many of these people we don't know and will never know until we get to heaven. Our church family cried out to the Lord daily, some with weeping, and the Lord heard all these prayers. "Call upon me in the day of trouble," says the Lord Almighty, and "I will deliver you."[1]

To the amazement of many, medical staff included, my condition began to improve. ICU nurses started calling me "the miracle boy." To this day, doctors familiar with my medical condition shake their heads in disbelief. Others see my recovery as a true miracle from God.

After two and a half weeks on the ventilator, I needed to learn how to breathe on my own again. What a slow, difficult, and tedious process! During this time I was finally able to open my eyes, and the hearing in my left ear began to slowly improve. To my great joy, I was transferred to a regular room ten days later, and after a week in the west wing, I was sent home after much begging and pleading.

Lessons Learned

After spending thirty-five days in the hospital, I was discharged on Monday afternoon, May 14, 2007.

An almost three month recovery followed, during which time I had to learn basic life skills again—brushing my teeth, combing my hair, and taking daily showers. After three weeks of intensive physical therapy at home, I could walk again. With an additional five weeks of outpatient physical therapy, much of my strength returned.

According to Dr. Whitlatch, what happened to me occurs in less than 5 percent of patients receiving adjuvant chemotherapy for colon cancer.

Four CT scans since my discharge from the hospital, including numerous CEA blood tests, have revealed no trace of cancer. During each of my last six quarterly visits with Dr. Whitlatch, she has enthusiastically reported to me that "everything looks fine." Those three words are like George Frideric Handel's *Messiah* to my ears. Again, I value nothing more than to be alive and well, and to be surrounded by my family whom I love dearly. This life is a truly great gift from God.

When it appeared there was little else doctors could do—when the situation seemed totally hopeless—God miraculously and powerfully intervened. Life is a precious gift from God. "[Our] times are in [His] hands."[2] In the book of Exodus and other places in the Bible, we read that the Lord is the One who heals.[3] Medical experts are only a means by which God works out His sovereign plan. He could have instantly and supernaturally healed me, and countless instances attest to this amazing act, but He chose the more conventional way for me.

> I remember my affliction and my wandering,
> the bitterness and the gall.
> I well remember them,
> and my soul is downcast within me.
> Yet this I call to mind
> and therefore I have hope:
> Because of the Lord's great love we are not consumed,
> for his compassions never fail.
> They are new every morning;
> great is your faithfulness.
> I say to myself, "The Lord is my portion;
> therefore I will wait for him."
>
> —Lamentations 3:19–24

Did God receive the glory as I had prayed? I believe so. I also pray that after reading this story, you too will give Him glory, just as many who witnessed God's power and grace in my life during my illness have.

Yes indeed. For all He has done we give God the glory!

                    Your friend,
                    John

Thirty-Two

On a Hill Far Away

My dear friend,

While serving as a young trooper at Fort Bliss many years ago, our platoon sergeant, maliciously called the "Bible Pounder," frequently visited us on Saturday afternoons. He wasn't there to inspect the barracks or to see how things were going with his soldiers. No, he was there with Bible in hand to preach a ten-minute sermon.

This man often spoke about the love of God, especially His love for sinners. He added that we were all sinners, himself included, and that we were all in need of forgiveness and salvation. My friends and I quickly dismissed what this man said because we were busily preparing to go out on the town.

I also had a hard time swallowing the fact that I was a sinner. After all, I treated everyone with common courtesy and respect. I considered myself a morally decent person. I didn't go around blatantly telling lies, stealing, cheating, plundering, raping, or killing. In fact, I worked hard, cared for others by lending a helping hand when necessary, and was always careful not to hurt or offend anyone.

I proudly considered myself a pretty good fellow, and everyone with whom I came into contact seemed to wholeheartedly concur with this self-assessment. The word *sin* was a strange and totally foreign concept to me. How anyone could suggest that I was a sinner in need of salvation was incomprehensible.

Perhaps you feel the same way.

The problem with my self-examination (and maybe yours as well) is that it is based solely on how I perceive myself and how I compare or appear to others. However, as you have journeyed with me through my story and as I have shared my life with you, you have discovered the hidden side of me. You've seen me as a wounded boy who harbored immense anger, hatred, and bitterness toward his stepfather. You know me as a young man who erected impenetrable fortifications around his heart, hid behind a thousand masks, and always pretended to be somebody he wasn't. You may also recall the scene in my foxhole at Kilroy Compound when I was terrified at the thought of dying and frantically tried to make a deal with a God I didn't know. Later, you watched me try to fill that great, God-shaped void in my life by looking for love and acceptance.

You joined me at Meisenweg 28, where everything seemed to be going my way. I enjoyed a great job, travels to exotic places, and a wonderful social life. Yet an invisible, unbearable weight pushed me down. Things looked good on the outside, but inside I was a deeply troubled young man. You saw how I carefully disguised my inner turmoil from those around me, but my lifestyle was a masquerade.

Have you ever felt the same way?

When I climbed those stairs to my little apartment on the third floor at Meisenweg 28 in Germany, I was suddenly overcome with that inexplicable crushing burden, a burden that had become so physically heavy that I barely had the strength to climb those five short flights. Finally making it into my apartment, my mind and heart were flooded with guilt, loneliness, and shame. I saw no way out of my desperate situation.

That night, as I despaired of life itself and poured out my guilt-ridden and broken heart before God, He transformed my life in an instant. He literally lifted the burden from my shoulders and flooded me with His love and peace. And I've never been the same. I was given a new life, a life only God can give.

Even though I had refused to listen because of the hardness of my heart, I now realize that God had used the words from my Bible-pounding platoon sergeant and many others to help me recognize that I was a sinner in desperate need of a Savior. You remember them . . . Aunt Julie and her Bible; Andy, our clerk in Vietnam; those long-haired and barefooted Jesus freaks on the campuses of Pasadena City College and Cal Poly; Steve in boot camp; my best friend from Romeoville; Martha Schulze and Colonel Skinner at Patch Barracks; and those army chaplains on AFN radio. But most of all, I needed the mighty hand of God to bring me to the end of myself.

I was hungering for something, but I knew not what. Couple that hunger with the fact that within me dwelled a desire and longing to know God and His truth. I can only conclude that what I really wanted—in fact, had lacked most of my life—was an intimate, loving relationship with God. But why was it so elusive?

SPIRITUALLY BANKRUPT

Years later, I heard an army chaplain speak about the holiness of God. He said that God dwells in unapproachable light; He is so holy, so incomprehensibly pure, even Mother Theresa would be blown away by His awesome presence. God is so absolutely good that He cannot even stand to look at sin. The Bible is clear about our problem:

> The Lord looks down from heaven on the sons of men to see if there are any who understand, any who seek God. All have turned aside, they have together become corrupt; there is no one who does good, not even one.[1]

Again, in the book of Romans, God speaks through the apostle Paul and says that "all have sinned and fall short of the glory of God."[2] *All* means all. It means me and it means you. We *all* fall short of the holiness that God requires. You see, many years ago I couldn't accept the fact that I was a sinner because my point of reference was off the mark. Sin isn't about my opinion or the opinion of others; rather it's about *God's* opinion. I'm judged based on *His* standard of measurement.

Jesus Christ is the only One who walked this earth and didn't miss God's standard. Even though I possessed an emptiness in my heart only God could fill, my sin nature created an impenetrable barrier to God's presence. I was eternally separated from Him. Though my body was alive, I was dead—dead to God, dead to His Spirit, and dead in my transgressions and sins. I was spiritually bankrupt![3] Elsewhere Romans says, "The wages of sin is death."[4]

The incredibly and utterly amazing fact is that in spite of our sinful condition, God still loves us! It doesn't matter who we are or what we've done; God loves each of us. The book of Romans says, "But God demonstrates his own love for us in this: While we were still sinners, Christ died for us."[5] John 3:16, a verse familiar to many, sums up this idea best: "For God so loved the world that he gave his one and only Son, that whoever believes in him shall not perish but have eternal life."

After journeying with me through much of my life, I'm now asking you to travel a bit further. The title of this chapter, "On a Hill Far Away," is based on an old, familiar hymn of the faith written by George Bennard. It's to that far-away hill I'd like to take you now—to the cross on that hill and to the One who "for a world of lost sinners was slain."

> On a hill far away stood on old rugged cross,
> The emblem of suffering and shame;
> And I love that old cross where the dearest and best
> For a world of lost sinners was slain.

This is exactly what the prophet Isaiah foretold concerning the suffering Messiah (Jesus Christ), saying that He takes the punishment you and I deserve:

> But he was pierced for our transgressions, he was crushed for our iniquities; the punishment that brought us peace was upon him, and by his wounds we are healed. We all, like sheep, have gone astray, each of us has turned to his own way; and the Lord has laid on him the iniquity of us all.[6]

This concept may be difficult to fathom, but God heaped all our sins on His Son when He hung on that cross in excruciating agony. The apostle Peter wrote, "He himself bore our sins in his body on the tree."[7] Jesus literally paid the "death penalty" for our sins. He died so you and I could live eternally. The following story helps to explain what happened.

A Story

A judge presided over his court. He had imposed a well deserved, hefty fine on an utterly destitute offender. The poor man faced the judge empty-handed; he had absolutely no way to pay the court his fine. Out of the kindness of his heart, however, the judge stepped down from the bench, removed his wallet, approached the bailiff, and paid the fine for the offender.

This story sounds simplistic. Of course, what the judge sacrificed for the guilty man was insignificant compared to what Jesus suffered for us when he paid the penalty for our sins. The similarity lies in the fact that the guilty party had no means to settle his debt and needed someone with the desire, the authority, and the ability to intervene.

Imagine

Imagine if you will, the scene that took place two thousand years ago on that hill far away. Before being nailed to the cross, Jesus had already been tortured and disfigured beyond recognition. The prophet Isaiah wrote that "his appearance was so disfigured beyond that of any man and his form marred beyond human likeness."[8] Between noon and three o'clock, complete darkness covered the face of the whole land, and the sinless Son of God experienced the crushing weight of all humanity's sins.[9]

Jesus became our sin bearer, and God, who is light and in whom there is no darkness at all, had to turn away from His own dearly beloved Son as He hung there on that cross. This rejection prompted Jesus to cry out in great anguish, "My God, my God, why have you forsaken me?"[10] At exactly three o'clock that afternoon, with His last breath Jesus cried out again—not in defeat but in victory: "It is finished."[11]

At the exact moment Jesus died, His work completed, something unusual happened. The temple curtain, which for centuries had symbolized the separation between a holy God and sinful man, tore into two pieces.[12] It was a picture of what Christ's work on the cross had accomplished for all mankind. No wall of separation exists between believers and their God. Jesus paid the price; He made the way for all of us. In fact, if you or I was the only person on earth, Josh McDowell wrote, Christ would still have died to pay the price.[13]

But wait. The story doesn't end there. Jesus didn't stay on the cross or in the grave. The best was yet to come. Three days later, the Lord rose from the dead. The whole of Christianity hangs on this one fact—that Christ died and was resurrected on the third day. This is the good news:

> That Christ died for our sins according to the Scriptures, that he was buried, that he was raised on the third day according to the Scriptures, and that he appeared to Peter, and then to the Twelve [His twelve disciples]. After that, he appeared to more than five hundred of the brothers at the same time.[14]

Do you remember that scene early one morning during my quiet time in Florida? It ended with my standing in the front yard of our home with my arms raised to heaven. The scene began with my reading this passage in the book of Acts: "Salvation is found in no one else, for there is no other name under heaven given to men by which we must be saved."[15] This is plain language. Jesus says of Himself in the gospel of John, "I'm the way and the truth and the life. No one comes to the Father except through me."[16] These verses sound pretty exclusive in today's inclusive society. But for those who truly want to know God, there is only one way.

Jesus desires a personal relationship with you. He says, "Here I am! I stand at the door and knock. If anyone hears my voice and opens the door, I will come in and eat with him, and he with me."[17]

These words express Christ's longing to have fellowship with you. This message distinguishes Christianity from other world religions. In those religions mankind is working and striving to reach up to an unknown and seemingly unconcerned God. In Christianity a loving God reaches down to us and seeks to restore us to Himself. Is He knocking on the door of your heart at this moment? Do you want to open the door? As soon as you open the door of your heart to Him, Jesus will come in. Just as He heard my cries for help on that dreadfully cold November night in 1977, He will hear you. He said, "I am come that they might have life, and that they might have it more abundantly" (KJV).[18]

My dear friend, do you want to experience that abundant life? Do you want to be set free from the burden of sin and experience God's transforming power to rid you of the baggage in your life you've been lugging around? Have you been searching for truth and can't seem to find it? Are you tired of looking for love in all the wrong places? Do you want to experience real and sweet fellowship with Jesus and the love of God in your life? Most importantly, do you want to live your life in full knowledge that when you die, God will welcome you to an eternal home in heaven with Him?

If your answer to any of the above questions is yes, then please believe that God exists and begin to earnestly seek Him. My prayer is that the stories of my life have helped you believe that God is real. Testimonies of His goodness fill these pages, and not just my own but also testimonies from those who have touched my life in so many ways. They all testify to the one true God.

Also, agree with God that you are a sinner; turn away from your sin and turn to God, and ask Him to forgive you. Acknowledge that Jesus is Lord and that He paid the penalty for your sins by dying on the cross. Know and believe that God raised Him from the dead. By faith receive the greatest gift from God by inviting Jesus into your heart and ask Him to become Lord of your life. "Yet to all who received him, to those who believed in his name, he gave the right to become children of God."[19]

You surely have noticed from the stories of how I came to faith in Christ that I didn't follow this formula. I didn't even know these truths on the night I was saved in my little apartment at Meisenweg 28. I don't blame my ignorance on anyone but myself. I stubbornly refused to listen to people who wanted to share these fundamental truths with me. I always pushed them away, saying, "Not today! Not today! Not today!" The point I'm making is that God didn't reject my pleas for help just because I didn't say just the right things in the right order.

God looks on the heart.[20] He doesn't work with a set of formulas. If we're truly sincere in wanting to know the one, true, and only God, He will meet us on our life's journey as He did in my case and as He has in countless other lives. What's important to remember is that God requires something on our part. We must take that first step; we must recognize our need and come to Him. This is what the Lord said:

Come to me, all you who are weary and burdened, and I will give you rest. Take my yoke upon you and learn from me, for I am gentle and humble in heart, and you will find rest for your souls. For my yoke is easy and my burden is light.[21]

Those who accept the invitation embark on a journey of faith and a blessed walk with the Lord. Will the journey always be easy? Will you still have problems and life issues to deal with? Certainly, but you will have a new friend at your side, one who sticks closer than a brother.[22] This friend will never leave you or forsake you, and His love will transform you in this life and for all eternity.[23]

THE WITNESS

I would like to conclude with one final story.

Several years ago I flew from Atlanta, Georgia, to the Netherlands to visit my dear, ailing mother. When I boarded the plane, I asked the Lord to give me an opportunity to share the good news of Jesus Christ with someone. After I took my seat, a young man from Holland, who appeared to be in his early twenties, sat next to me.

We immediately struck up a conversation. The young man was flying home to spend the Christmas and New Year's Day holidays with his family. A recent graduate of the Technical University of Delft in the Netherlands, he was now working as a contract engineer for one of the U.S. military service academies. During the conversation, I heard an all-too-familiar story: he had left the church at a young age because it had failed to provide what he was looking for in life.

About two hours into the flight, he shared an interesting tale about his boss, who wasn't an easy man to work for. One day, however, he noticed a sudden change in the man. Almost overnight his supervisor seemed like a totally different person; he now appeared genuinely kind and friendly to everyone. When he asked his boss about his changed behavior, his boss replied that he had become a born-again believer. His boss told a compelling story about his life and about one day having an encounter with the Lord Jesus Christ.

My fellow passenger was puzzled by this change. The testimony of his boss, coupled with the sudden improvement in his behavior, had made a profound effect on this young man. That's all I needed to hear—this was the answer to my prayer.

I shared with my new friend my life's story and my miraculous encounter with the living God. Early the next morning after our arrival at Schiphol International Airport in Amsterdam, we parted company. Later, after retrieving my suitcase, I noticed that he was making a special effort to find me among hundreds of passengers, many of whom were loaded down with their luggage. He shook my hand with a smile from ear to ear, said good-bye a second time, and wished me well. He didn't need to say anything else; I could tell by his demeanor that he had enjoyed our long conversation and that my story had touched him in a heart-stirring way. When he turned and walked away, I sensed deep in my heart that I would see him again, perhaps not in this life but most assuredly in the life to come.

And so, my dear friend, I have finally reached the end of my story. Although we may have never met, I feel to some degree that you are like that young man who sat beside me on my flight across the Atlantic Ocean. I have shared with you my true confession. Now I close with the sincere hope that you will not dismiss but rather take to heart all that I have written and that someday you and I will meet—if not in this life, definitely in the life to come. I look forward to hearing about all the wonderful things God has done in your life.

> You will seek me and find me when you seek me with all your heart.
>
> —Jeremiah 29:13

> All that the Father gives me will come to me,
> and whoever comes to me I will never drive away.
>
> —John 6:37

Thank you for allowing me to share my life with you. May the Lord richly bless you in ways you cannot dream or even imagine.

Your friend,
John

Supplement to "The Miracle Boy"

THE STORY OF my struggle with stage III colon cancer would be incomplete without my recognizing many very special people.

To begin with, I want to express my deep love and affection to Janneke, who didn't leave my side from the moment I was diagnosed with cancer. Room 1 in the ICU became her virtual campground. My sweet wife and best friend was a constant source of strength, comfort, and encouragement throughout this difficult time in my life.

Only wonderful, caring, and professional people make up the staff of the oncology clinic in South Hill, Virginia. Their names are too numerous to mention here. However, I do wish to acknowledge those who were and still are directly involved in my treatments and follow-up visits. Nicole Whitlatch, MD, my oncologist, is an extraordinary, kindhearted, gentle soul who cares deeply for her patients. She made it clear to me from the onset that in time of need she was available 24-7.

Four other special people I do not wish to overlook: Susan Baird, Wendy Bohannon, Julie Hamby, and Donna Robertson. They are exceptionally skilled, courteous, friendly, and energetic nurses who have enabled me to maintain a sense of humor in the face of adversity. Each time I saw Dr. Whitlatch, or when I reported to the clinic to have my blood drawn or chemotherapy administered, I felt like I was in the company of very good friends.

One evening during the early stages of my chemotherapy, friends from the Southside Virginia Emmaus Community orchestrated a healing service at Crenshaw United Methodist Church in Blackstone, Virginia. The service was held not only for me but also for others who had been stricken with cancer. Janneke and I will always remember this special time of prayer and the celebration of Holy Communion with dear friends.

I also wish to convey to my pastor, Paul Montanye, my deep appreciation for being there for me and my family, especially during my hospitalization. Despite a busy schedule, Paul spent long hours nearly every day at my bedside, praying for me, reading Scriptures, encouraging Janneke, and constantly staying abreast of my situation by speaking with the doctors.

Words cannot express how grateful I am to Christopher J. Ackerman, MD, my primary care physician. He rushed to the ICU when my heart had slowed to a dangerously slow pace; he corrected a dislodged ventilator and administered CPR. A month after my discharge from the hospital, Dr. Whitlatch told me, "Dr. Ackerman saved your life!"

I would be negligent if I failed to acknowledge two good friends with big hearts, Tom and Janet Hunter from Blackstone. While I was in the hospital and without our knowledge, they orchestrated a project to replace the old roof on our house. It entailed organizing a fundraising effort, finding an affordable and reputable roofing contractor, and recruiting others to do chores around our house I had neglected for some time, partly because of my illness. Thanks to Tom, Janet, and all those who so generously gave of their time and money, our roof no longer leaks!

Mounted on the wall only inches from my computer monitor is a twenty-eight-inch-by-twenty-two-inch, color photograph of my church family. The arms of both young and old are raised to heaven. That picture is a symbol of how God used the Body of Christ to bring about a miracle in my life. Printed on the upper left-hand side in big, bold letters is the caption "We're Praying for You!" Presented to me when I was a patient in the ICU, the photograph is a gift that has touched my heart deeply. Thank you, Barbara Wine, as well as Helmut and Janet Loeser, for your loving kindness. I never tire of looking at that picture.

It serves as a constant reminder that I serve a kind and most merciful God who answers prayers.

To all those whose names are recorded herein, including countless other wonderful, kind, and gentle people whose names are not mentioned, I owe a debt of gratitude I can never hope to repay.

Endnotes

10. Life at Kilroy Compound

1. Erik Villard, *The 1968 Tet Offensive Battles of Quang Tri City and Hue* (Washington, D.C.: U.S. Army Center of Military History, 2008), 5.

11. The Snare of Death

1. Erik Villard, *The 1968 Tet Offensive Battles of Quang Tri City and Hue* (Washington, D.C.: U.S. Army Center of Military History, 2008), 13.
2. Memorandum, "Quang Tri Victory," Senior Province Advisor, Advisory Team 1, 4 February 1968.
3. Erik Villard, *The 1968 Tet Offensive Battles of Quang Tri City and Hue* (Washington, D.C.: U.S. Army Center of Military History, 2008), 8.
4. Jeffrey J. Clarke, Foreword to *The 1968 Tet Offensive Battles of Quang Tri City and Hue,* by Erik Villard (Washington, D. C.: U.S. Army Center of Military History, 2008).

15. A Long, Sweet Honeymoon

1. Joel 2:32; Acts 2:21; Romans 10:13
2. John 5:24; Ephesians 2:1–5; 1 John 3:14

3. 1 Samuel 16:7; 1 Chronicles 28:9; 2 Chronicles 6:30; Psalm 44:21; 139:23
4. Psalm 127:3
5. Psalm 139:14

16. A Flower in the Desert

1. Romans 8:28

17. End of a Honeymoon

1. Acts 17:25; 1 Timothy 6:13

18. Not-So-Quiet Time

1. Psalm 5:3; 88:13
2. 2 Kings 5:14–15
3. Deuteronomy 4:35, 39; 6:4; Isaiah 43:10; 44:6, 8; 45:5–6, 18, 22; 46:9; Mark 12:29; 1 Corinthians 8:4; Ephesians 4:6
4. Matthew 13:42, 50; Luke 13:28; Revelation 21:8
5. Proverbs 24:11; Jude 23

19. When Johnny Comes Marching Home

1. Proverbs 3:5–6

20. My Golden Calf

1. Exodus 32:1–4
2. 1 Corinthians 10:14; 2 Corinthians 7:1

21. An Opportunity Squandered

1. Lamentation 3:22–23
2. 2 Timothy 2:13
3. Hebrews 13:5 (also see Deuteronomy 31:6)

22. The Fire of Affliction

1. Psalm 25:4–5
2. James 4:4

23. A Spiritual Transformation

1. Psalm 19:9–10
2. Luke 6:46–49

24. A Church in Peril

1. John 3:16
2. John Ankerberg and John Weldon, *Cult Watch: What You Need to Know About Spiritual Deception* (Eugene, OR: Harvest House Publishers, 1991), 302.
3. Psalm 102:17
4. Proverbs 6:16, 19

25. No Place Like Home

1. See Philippians 4:6.
2. See Matthew 19:26; Mark 10:27; Luke 1:37; 18:27.

26. A Time to Cry

1. Psalm 133:1
2. Philippians 2:14

27. This Thing is from Me

1. Mrs. Charles E. Cowman, *Streams in the Desert*, Vol. 1 (Grand Rapids, MI: Zondervan Publishing House, 1965), 35

28. Jehovah Jireh

1. Genesis 22:2
2. Genesis 22:7–14

29. No Fear of Death

1. Hebrews 2:15
2. 2 Timothy 1:10
3. 1 Corinthians 15:54

30. A Rude Awakening

1. James 5:14–15

31. The Miracle Boy

1. Psalm 50:15
2. Psalm 31:15
3. Exodus 15:26; Psalm 103:3; Jeremiah 17:14; Mathew 8:7; 10:1

32. On a Hill Far Away

1. Psalm 14:2–3
2. Romans 3:23
3. Ephesians 2:1; Colossians 2:13; James 2:26
4. Romans 6:23
5. Romans 5:8
6. Isaiah 53:5–6
7. 1 Peter 2:24
8. Isaiah 52:14
9. Matthew 27:45; Mark 15:33; Luke 23:44
10. Matthew 27:46; Mark 15:34
11. John 19:30
12. Matthew 27:51; Mark 15:38; Luke 23:45
13. Josh McDowell, *The New Evidence That Demands a Verdict* (Colorado Springs, CO: Thomas Nelson, 1999), XXV.
14. 1 Corinthians 15:3–6
15. Acts 4:12
16. John 14:6
17. Revelation 3:20
18. John 10:10
19. John 1:12
20. 1 Samuel 16:7; 1 Chronicles 28:9; 2 Chronicles 6:30; Psalm 7:9; 44:21; Revelation 2:23
21. Matthew 11:28–30
22. Proverbs 18:24
23. Deuteronomy 31:6; Joshua 1:5; Psalm 94:14; Hebrews 13:5

I will exalt you, my God the King;
I will praise your name for ever and ever.
Every day I will praise you
and extol your name for ever and ever.
Great is the Lord and most worthy of praise;
his greatness no one can fathom.
One generation will commend your works to another;
they will tell of your mighty acts.
They will speak of the glorious splendor of your majesty,
and I will meditate on your wonderful works.
They will tell of the power of your awesome works,
and I will proclaim your great deeds.
They will celebrate your abundant goodness
and joyfully sing of your righteousness.
The Lord is gracious and compassionate,
slow to anger and rich in love.
The Lord is good to all;
he has compassion on all he has made.

—Psalm 145:1–9

Contact Information

REDEMPTION PRESS

To order additional copies of this book, please visit
www.redemption-press.com.
Also available on Amazon.com and BarnesandNoble.com
Or by calling toll free 1 (888) 305-2967.